GUN CONTROL

*What Australia did,
how other countries do it &
is any of it sensible?*

DAVID LEYONHJELM

With contributions by: Grant Bayley,
Frank Brophy, Chaz Forsyth, David Karasek, Richard Law,
Abhijeet Singh and Peter Whelan

Copyright © 2020, David Leyonhjelm

Published by Connor Court Publishing Pty Ltd

ALL RIGHTS RESERVED. This book contains material protected under International and Federal Copyright Laws and Treaties. Any unauthorised reprint or use of this material is prohibited. No part of this book may be reproduced or transmitted in any form or by any means, electronic or mechanical, including photocopying, recording, or by any information storage and retrieval system without express written permission from the publisher.

CONNOR COURT PUBLISHING PTY LTD
PO Box 7257
Redland Bay QLD 4165
sales@connorcourt.com
www.connorcourtpublishing.com.au

ISBN: 978-1-925826-96-8 (pbk.)

Cover design by Ian James

Photos in book taken from Wikipedia Commons.

Printed in Australia

CONTENTS

1: Introduction	5
2: Why Australians own guns	9
3: Background to Australia's gun laws	23
4: The Howard gun laws	33
5: Guns 101	49
6: How to legally own a gun in Australia	79
7: Did the Howard gun laws work?	87
8: Gun Control in Other Countries	133
New Zealand	134
Switzerland	158
United Kingdom	168
Ireland (Eire)	196
India	207
Czech Republic	216
Malaysia	233
9: Gun Control in America	235
10: Moral and philosophical arguments for gun ownership	263
11: Gun myths	305
12: Sensible gun laws	321
Acknowledgements	339

1

INTRODUCTION

The gun debate in Australia barely qualifies as a debate at all. It is more like opposing sides at a rally hurling insults at each other. The two sides each have firmly held convictions and there is little interest in reconsidering them.

On one side are firearm owners – hunters, sporting shooters and collectors – who know what it is like to live under Australian firearms laws. Having done nothing wrong, they feel victimised because of their chosen sport or hobby.

On the other side are the anti-gun people, who regard guns as fundamentally evil and whose ultimate goal is complete civilian disarmament.

In the middle are the majority of Australians, few of whom have ever held or fired a gun and whose opinions are largely informed by the news media, movies and television. Beyond knowing they are "tough", they have little understanding of Australian gun laws and know next to nothing about gun laws in other countries.

They are nonetheless inclined to accept the assertion that Australia has found the solution to gun violence and, unless it maintains its current approach to gun control, it will end up like America, which they believe is a violent country.

Politicians are no different, as I know from personal

experience. Few have any direct experience with firearms or their regulation, and quite a few genuinely believe Australia's gun laws are an example to the rest of the world. The bureaucrats who advise them are no better informed.

This book is written primarily for those who are willing to form an opinion based on facts and reason rather than fear and ignorance. What they are missing is a source of information, which the book aims to provide.

What the facts show is that gun availability and violent crime are independent variables. That is, they are unrelated. A high level of gun control does not reduce violence, and a low level of gun control does not increase it. Countries with stringent gun control would not become violent if their gun laws were relaxed, and countries with relaxed gun laws would not become less violent if they adopted stringent gun laws.

This is difficult for Australians to accept, as they have been repeatedly told that our gun laws have made us safer. It is a classic example of truthiness – it is not true, but it sounds like it ought to be true.

Fairly obviously, this book will not influence those who are afraid of guns and refuse to reconsider their fear. Opinions based on emotion are not usually revised except when more powerful emotions intrude.

It will also not influence those who believe all government authority is legitimate, irrespective of its consequences.

On the other hand, among those who harbour the feeling that governments are not always right, that unbridled power is a threat to a free and democratic society, and that shooting guns just might be fun, perhaps it will prompt some to reconsider their views.

The book is intended to be informative rather than creative.

It reproduces data and text from many sources, quite a few of which are online. Attribution is acknowledged as much as possible and there is no deliberate plagiarism, but reproduction of work by unidentified authors is included where appropriate.

2

WHY AUSTRALIANS OWN GUNS

It is common to hear people ask "Why do you need a gun anyway?", sometimes followed by "especially in the city."

This reveals a lack of understanding of the legitimate reasons for owning firearms, beyond a vague notion that there is some justification for owning them in rural and regional areas.

This chapter describes the reasons Australians currently own guns. As is obvious, many reasons apply to metropolitan areas just as much as to rural or regional areas. Indeed, superior facilities in the cities makes ownership more understandable in some cases.

SPORT

There are sporting uses for every type of pistol, rifle and shotgun available. When a greater range of firearms was permitted, before 1997, there were sporting uses for them as well. Even machineguns and submachine guns, which could be legally owned by collectors in Tasmania prior to 1996, have sporting matches.

Firearms are used in the Olympic Games, Commonwealth Games and World Championships, plus numerous other international and domestic competitions. Shooting was one of the sports included in the first modern Olympics, beginning in Athens in 1896.

Sports shooting occurs on a shooting range. For some matches (eg air pistol, air rifle) the range is normally inside. For others, it can only be located outdoors. There are thousands of shooting ranges all over Australia.

The design of shooting ranges is typically quite sophisticated, taking into account factors such as where the projectiles land, safety to users, bystanders and neighbours, and the potential for adverse levels of noise to users and surrounding areas.

In countries that have a rich tradition of target shooting, such as Switzerland, both outdoor and indoor shooting ranges are found in many towns and villages, often close to houses. These are extremely well designed to ensure the safety of both participants and neighbours. Baffling is ubiquitous and the use of suppressors (inaccurately also known as 'silencers') is common.

In Australia, outdoor ranges tend to be established at relatively low cost, away from housing. However, urban encroachment is a common problem in large cities and growing in country towns.

As a sport, shooting is virtually unique. Males and females can compete on equal terms in most disciplines, as can the young and the old, the able bodied and the disabled. The skills required, in particular adequate vision and a steady hand, are also not limited to elite athletes.

Sports shooting is also one of the safest sports, with accidental injuries and deaths almost unknown.

Pistols (Handguns)

Air, rimfire (.22) and centrefire pistols are used in sporting competitions over distances ranging from 10 to 200 metres. Pistol types include semi-automatic, revolvers and single shot.

Most targets are paper or cardboard, although some matches use wooden panels or steel plates. Electronic targets are also increasingly popular.

Rifles

Rifles are used in sporting competitions over ranges from 10 metres to more than 1,000 metres. Air, rimfire and centrefire rifles are used.

Targets may be paper, electronic, steel or wood.

Rifles can be bolt action, break action, lever action, pump action and single shot. Prior to 1996, semi-automatic rimfire and centrefire rifles were used in sporting competitions as well.

Shotguns

Shotguns are used in sporting competitions at ranges from 20 to approximately 90 metres. Clay targets are used or, in a few matches, metal plates.

The majority of shotguns are break action, mostly double barrelled. Semi-automatic shotguns may only be used with special permits. There are also bolt action and lever action shotguns.

Most shotguns are 12 gauge although 20 gauge and 410 are also available.

More information

For more information on shooting disciplines, these websites are useful.

https://shootingaustralia.org/
https://ssaa.org.au/disciplines/

HUNTING

By far the most popular reason for owning a firearm in Australia is hunting. Native animals are protected and may not be hunted except with a permit. However, there is quite a range of feral animals that may be hunted subject to safety, location and the permission of the property owner.

Feral animals are all, to varying degrees, harmful to the Australian environment. The least harmful compete for pasture with farmed livestock and native animals (eg deer), while the most harmful are those that prey on livestock (eg pigs, dogs, foxes) or native animals (cats and foxes). Some native animals are now extinct and others are seriously endangered because of feral animal predation.

The animals that may be hunted are:

> Feral pigs, foxes, feral cats, wild dogs, rabbits and hares goats, deer, buffalo, camels, donkeys, ducks (certain species), quail, pheasants, pest birds eg Indian Mynas, sparrows, pigeons

Most of these may be hunted year-round. Deer and ducks are subject to hunting seasons in some states.

Recreational duck hunting is permitted in Victoria, South Australia, Tasmania and the Northern Territory. In Victoria, South Australia and Tasmania hunters must pass a Waterfowl Identification Test (WIT) before being permitted to hunt ducks. This helps licensed duck hunters to identify game and non-game waterbirds while in the field.

In NSW, recreational hunting of ducks is not permitted. However, many hunters help farmers to control ducks in rice-growing areas.

Deer hunting seasons vary between the states depending on whether they are categorised as a pest animal or a game animal. Restrictions are intended to avoid hunting during the breeding season when baby deer are common. In Victoria, for example, Hog deer may only be hunted between 1 April and 30 April each year and there is a bag limit of one male and one female.

Also in Victoria, Sambar deer may be hunted by stalking all year round but only between 1 April and 30 November if hunting with hounds. Rusa, Chital and Fallow deer, on the other hand, may be hunted all year.

Some pest animals are quite numerous in metropolitan and semi-urban areas but cannot be controlled by shooting due to blanket restrictions on the use of firearms. Examples include foxes, rabbits, Indian Mynas and pigeons.

Kangaroos may only be hunted by commercial shooters subject to a permit system, and by farmers and others with a pest control permit. In both cases there are strict quotas.

OCCUPATIONAL

Australians are permitted to own firearms for certain occupational reasons. These include:

- Professional pest control
- Farmers, for destruction of livestock and feral animals
- Security guards for protection of property

COLLECTING FIREARMS PRESERVING OUR HERITAGE[1]

Australia has a rich history involving firearms, from the colonial period through to its various wars. Private collectors are almost entirely responsible for the preservation of this history.

Collecting is a serious hobby for many gun enthusiasts. This has seen prices escalate during the past couple of decades, as older guns migrate from grandpa's toolbox to collector's display case.

Many such guns have achieved 'classic' status and are highly sought after. High on the list of collectible pistols, for example, are the Model 1896 Mauser ('Broomhandle') and its derivatives and the many variations of Imperial German P-08 ('Luger') pistols. Among dozens of others, collectors might seek various Astras, Berettas, Colts, Smith & Wessons, Tokarevs and Webleys.

Collectors often follow a particular theme. While the military theme is popular, there are many other possibilities, such as chronological collections of particular manufacturers, countries or styles. Some collectors concentrate on Colts or Rugers; others might specialise in designs copied from the self-loaders of JM Browning. One person may choose to collect Belgian purse pistols, while another might look for colonial firearms from Australia's early days.

Flintlock and percussion firearms command high prices and are very popular. Breech-loading pistols are much more widely available than the real old-timers and some of the earlier breech-loaders may not require registration. This influences those collectors who do not wish to bother with licences.

---

[1] Adapted from *Motives of a handgun collector,* Geoff Smith: https://ssaa.org.au/stories/historical-motives-of-a-handgun-collector.html

Collectors have often stepped in to preserve Australia's firearms history when it was neglected by governments. In his book Service Arms of the SA Police (Antique and Historical Arms Association of SA Inc, 1988) Max Slee tells the now heartbreaking tale of how the SA Police divested itself of its old weapons back in 1952. A consignment including 82 Adams .450 and 233 S&W .44 Russian revolvers, 293 Martini Henry .577-.450 rifles and 177 carbines of like calibre (plus a vast quantity of ammunition, bayonets, holsters, scabbards and other surrendered pistols) were virtually dumped onto the US market as a bulk lot for a total of just $2,506.

On today's market (based on recent auction prices) this little lot would bring roughly $800,000 in Australia and maybe twice this in the USA.

In more recent times an ignorant and barbaric process of obsessively melting down 'surrendered and seized weapons' purely because they are guns has destroyed rare and, in some cases, irreplaceable firearms. The fact that they could command astonishing prices overseas is ignored. That those firearms associated with criminal activity might be of great interest to historians and scientists in the future is also ignored.

A collection of any kind obviously begins with one single item. Having somehow obtained this item, the owner commences a process of research. This process is often informal and sometimes even subconscious. The curiosity evoked by possession of this particular firearm may initially relate to the person from whom it was obtained rather than from the gun itself.

Perhaps one inherits an old Luger that the late lamented Uncle Fred liberated from Villers Bretonneux in 1918. Old Fred probably kept it, knowing the law restricted his possession of it after about 1930, perhaps wilfully and defiantly avoiding licensing and registration of it for his entire life. Perhaps he took somebody else's life to obtain it in battle. Possibly he simply found it lying on the ground or won it in a two-up game.

Whatever the circumstances, Uncle Fred clearly valued it as a keepsake because he kept it for so long. Perhaps for him it was tangible evidence of another time, a dreadful, terrifying time probably, but one that was also the greatest adventure of his life. From family information, you might be privy to some of these personal details, which add to its individual family heritage value. As the new legal owner, maybe you log onto the bibliographical section of the Australian War Memorial in Canberra and check out Uncle Fred's army records. You enter his name and the state from which he enlisted and discover a brief summary of his service details.

From a few of these details (such as the unit in which he served and his service number), you find you can purchase a full transcript of his service record. Having established that he was with a particular unit, it is likely that a history of this unit, coupled with Uncle Fred's service records, will enable a great deal of information to be gathered in relation to this pistol. The pistol has thus become a part of living history to you as the owner, and to the whole nation in general.

So now you carefully dismantle Uncle Fred's Luger and then get out the books. The marks on the gun will reveal when and where it was made, how much it cost at the time and how many others like it were bought. The serial number and proof markings will, with detailed study, tell the physical history of the gun. The military records might also show the range of enemy units from which it was possibly souvenired.

The process of determining the above information often leads the beginning collector to other people who own similar items. These days, to even be regarded as a firearms collector, one must belong to a collectors club and meet the minimum attendance requirements each year. But even if this were not the case, most collectors seek out other like-minded people if for no other reason than to compare notes about the items being sought. Often where a person has one item, interested fellow club members will say that they know where there is another such item or perhaps a related item that might be for sale.

Assume, for example, that you acquire a Japanese Nambu pistol through a family connection. You are intrigued by the peculiar markings, the crudely executed wooden grips and the remarkable rust blued finish and nickel-plated magazine. At this point you know very little about the weapons of Imperial Japan, but after making a few inquiries at the club, it turns out that a fellow club member has a magazine and some parts, somebody else has a holster and yet another person invites you to come and inspect his collection of WWII Japanese militaria. He gives you a brief rundown on General Kijiro Nambu, Japan's most famous small-arms designer.

You take the pistol along to a meeting and discover that the numbers on the right-hand side of the receiver tell you the year and month in which it was made. That funny "Mickey Mouse head with three ears" symbol, in fact, represents the top view of a pile of four cannonballs. It is the mark that, on this firearm, symbolises the Kokura Arsenal near Tokyo. It could just as easily have featured three circles depicting the 'fighting fish' symbol of the Nagoya Arsenal. A club member shows you how, on firing the last shot, the bolt locks open, not on a separate catch like many other military pistols, but on the actual magazine, which tells nearby enemy forces you are out of ammo because you need two hands to change magazines.

Not long afterwards you find a Japanese Arisaka rifle for sale at the local gun shop. It has similar arsenal markings to the pistol so you purchase this too. Now that you are hooked, you start to really become keen on anything to do with weapons and militaria of this period.

From being the novice at the club who wanted to find out more about an inherited pistol, now, a few years down the track, you are the person others come to see in order to find out how to identify those funny marks and numbers on such firearms. You have obtained books and photocopied articles relating to this area of conflict.

Perhaps you have set up some web pages with your findings and made contact with fellow collectors in other states or overseas. Your collection could extend to other items of militaria, such as Japanese swords, flags, helmets, medals and such. Other collectors might focus more specifically on handguns but spread the interest out to obtain examples of other handguns from the same conflict.

The student of firearms is as much interested in shape, appearance, the combination of ideas and utility, as in history, technology and engineering. Many find fascinating the hand crafting of many aspects of firearms, their fine mechanical engineering and mass production techniques pioneered long before the likes of Henry Ford applied similar techniques to automobiles in the 20th century.

The study of guns helps keep many aspects of history alive. Like all forms of recreation, it brings serious and tangible rewards to all of society.

SELF DEFENCE AND PROTECTION OF PROPERTY

Prior to 1997 it was possible for people faced with a realistic threat of violence to obtain a permit to carry a concealed pistol. The police in Australia would regularly recommend to wives pursued by violent ex-husbands and celebrities hounded by crazed fans, amongst others, that they should apply for a permit. And of course jewellers and gun shop owners were able to carry a gun to protect themselves and their merchandise.

Self-defence remains available as a defence to a charge of causing injury or death in defence of the person or, to a limited extent, property. It is also a partial defence to murder if the degree of force used was excessive. In other words, self defence is a recognised legal right.

Furthermore, the law regarding self defence is statutory in NSW, which means the common law concepts of retreating and proportionality do not apply. A person is not criminally responsible for an offence if the person carries out the conduct constituting the offence in self-defence *if and only if the person believes the conduct is necessary:*

- *(a) to defend himself or herself or another person, or*
- *(b) to prevent or terminate the unlawful deprivation of his or her liberty or the liberty of another person, or*
- *(c) to protect property from unlawful taking, destruction, damage or interference, or*
- *(d) to prevent criminal trespass to any land or premises or to remove a person committing any such criminal trespass, and the conduct is a reasonable response in the circumstances as he or she perceives them.*

The law in the other states is very similar.

However, since 1997 Australians have not been permitted

to own firearms to protect themselves, their families or their property. Certain VIPs, including the Prime Minister, are protected by armed plain clothes police, while guards transporting cash in armoured vans are permitted to carry firearms.

Nobody else is permitted to carry a firearm for protection or even to own one for that purpose, either in the home or elsewhere. Even those facing an imminent threat (for example, an obsessive former partner) or who work in occupations involving substantial risk (eg jewellers and gun shop owners) are not permitted to protect themselves with firearms. In some States jewellers and others can acquire licences to carry firearms, but only for protecting valuable property, not to protect themselves or others.

In NSW it is actually illegal to use a firearm for self-defence as it is contrary to the "genuine reason" for granting the firearms licence or permit. Even when used by the victim of a home invasion (irrespective of whether it is fired or even loaded), it is routine for a firearms owner to have their firearms seized by police and their licence status reviewed.

It is also illegal to carry any items specifically for self-defence. That includes pepper spray, mace and tasers, which are prohibited weapons, as are bullet proof vests. Knives, canes, hat pins, hair spray and other items that have the potential to be used for self defence may not be lawfully carried for that purpose. They may only be carried for another purpose, such as recreation or occupational use. Anyone found in possession of such items without such a reason may be prosecuted for carrying an offensive weapon.

The only exception is WA, where pepper sprays are legal:

> *If it is carried or possessed by a person for the purpose of being used in lawful defence in circumstances that the person has reasonable grounds to apprehend may arise.*

Self defence in the home is marginally less restrictive, but only because potential weapons tend to be readily available and do not require an alternative justification for possession.

If you had the right to vote but there were no ballot boxes, the right would be academic; it would not exist as a reality. It would be the same if you have a right to freedom of religion but churches were all banned. A right that cannot be exercised is not really a right at all.

Fit young men and noisy social commentators often scoff at the idea that they need a weapon for self-defence, but seem to forget about their grandmother, sister or frail old uncle. For those prepared to learn how to use them, the most practical means of self-defence is often a gun. Guns do not favour the strong over the weak, the fast over the slow, or the able-bodied over the disabled. Most people will never need one, but there's no doubt that if you really need to defend yourself, a gun is often the best option. In fact, many claim a shotgun is overall the best option at home and a concealed pistol outside the home.

In practical terms a firearms owner in Australia faced with a dire threat would be tempted to use a firearm for self-defence and worry about the consequences later. Depending on the circumstances they may not be prosecuted, and juries are reluctant to convict even if they are, but there is a strong chance their firearms licence will be revoked.

Australia's prohibition on guns for self defence is not unique, but it is rare. Very few countries prohibit ownership of firearms for self-defence in the home, and not all that many prohibit firearms for self-defence when there is a clear, identifiable threat.

3

BACKGROUND TO AUSTRALIA'S GUN LAWS

By international standards Australia is a peaceful, law-abiding country with a low level of crime involving guns. Furthermore, its homicide rate has been on a downward trend since at least the 1980s. Mass murders, including public shootings, are very rare.

Two incidents involving mass murders are of particular relevance to this chapter.

First is the Sydney Hilton Hotel bombing in 1978[2], which killed three and injured 11. It was an attempt to assassinate the Indian Prime Minister, part of a campaign to free the head of Ananda Marga, an Indian sect, who was imprisoned in India.

Evan Pederick, a sect member, confessed to planting the bomb although his confession was later described as unreliable.

Controversies and conspiracy theories continue to circulate around what has been described as Australia's first case of domestic terrorism. There are still many unanswered questions including allegations that Australian security forces, such as the Australian Security Intelligence Organisation, may have been involved.

---

[2] https://en.wikipedia.org/wiki/Sydney_Hilton_Hotel_bombing

A coronial inquest into the bombing was eventually held in 1982 but all applications by witnesses to subpoena evidence were rejected and potentially important witnesses were not called. The inquest was terminated prematurely due to the finding of a *prima facie* case of murder. However, those accused were later acquitted on appeal.

In 1991 and 1995 the New South Wales parliament unanimously called on the Commonwealth to hold an inquiry. The federal government refused.

The second was a deliberately lit fire in the Whisky Au Go Go nightclub in Fortitude Valley, Brisbane, in 1973.[3] Part of an extortion-terror campaign aimed at Brisbane nightclub operators, it was the worst mass murder in modern Australian history prior to Port Arthur. There were 15 people killed.

Two career criminals, James Finch and John Stuart, were convicted of the murders. Both loudly protested their innocence, claiming they had been "verballed" and convicted based on false confessions. Finch repeatedly appealed, including to the Privy Council. He was deported to England upon release on parole, where he confessed to the crime. He also repeated claims that he had been "verballed" by the original police investigators.

In 2017 the Queensland Attorney-General announced that the government would re-open the coronial inquest into the fire[4], stating:

> *There is no doubt there is significant public interest in getting answers in relation to the Whiskey Au Go Go firebombing in 1973 in which 15 people died. Given recent events, witnesses who have previously not been willing to come forward, might now be willing to provide new information that will give us those answers.*

---

[3] https://en.wikipedia.org/wiki/Whiskey_Au_Go_Go_fire
[4] http://statements.qld.gov.au/Statement/2017/6/2/statement-from-attorneygeneral-yvette-dath-on-whiskey-au-go-go-inquest

The significance of these two events is that, without full public inquiries, they remained controversial and a source of speculation as to malfeasance by both the government and the police.

Commencing in 1984 there were four public mass shootings. When the fifth occurred in 1996, at Port Arthur, the perception emerged that there was a problem with firearms. A newly elected Prime Minister with an emotional attitude to guns provided the "solution" in the form of the National Firearms Agreement.

The first such public shooting was a gunfight between rival motorcycle gang members in a hotel car park in Milperra, an outer Sydney suburb, on Father's Day 1984. The participants were 19 armed Comancheros and 34 armed Bandidos. Although never mentioned by the media or charged, it is claimed that several wives and girlfriends of club members also took part.[5]

The fight led to seven fatalities, comprising six motorcycle club members and a bystander. There were also 28 wounded.

Firearms used in the fight were mostly shotguns, with reports of one rifle and a pistol also involved. All were apparently legally owned. No semi-automatic rifles were used.

The incident led to changes in the law in NSW, with the introduction of a "good reason" for issuing a firearms licence and provisions allowing the police to refuse a licence to those convicted of violent or drug crimes.

The second public shooting occurred in Melbourne in 1987, and is known as the Hoddle Street massacre.

Seven people were killed and 17 wounded by 19 year old Julian Knight, a former army officer cadet. He initially used

---

[5]   https://en.wikipedia.org/wiki/Milperra_massacre

a .22 rifle, wounding a number of people, before switching to a shotgun and a Chinese copy of the M14 rifle in .308 calibre.

Chased by the police and realising he had lost his 'suicide' bullet, Knight surrendered and was arrested. He is serving an indefinite prison term.

Knight was on bail for stabbing a fellow officer cadet, had financial difficulties and had been rejected by his girlfriend and drifted apart from friends. He was heavily intoxicated at the time of the shooting.[6]

The third public shooting was also in Melbourne, later in 1987, and is known as the Queen Street massacre. There were nine fatalities, including the perpetrator, Frank Vitkovic, plus five wounded.

The shooting ended when a male office worker, Donald McElroy (who had been shot once) and Tony Gioia tackled Vitkovic, while Frank Carmody, who had been shot several times, wrestled the rifle from him. Vitkovic climbed through an open window, apparently trying to escape, but Gioia held him by the ankles. Vitkovic kicked free and fell to his death on the pavement below.

A search of Vitkovic's room after the killings revealed that Vitkovic kept press clippings of the Hoddle Street massacre, with extracts underlined in red. His rampage had been planned well in advance, obtaining a shooter's licence and buying the gun a few weeks before the shooting.

The gun used was a sawn-off .30 M1 carbine which, because of the modification, was no longer capable of semi-automatic operation. It had to be cocked between each shot, the same as a bolt action.

---

[6] https://en.wikipedia.org/wiki/Hoddle_Street_massacre

The contents of Vitkovic's diary were read to the inquest. The diary included apologies to his family for his planned actions and a suicide note. Among his comments to his sister he wrote "It's time for me to die. Life is just not worth living." The final diary entry, written on the day of the shooting, read "Today I must do it, there is no other way out."

Forensic psychologist Dr Alan Bartholomew told the inquest that Vitkovic would have been eligible at the time to be certified insane under the Mental Health Act. After studying Vitkovic's diaries, Bartholomew concluded he was a paranoid schizophrenic and criminally insane at the time of the shooting.[7]

The fourth shooting occurred in 1991 in Strathfield, a suburb of Sydney, with eight dead in total and six wounded. One death and one wounding were caused by stabbing with a knife, while six people were shot with a semi-automatic Chinese SKS rifle in 7.62x39 calibre. With the police closing in the perpetrator, Wade Frankum, then killed himself with a single shot to the head.[8]

Frankum had a firearms licence and the rifle was legally owned. He was seeing a psychologist for depression but had no criminal convictions.

The Port Arthur massacre occurred at Port Arthur, south of Hobart, Tasmania, on 28 April 1996. There were 35 people killed and 23 wounded.

The confessed perpetrator was Martin Bryant. At the time, Bryant was 28 years old. He was intellectually disabled, with a history of erratic behaviour. He left school early and later received a disability pension following a psychiatric evaluation.[9]

---

[7] https://en.wikipedia.org/wiki/Queen_Street_massacre
[8] https://en.wikipedia.org/wiki/Strathfield_massacre
[9] https://www.britannica.com/event/Port-Arthur-Massacre

Bryant initially pleaded not guilty to the 35 murders and did not provide a confession. He claimed that the guns found by police were not his, although he admitted to owning the shotgun that was found with his passport in his own car.

However, after weeks in solitary confinement and with a new court-appointed lawyer (due to the fact that his entire estate had been seized by the Tasmanian government so he could not afford a lawyer), he changed his plea to guilty for a court hearing on 19 November 1996. The judge then ordered that all evidence in the case be sealed.[10]

Bryant was sentenced to 35 terms of life imprisonment for each count of murder and 25 years for other offences (20 attempted murders, three counts of infliction of grievous bodily harm, the infliction of wounds upon a further eight persons, four counts of aggravated assault and one count of unlawfully setting fire to property). All sentences are being served concurrently in Hobart's Risdon Prison where he remains in solitary confinement and is not permitted any visitors other than his immediate family.

His prison papers indicate that he is never to be released, and he continues to serve his term without the possibility of parole. This is very rare in Australia, where the majority of murder sentences allow for parole after a long prison term.

Despite much written about it, there are aspects of the Port Arthur massacre that remain troubling. This is compounded by the fact that a full public inquiry has never occurred. An inquest was commenced but suspended once Bryant had been charged. The coroner explained that the law prevented him from making a finding that was different to a ruling of the court.

This would not prevent a subsequent inquiry. Moreover, it does not explain why the evidence presented to the court

---

[10]   https://en.wikipedia.org/wiki/Port_Arthur_massacre_(Australia)

in Bryant's trial remains sealed, or why nobody is allowed access to Bryant, something that does not apply to other murderers. This has led to assertions that the official version of events cannot be relied upon, with the development of alternative theories including conspiracies.[11]

A conspiracy requires not only coordination and planning, but also the ability to maintain confidentiality on an indefinite basis. That makes it unlikely, even before considering whether there may be plausible explanations for many of the uncertainties.[12]

Nonetheless, like the Hilton bombing and Whisky Au Go Go arson case, an inquiry would potentially resolve a number of obvious difficulties with the official version and ensure the full story is finally told. Here are just a few of them.

1. Was the police response appropriate? Could earlier police intervention have saved lives?

    This is not a trivial point - it was only through an inquiry that it was shown the police were responsible for the death of one of the two victims in the Lindt Cafe siege. Controversy continues over whether they should have acted earlier.

    Just before the Port Arthur shootings, the only two police officers in the region were called to investigate a report of a heroin stash which turned out to be soap powder, taking them too far away to be of any use at saving lives. At the very least, they would have been able to block access into and out of the area if they had remained in the area.

    Who was responsible for this false report? Was it a decoy, to lure police away, or was its timing simply coincidental? Was the soap powder analysed and its container checked

---

[11] For example: *The 2nd Empty Chair: The Port Arthur Paradox* by Oskar Zimmerman ISBN-13: 978-1983147142.
[12] https://skeptoid.com/episodes/4253

for fingerprints? If so, where are the reports?

Who ordered the responding armed police to stop at Tarana, where they had a barbeque? Who ordered the police who arrived by boats and were quite close to the main crime scene to hold back and not enter? Why?

A Tasmania Police officer, Sergeant Gerard Dutton, is said to have told an audience in America: "There is no evidence to link Bryant to the [Broad Arrow] cafe." Some say he admitted to the media that there was no forensic evidence to place Martin Bryant at the Broad Arrow Cafe: no fingerprints, no DNA, no blood splatter.

2. Could legally armed and trained citizens have intervened earlier, saving the lives of Nanette, Alannah and Madeline Mikac?

Although many were killed within a short period in the Broad Arrow Cafe, later victims were shot sporadically over a longer period, including the Mikac family. What if there had been an off-duty police officer with a firearm among the crowd? Or a former soldier or skilled civilian sporting shooter?

3. How was Bryant able to kill so many people with such accurate shots to the head?

The Crown Prosecutor, Mr Damian Bugg, told the court at Bryant's trial:

I would put to this court that he was in there for approximately one and a half minutes to, at the outside, two minutes, whilst he was firing his gun. In that time he killed twenty people, attempted to kill four, wounded six, and caused grievous bodily harm to one. He fired twenty-nine shots, very few of them missed a target, and most of them struck targets when fired at either point blank or close range. There is absolutely no doubt as to his intent and his desire to cause maximum carnage.[13]

Point shooting like this is extraordinarily difficult. In specialist military units that teach the technique, it must be regularly practised. While it is true that most of these people were shot at very short range, it is still remarkable accuracy. An inquiry could objectively consider this.

4. Was Martin Bryant the only perpetrator?

    Witnesses vary in their identification of Bryant as the perpetrator. One said he had a freckled face, while another said it was pock-marked or acne spotted. Neither description fits Bryant, who has a very smooth complexion. Jim Laycock had known Martin Bryant for a decade, banning him from the Broad Arrow Cafe for nuisance. His witness statement says that he did not recognise the shooter as Martin Bryant. One witness (Graham Collyer) says it was not Bryant who shot him in the neck.

    The murders in the Broad Arrow Cafe were said to have been committed by a right handed shooter. Martin Bryant is left eye dominant and on the police interview tape can be seen demonstrating firing a rifle from his left shoulder

    Three more shots were fired at Port Arthur at 6:30 pm while Bryant was at Seascape. Who fired those shots?

    Semi-automatic rifles were found at the guesthouse from which Bryant emerged the morning following the massacre which did not belong to him. Where did they come from?

    Shots were fired from the guesthouse while someone, assumed to be Bryant using a false name, was talking to police. Who fired them?

---

[13] https://web.archive.org/web/20010508013225/http://www.shooters-news.addr.com/cttranscript.htm

5. On the morning of the massacre, two hours before the murders, ten of the senior managers of Port Arthur Historic Site were taken to a seminar many miles away.

   Some have suggested it was no coincidence they were out of harm's way at the crucial time. An inquiry would clarify the circumstances that led to them being away from the site at a crucial time.

6. Before the massacre a specially built 22-person mortuary truck was acquired in Hobart. Although it attracted some derision at the time, its value at Port Arthur was obvious. However, after the massacre it was advertised for sale and then converted for another purpose.

   Why was it acquired prior to the massacre and then disposed of after the massacre? An inquiry would establish the facts.

A Royal Commission can be conducted into decades-old sexual abuse by the Catholic Church, the Whiskey Au Go Go inquest can be reopened after 44 years, and the first Lindt Café inquiry can begin six days after the event, but the biggest mass shooting in modern Australian history has not been subject to a single inquiry.

Given that it prompted the most draconian infringement of individual rights in the country's history, a thorough review into the circumstances and whether it can indeed be blamed on lax gun control is thoroughly justified.

The victims' families deserve it; the Australian public deserves it, and over a million firearm owners deserve it.

Finally, it is worth noting that of the five public shootings, only three involved the use of semi-automatic rifles.

4

THE HOWARD GUN LAWS

BACKGROUND

Under the Australian Constitution, any power not assigned to the Commonwealth remains with the States. With no provision in the Constitution that relates to firearms apart from a general responsibility for imports, their regulation falls within the jurisdiction of state governments.

In 1996 following the Port Arthur massacre, Prime Minister John Howard convinced the States to commit to implement major changes to their gun laws, consistent with what became known as the National Firearms Agreement.

The Agreement is a product of political negotiation involving nine jurisdictions – the Commonwealth, six states and two territories. The process was driven by Howard, whose government had been elected in a landslide just a few weeks prior to the massacre.

Although both Howard and the leader of the National Party, Tim Fischer, had mentioned the prospect of reducing the number and availability of firearms in the community in the previous year, gun control had not been an issue during the election and neither the Coalition nor Labor had a policy to radically control firearms. Law-abiding firearm owners had no reason to believe the new government would do anything that would directly affect them. With the exception of imports, the issue was assumed to be one for the states.

What happened at Port Arthur was legally a matter for the Tasmanian government. Nonetheless, driven by his personal antipathy to firearms, Howard resolved to address what he considered to be major deficiencies in Australia's gun laws using the authority of his office.

He knew very little about firearms and his perception of so-called "American gun culture", like that of most Australians, was informed more by movies and the news media than by objective reality. He nonetheless resolved to ensure Australia did not:

> Go down the American path …. Ours is not a gun culture, ours is a culture of peaceful cooperation.

Just eight days after the massacre, on 6 May, a draft national agreement based on proposals prepared following the Hoddle Street and Queen Street massacres was approved by Federal Cabinet. This was then taken to a hastily convened meeting of all the state police ministers on 10 May, where it was endorsed.

The media generated a chorus of support for major change, with public opinion heavily in favour of doing something. Few people had any knowledge of the current laws with regard to firearms, but were nonetheless convinced of the need for change.

Firearm owners, despite having done nothing wrong, were left with few supporters.

The opposition Labor Party and minor parties offered unconditional support for Howard's proposals. Law enforcement agencies voiced approval as did farming organisations. The anti-gun lobby was jubilant.

Deputy Prime Minister and leader of the National Party, Tim Fischer, gave Howard his full support, prompting a backlash within his party from members concerned at both the expected political response and the fact that many were firearm owners themselves. In NSW, state by-elections were held on 25 May at which the Nationals vote declined by almost 14 percent.

A variety of compromises was canvassed but Howard would not budge. Fischer survived and his party reconciled to his position, but it was permanently politically damaged.

Queensland and Western Australia continued to resist the proposal to prohibit semi-automatic firearms. Howard agreed the Commonwealth would fund the 'buyback'. Queensland and Victoria protested the prohibitive cost and dubious benefit of a firearms register, declaring that since criminals did not register their firearms, scarce police resources would be better used elsewhere. Howard cynically threatened to withhold federal funding unless the states complied.

Sporting shooters held rallies around the country, with approximately 70,000 attending a rally in Melbourne. Howard addressed one such rally in Gippsland, eastern Victoria, attended mainly by farmers, where he wore a bulletproof vest which was visible in media photos. Law abiding firearm owners were disgusted and offended.

There were further meetings of police ministers but Howard prevailed. All states passed legislation to translate the National Firearms Agreement into law and the buyback and amnesty commenced nationally in October.

At the subsequent election in 1998 the Howard government's majority was slashed from 45 to 13 seats, in part due to the backlash from shooters.

Two subsequent events prompted changes to the Agreement. In 2002 an international student at Monash University killed two people and wounded five with a pistol. The student's mental state had concerned other students and he was later diagnosed with paranoid delusional disorder, although he had managed to obtain a licence and legally purchase a pistol.

Howard again reacted by insisting on changes to gun laws, declaring he did not like guns and did not believe anyone other than the police, military and security industry should possess them.

The outcome was an amendment to the National Firearms Agreement to make ownership of pistols more difficult, with another Commonwealth funded buyback. Pistols were prohibited in calibres greater than .38 calibre or with short barrels or large capacity magazines. Such pistols were not used in the Monash murders and are no more likely to be used for criminal purposes than any other kind, but that was not considered relevant. It has been claimed that Howard was actually determined to achieve a complete ban on pistols but was thwarted because he could not generate the same level of support he had enjoyed in 1996.

In 2017 there were further changes as the outcome of a review prompted by the 2014 siege in the Lindt Cafe in Sydney in which a mentally ill man advocating Islamic extremist views held customers hostage with a shotgun. A hostage was killed by the perpetrator, Man Monis, another hostage and Monis were killed by police, and three other hostages and a police officer were injured by police gunfire. The police fired 22 shots, of which 13 hit Monis.

The firearm Monis used was an unregistered, sawn-off, pump action shotgun. He did not have a firearms licence.

The National Firearms Agreement was amended to reclassify lever action shotguns to make them harder to obtain, based on the claim that they are 'new technology'. This is nonsense – lever action shotguns have been in use for over a century – and in any case were not relevant to the siege. Nonetheless, all jurisdictions approved the change and as a result, all lever action shotguns require a higher level of 'genuine reason' while those with magazines containing more than five rounds are effectively prohibited.

Despite all that, the Agreement has no formal legal standing and remains a purely voluntary arrangement between the states. It only operates as long as the states choose to abide by it. While that remains the case, the laws in each state differ in minor details only.

The National Firearms Agreement is available online.[14]

---

[14] https://www.dnrme.qld.gov.au/__data/assets/pdf_file/0010/1399510/17-257.pdf

IN PRACTICE

With few exceptions, civilians are not permitted to own semi-automatic rifles (centrefire or rimfire) or shotguns, or pump action shotguns.

Clay target shooters with a medical reason for inability to use a double barrel shotgun may be permitted to own a semi-automatic shotgun but cannot have a spare in case the first one breaks. Furthermore, they are prohibited from loading more than two rounds into the firearm, even if it can accept more.

NSW farmers can own a single semi-automatic rimfire rifle or shotgun for destroying vermin such as rabbits, foxes and pigs, or injured livestock, but are also not permitted to own a spare one. Their employees, family members or contractors cannot own or use these rifles.

Magazine capacity is restricted on everything and there is individual registration of rifles and shotguns (pistols were already registered in all states as were semi-automatic rifles in Victoria and Western Australia).

All firearm owners must be licensed with licences issued subject to a "genuine reason", for which there are ongoing obligations. Participation in sport shooting (rifles, pistols or shotguns) requires membership of an approved club. Firearms collectors must belong to an approved collectors club and attend at least one meeting a year. In NSW, hunters must belong to a hunters club if they do not have written authority to hunt on private land, despite hunting being necessarily a somewhat solitary activity.

When the gun laws were implemented a special tax was introduced via the Medicare levy to fund a confiscation with compensation scheme, inaccurately referred to as a "buy-back" (you can't buy back something that was never yours to start with). The cost was about $700 million plus State costs (in 1997 dollars), with about 700,000 firearms surrendered.

Changes in 2002/03 meant pistols with short barrels (< 120mm for semi-autos, <100mm for revolvers), pistols with calibres greater than .38 inches (9mm) and pistol magazines holding more than 10 rounds were prohibited. A "buy-back" of newly-prohibited pistols, magazines and accessories was implemented.

Target pistol shooters who wanted to leave the sport for a minimum of 10 years were offered a "buy back" of their entire collection including ancillary equipment (such as holsters and reloading equipment).

For target pistol shooters remaining in the sport, additional participation and licensing obligations were imposed. New shooters were subject to probationary licences and limits on initial pistol purchases for a period of 12 months.

The new laws were profoundly coercive. A firearm owner could be liable for 15 years in prison simply by doing nothing. An Australian Rip van Winkle who fell asleep in 1996 with a totally legal semi-automatic rifle and awoke in 1998 owning an unregistered prohibited firearm would be a criminal. An Australian living and working overseas would have had a similar problem.

The shooting sports had to abandon or restructure popular disciplines. Rifle matches were forced to make do with technology developed prior to World War I, because most developments since then have been semi-automatic.

In some disciplines pistol shooters became internationally uncompetitive because of the restrictions on calibres or magazine capacity.

A maze of legal traps was created relating to things such

as having your licence with you, storage and transport of firearms and ammunition, and licence conditions including minimum attendance at club events.

Any police officer can look up the police computer and see who has a firearms licence and legally owns guns. When police come to a firearm owner's house, they typically arrive in pairs. While one comes to the door, the other stands back with a hand near his/her pistol, just in case the owner bursts out the door and sprays them with bullets. They know, before arriving, that the occupant has a firearms licence and owns firearms. They claim it is important to know this, for "operational reasons".

Of course they are far more relaxed when they visit someone who does not have a firearms licence. There are probably hundreds of thousands of Australians who have a gun but no licence, but the police do not know who they are. Thus they assume such people are unlikely to spray them with bullets.

It is very easy to break the law if you are a firearm owner. Many regulations were written to make compliance difficult in the hope it will discourage licence applications. For example, in NSW the safe in which guns are stored at home is subject to inspection at virtually any time. If a single .22 bullet or air pistol pellet is found that is not locked up, the licence may be suspended or revoked. Moreover, while revocation of a licence can be challenged in a court, suspension of a licence cannot be challenged; police have complete discretion.

In Queensland the storage regulations have become so convoluted that the police website has several errors and contradictions.

The police also have significant discretion to declare that anyone is not a 'fit and proper' person to possess firearms or ammunition. Prosecution for a criminal offence, even without conviction, commonly results in licence suspension and seizure of guns. Apprehended violence orders or their equivalent, even when taken out frivolously by neighbours or angry wives and husbands in divorce or custody disputes, always result in the loss of licence and guns.

The sheer bastardry of the gun laws is one reason why law-abiding gun owners never "get over" or even "get used to" the gun laws. They live with the constant reminder of the injustice of being viewed as criminals in waiting.

Illegal gun owners, naturally enough, have no such concerns.

THE NATIONAL FIREARMS AGREEMENT[15]

The National Firearms Agreement adopted a system of classifying firearms which forms the basis for control of ownership and use by the states and territories. The relevant categories are A, B, C, D, G and H.

In practical terms, Category A and B firearms are available to sporting shooters, Category C firearms may only be owned in restricted circumstances, while Category D firearms are effectively unobtainable. Category G is for collections while Category H firearms (pistols) are available subject to specific conditions.

Category A:
Air rifles (including semi-automatics)
Blank-fire firearms at least 75 cm in length
Rimfire rifles (other than semi-automatic)
Shotguns (other than pump-action, semi-automatic or lever-action)

---

[15] https://www.dnrme.qld.gov.au/__data/assets/pdf_file/0010/1399510/17-257.pdf

Break-action shotgun/rimfire rifle combination firearms
Paintball guns

Category B firearms:
Muzzle-loading firearms made after 1 January 1901
Single-shot centrefire rifles
Double barrel centrefire rifles
Repeating centrefire rifles (ie bolt action, pump action and lever action)
Break action shotgun/centrefire rifle combination firearms
Lever action shotguns with a magazine capacity no greater than 5 rounds

Category C
Semi-automatic rimfire rifles (with a magazine capacity no greater than 10 rounds)
Semi-automatic shotguns (with a magazine capacity no greater than 5 rounds)
Pump-action shotguns (with a magazine capacity no greater than 5 rounds)
Primary producers, farm workers (not in NSW), firearm dealers and clay target shooters may own functional Category C firearms, subject to a permit. Collectors may also own them if rendered temporarily inoperable.

Category D
Semi-automatic centrefire rifles
Semi-automatic shotguns with a capacity greater than 5 rounds of ammunition
Pump action shotguns with a capacity greater than 5 rounds of ammunition
Semi-automatic rimfire rifles with a magazine capacity greater than 10 rounds
Lever action shotguns with a magazine capacity greater than 5 rounds

A Category D licence is only available to professional shooters who can prove their principal occupation is the controlling of vertebrate pest animals, or a bona fide firearms collector subject to certain conditions including permanent deactivation of the firearms.

Category H
Handguns (including air pistols), no greater than .38 calibre, including deactivated handguns.
Underwater explosive devices
Magazine capacity is limited to 10 rounds for all handguns. Barrels must be at least 100mm (3.94") long for revolvers, and 120mm (4.72") for semi-automatic pistols unless the pistols are clearly ISSF target pistols.
Permits are available for handguns of up to .45 calibre to be used in certain competitions with approved clubs, at approved ranges. This is currently Single Action Shooting and Metallic Silhouette.
IPSC shooting is approved for 9mm/.38/.357 SIG handguns that meet IPSC rules; larger calibres up to .45 were approved for IPSC shooting in 2014 but this only applies in Victoria so far.

Category R/E
Restricted firearms include military weapons such as machine guns, rocket launchers, fully automatic self loading rifles, flame-throwers and anti-tank guns. These are limited to collectors and must be permanently deactivated.

Category G
This is for collections and is a licence category rather than a firearms category.
Firearms in Categories A, B, C and H held on a Category G licence must be rendered temporarily inoperable.
Firearms in Category D held on a Category G licence

must be rendered permanently inoperable.[16]

Certain antique firearms (generally muzzle loading black powder flintlock firearms manufactured before 1 January 1901) can in some states be legally held without a licence. In other states they are subject to the same requirements as modern firearms.

Single-shot muzzle loading firearms manufactured before 1 January 1901 are considered antique firearms. Four states require licences for antique percussion revolvers and cartridge repeating firearms, but in Queensland and Victoria a person may possess such firearms without a licence so long as the firearm is registered (percussion revolvers require a licence in Victoria).

HISTORY OF GUNS IN AUSTRALIA[17]

Firearms were introduced to Australia with European settlement on 26 January 1788, though other seafarers that visited Australia before settlement also carried firearms. The colony of New South Wales was initially a penal settlement, with the military garrison armed.

Firearms were used for hunting, protection of persons and crops, in crime and fighting crime, and in many military engagements. From the landing of the First Fleet there was conflict with Aborigines over game, access to fenced land, and taking of livestock.

Firearms were used to protect explorers and settlers from Aboriginal attack and a number of punitive raids and massacres of Aboriginals were carried out in a series of local conflicts.

---

[16] https://www.police.nsw.gov.au/__data/assets/pdf_file/0015/133134/GR_TABLE.pdf
[17] Initial draft by Peter Whelan

Australian colonists also used firearms in conflict with bushrangers and armed rebellions such as the 1804 Castle Hill convict rebellion and the 1854 Eureka Stockade.

From the beginning there were attempts to keep firearms out of the wrong hands. The firearms issued to convicts (for hunting meat) and settlers (for hunting and protection) were stolen and misused, resulting in controls.

In January 1796, David Collins wrote that "several attempts had been made to ascertain the number of arms in the possession of individuals, as many were feared to be in the hands of those who committed depredations; the crown recalled between two and three hundred stands of arms, but not 50 stands were accounted for".[18]

Firearms nonetheless remained a key part of our culture. Military rifle clubs were formed from the mid 1800s, highly regarded as a way of bringing communities together and promoting civilian marksmanship programs. These developed into variations of a Volunteer Defence Force, organised initially on a local basis and, after Federation, on a State by State basis in cooperation with the Department of Defence and later the Army.

When the Melbourne Cricket Club was established in 1838 it had shotgun shooting as an affiliated sport. The ANZAC rifle range at Malabar, NSW, was established in the 1850s and is still in operation, as the largest shooting range in the Southern Hemisphere.

Most towns and cities had a gun club and rifle range, as evidenced by street signs such as "Rifle Range Rd" in suburbs and country towns.

Henry Lawson's poem "Every Man should have a Rifle"

---

[18] Christopher Halls, 1974, *Guns in Australia*, Paul Hamlyn Pty Ltd Dee Why NSW.

(1907) expressed the sentiments of the time, that firearms were an important part of civil defence.

Olympic Games featured shooting events from the beginning and, over the years, Australia has had many Olympic shooting champions.

Further evidence of Australia's gun culture is the film "Smiley gets a Gun", a popular 1950s film starring Chips Rafferty as the friendly local policeman and Keith Calvert as "Smiley", the cheeky local rascal. The film showed how normal it was to want a gun or rifle, but also emphasised the close cooperation between local police and kids.

Firearms ownership was also a well accepted means of promoting personal responsibility.

Immigration in the years after the second world war, from European countries such as Italy, Greece and Poland, brought with it a love not only of shooting and hunting, but also of the importance of personal gun ownership for safety and defence of family, community and country.

Regulation of firearms varied from state to state. In New South Wales handguns were effectively banned after World War II, until the 1956 Melbourne Olympic Games sparked a new interest in the sport of pistol shooting and laws were changed to allow the sport to develop.

New South Wales also restricted ownership of firearms "of a military calibre", interpreted to mean the .303 cartridge then in use by the Australian military. This encouraged the conversion of rifles used by the military during the war to other calibres, a process known as sporterisation.

Lee Enfield rifles (particularly SMLE MkIII), the military rifle of the time, were particularly popular for sporterisation in Australia, New Zealand, and South Africa, with many being converted to wildcat calibres such as .303/25 or .303/22.

The .303/22, sometimes known as the .22/303, is a centrefire rifle cartridge based on the .303 case necked down to fire a .224 projectile. It originated in Australia in the 1930s, although similar versions also appeared in Canada around the same time.

The .303/22 had several advantages; the smaller .22 projectile was better suited to small game than the .303, the rifles were cheap and plentiful, and ammunition was neither restricted nor unduly expensive. In addition, sporting shooters at the time found it expedient to cut down their ex-military SMLEs in the interests of reducing weight or improving handling.

Large numbers of military surplus rifles were sporterised in the 1950s and 1960s.

From the 1970s the police in the eight jurisdictions in Australia began to routinely carry firearms while on duty. Before then the norm was for police to carry a baton, with only NSW police carrying firearms. Police firearms were initially carried in an enclosed holster but this was later changed to carrying them exposed.

Although semi-automatic rifles were used by the Americans during WWII, the Australian military persisted with the bolt action Lee Enfield until the adoption of an Australianised version of the FN/FAL, known as the SLR, in the 1960s.

Nonetheless, semi-automatic rifles and shotguns were available to the public. For example, many thousands of the Browning Auto 5 shotgun were imported into Australia. This was the first mass-produced semi-automatic shotgun, designed by John Browning in 1898. This shotgun was produced continually for almost 100 years by several makers, with production only ending in 1998.

A diverse range of semi-automatic rifles was also available. Some, such as the M1 Garand in 30.06 calibre, were too large for hunting in Australia unless for deer or buffaloes. M1 carbines, mostly from the Korean War, were used for hunting pigs. Semi-automatic .22 rifles were hugely popular for hunting rabbits and foxes.

From the 1970s hundreds of thousands of Chinese made semi-automatic rifles in 7.62x39 calibre were imported, particularly the SKS and SKK models. These were relatively inexpensive with ammunition readily available. A wide range of more expensive European and American semi-automatics was also imported.

There were also some semi-automatic rifles produced in Australia. The Australian Automatic Arms company, originally located in Smithfield, NSW and later Tasmania, produced high quality rifles and carbines in .223 calibre known as the Leader.[19] The company was closed down at the insistence of the government in the wake of the Howard gun laws.

---

[19] https://en.wikipedia.org/wiki/Leader_Dynamics_Series_T2_MK5

5

GUNS 101

AIR POWERED

Air-powered guns use compressed air or other gas as a source of propulsion.

Air-powered firearms include pistols and rifles (there are no air-powered shotguns). Those used for hunting or target shooting use small metal pellets, mostly in either .17 or .22 calibre. Many are single shot (that is, they are loaded with a single pellet between each shot) although some have a magazine for pellets and there are semi-automatic versions.

The firearms used in Airsoft (which is not permitted in Australia) and Paintball (which is permitted) are also air-powered. Their projectiles are small plastic balls approx 6mm in diameter (Airsoft) or gel balls containing paint (Paintball).

Australia treats air-powered guns the same as other kinds of firearms. This is rare in international terms; many countries do not regulate air-powered firearms at all and almost no other country restricts them as severely.

It is even more uncommon to prohibit Airsoft. Australians wishing to play Airsoft generally travel to New Zealand.

RIMFIRE AND CENTREFIRE

Rimfire refers to the fact that the cartridge is detonated by the firing pin striking the rim of the base of the cartridge, which contains priming compound. This ignites the propellant powder, forcing the projectile (bullet) out of the case.

Rimfire cartridges have a thin case so the firing pin can crush the rim and ignite the primer. This limits them to low pressures. Although rimfire cartridges of .44 calibre up to .56 calibre were once common when black powder was used as a propellant, modern rimfire cartridges use smokeless powder which generates much higher pressures. As a consequence they are mostly limited to .22 calibre (5.5 mm) or smaller, although a few larger calibres remain.

Centrefire refers to the fact that the cartridge is detonated by the firing pin striking a primer located in the centre of the base of the cartridge. This ignites the propellant powder, forcing the projectile out of the case.

A rimfire (.22) and centrefire (.45) case The indentations show where the firing pin struck the base.

Centrefire cartridges are more reliable and safer because the thicker metal cases can withstand rougher handling. The stronger base is also able to withstand higher pressures, giving the projectile greater velocity and energy.[20]

Centrefire cases range up to .50 calibre with many hundreds of lesser sizes, projectiles and powder charges.

Centrefire cartridges come in a wide range of sizes. These are for rifles; pistol centrefire cartridges are mostly smaller.[21]

SHOTGUNS[22]

A shotgun typically fires a number of small spherical lead or steel pellets called shot. However, they can also be used to fire a single solid projectile called a slug.

The pellets from a shotgun spread out after leaving the barrel, with low energy in each one. In a hunting context this makes shotguns useful primarily for hunting small game (rabbits, foxes, ducks, etc) at relatively short range.

---

[20] https://en.wikipedia.org/wiki/Centerfire_ammunition
[21] https://ronspomeroutdoors.com/blog/ideal-hunting-bullet-how-to-choose/_mg_0186/
[22] https://en.wikipedia.org/wiki/Shotgun

Shotguns are also used for target shooting sports such as skeet, trap, and sporting clays. The targets are clay discs, known as clay pigeons. Both skeet and trap competitions are included in the Olympic Games.

Shotguns come in a wide variety of sizes (bores), ranging from 5.5 mm (.22 inch) bore up to 5 cm (2.0 in) bore, and in a range of firearm operating mechanisms including breech loading, single-barrelled, double or combination gun, pump-action, bolt action, straight pull, lever action, revolver and semi-automatic variants.

The most common size by far is known as 12 gauge, which has a bore of 0.729 in (18.5 mm).

Modern shotgun shells from 12-gauge (LHS) to .410-bore (RHS).[23]

SUPPRESSORS (SILENCERS)

A suppressor, also known as a silencer or sound moderator, is a muzzle device that reduces the noise when a gun (firearm or air gun) is discharged. It operates by modulating

---

[23] https://blog.cheaperthandirt.com/understanding-shotgun-shells/

the speed of gas ejection from the muzzle.[24]

A suppressor can be a detachable accessory mounted separately onto the muzzle, or an integral part of the barrel.

A typical suppressor is a metal cylinder with internal sound baffles that slow and cool the escaping propellant gas, dissipating its energy over a longer time and over a larger area, thus reducing the blast intensity and decreasing both the sound volume and recoil generated during shooting.

There is no such thing as a silent firearm. A suppressor will diminish the report of a discharged round, or make its sound unrecognizable, but other sounds remain unchanged. Even subsonic bullets make distinct sounds by their passage through the air and striking targets, and supersonic bullets produce a small sonic boom resulting in a "ballistic crack". Semi-automatic and fully automatic firearms also make distinct noises as their actions cycle, ejecting the fired cartridge case and loading a new round.

Silencers are particularly useful in enclosed spaces where the sound, flash and pressure effects of a firearm discharge are amplified. Such effects may disorient the shooter, affecting situational awareness, concentration and accuracy, and can permanently damage hearing very quickly.

The most important advantage of a suppressor is hearing protection for the shooter and those close by. Many hunters and target shooters have suffered permanent hearing damage due to someone else firing a high-calibre gun too closely without warning.

By reducing noise, recoil and muzzle-blast, it also enables the shooter to follow through calmly on the first shot

---

[24] https://en.wikipedia.org/wiki/Silencer_(firearms)

and fire a further carefully aimed shot without delay if necessary. Wildlife are often confused as to the direction of the source of a well-suppressed shot.

In 2011 the US National Rifle Association began a campaign to increase the civilian use of suppressors for hunting and sport shooting in order to protect the hearing of shooters and bystanders, to counter the perception that silencers are associated with espionage, assassination, crime or military special operations, and to debunk the myth that suppressors are so effective that gunshot sounds can go totally unnoticed, such as by people in the next room of a building.

Improvised suppressors are relatively easy to construct. In 2015, Los Angeles County Sheriff deputies recovered a ZB vz. 26 light machine gun with an automobile oil filter attached. PVC pipes, plastic water bottles and foam-filled pillows are also used.

Suppressors are prohibited in Australia. However, they are legal in New Zealand where their use is regarded as considerate of neighbours and fellow shooters. They are also legal in many other countries and most US states.

CZ 452 bolt-action rimfire rifle with suppressor.[25]

---

[25] https://commons.wikimedia.org/wiki/File:CZ_452_A_silencer_large.jpg

Firearm suppressor disassembled to show blast chamber, baffles, and sections of the outer tube.[26]

A Glock pistol with suppressor, light and red dot sight.

---

[26]   https://commons.wikimedia.org/w/index.php?curid=30690344

FIREARM ACTIONS

Automatic

An automatic gun fires continuously as long as the trigger is pressed and there is ammunition in the magazine or chamber.[27] A semi-automatic firearm fires one round with each individual trigger-pull.

The first automatic firearms were machine guns, developed in the late nineteenth century and used in the First World War. A key development was the use of recoil energy for reloading, adopted in the Maxim machine gun. Others based on this included the famous British Vickers.[28]

Machineguns are large, heavy and designed to be used as support weapons. They are generally used when attached to a mount or fired from the ground on a bipod or tripod.

M60 machinegun 7.62 mm NATO.

---

[27] https://en.wikipedia.org/wiki/Automatic_firearm
[28] https://en.wikipedia.org/wiki/Machine_gun

A submachine gun is a short, hand-held automatic firearm which fires pistol cartridges.[29] Its range is limited and military application declined as selective fire (automatic) rifles were adopted. They nonetheless remain popular for close quarters combat (particularly by special forces) and with law enforcement.

One of the most famous submachine guns is the .45 calibre Thompson, used during the Prohibition era by various organized crime syndicates in the United States. It was also popular for jungle fighting during the Second World War.

Thompson submachine gun.

The Owen Gun is an Australian submachine gun in 9mm Parabellum, designed in 1939 and used by the Australian Army from 1943 until the mid-1960s when it was replaced by the F1 submachine gun.

---

[29] https://en.wikipedia.org/wiki/Submachine_gun

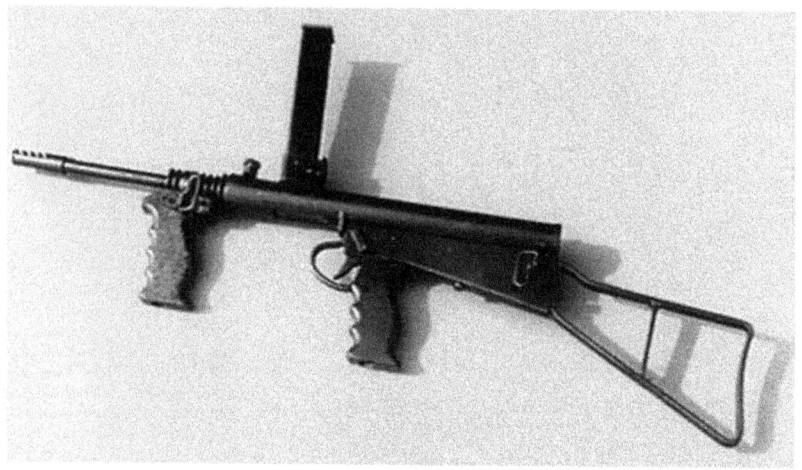

The Owen Gun

Standard service rifles in most modern armies are capable of selective fire, meaning they have a selector switch allowing the user to switch between semi-automatic and full automatic fire. That includes the service rifle issued to Australian troops – the Austrian designed Steyr AUG, designated the F88 Austeyr.

Due to the inherent inaccuracy of fully automatic fire, many such rifles limit the number of rounds fired in a burst. In the US M16/M4 rifles, for example, the burst mode is three rounds. That is, pulling and holding the trigger results in three rounds being fired. The gun will not fire again until the trigger is released and pulled again.

M4 rifle with M68 Close Combat Optic (CCO). [30]

Semi-automatic

A semi-automatic firearm fires one shot each time the trigger is pulled as long as there is ammunition in the magazine or the chamber.

There are semi-automatic pistols, rifles and shotguns. A double-action revolver also requires a trigger pull for each round to be fired but is not considered semi-automatic since the manual action of pulling the trigger advances the cylinder, not the energy of the preceding shot.

As with fully-automatic firearms, accuracy suffers substantially when a semi-automatic is fired rapidly.

Walther P99 semi-automatic pistol in 9mm.

---

[30] https://commons.wikimedia.org/w/index.php?curid=11309070

TriStar Raptor semi-automatic 12g shotgun 28" barrel, 5 round magazine.[31]

Ruger Mini 14 semi-automatic rifle (.223 calibre).[32]

AR-15 rifle with wooden stock. Uses the same ammunition as the Mini 14 above.

Bolt action

Bolt action is a type of action where the movement of cartridges into and out of the firearm's chamber is achieved

---

[31] https://www.sportsmansguide.com/product/index/tristar-raptor-semi-automatic-12-gauge-28-barrel-51-rounds?a=1808981
[32] https://commons.wikimedia.org/w/index.php?curid=78319233

by directly manipulating the bolt via a handle.[33]

When the handle is lifted, the bolt is unlocked from the receiver and pulled back to open the breech, allowing the spent cartridge case to be extracted and ejected, the firing pin within the bolt is cocked (either on opening or closing of the bolt depending on the gun design) and engages the sear, then upon the bolt being pushed back a new cartridge (if available) is loaded into the chamber, and finally the breech is closed tight by the bolt locking against the receiver.

Most bolt-action firearms are rifles, although there are some bolt-action variants of shotguns and a few handguns as well.

From the late 19th century through both World Wars until the 1950s and 1960s, the bolt-action rifle was the standard infantry firearm for most of the world's military forces. They are now only used by the military as sniper rifles.

Bolt action rifles are the choice of many hunters and target shooters due to their inherent accuracy.

Winchester Model 70 bolt action rifle.[34]

---

[33] https://en.wikipedia.org/wiki/Bolt_action
[34] https://commons.wikimedia.org/w/index.php?curid=11407919

A variant of the bolt action is the straight pull. In a straight-pull action, the bolt can be cycled back and forward without rotating the handle, reducing four movements to two. This enables a higher rate of fire.

The straight pull is also potentially more accurate as the bolt's movements are in line with the gun's barrelled action, unlike the turn-bolt designs whose bolt rotations can exert torque that can throw the gun off aim.

Lever action

Lever action uses a lever located around the trigger guard area (often including the trigger guard itself) to load fresh cartridges into the barrel chamber.[35]

The earliest lever action rifles were sold in 1837. By the 1890s, lever-actions had evolved into a form that would last for over a century. Both Marlin and Winchester released new model lever-action rifles in 1894, with the Marlin rifle still in production. The Winchester Model 94 ceased production in 2006.

While lever-action rifles have always been popular for short and medium range hunting in scrub or bushland, they have not been widely accepted by the military. One reason is that it is harder to fire from the prone position with a lever-action rifle than it is with a straight-pull or bolt-action rifle.

Another reason is ammunition. While lever-action rifles generally possess a greater rate of fire than bolt-action rifles, they are normally fed from a tubular magazine. This restricts the type of ammunition that can be safely used and the length of the tubular magazine relative to the length of the barrel above it.

---

[35] https://en.wikipedia.org/wiki/Lever_action

Lever action shotguns have been available for almost as long as lever action rifles. The earliest was the lever-action Winchester Model 1887, designed by John Browning in 1885.

Lever action shotguns are not especially popular relative to semi-automatic or pump action shotguns except in Australia, where semi-automatics and pump action shotguns are prohibited.

A modern reproduction of the Winchester Model 1887 lever-action shotgun.[36]

Pump action

A pump-action or slide-action firearm is one in which the fore end is moved forward and backward in order to eject a spent round of ammunition and chamber a fresh one. After firing, the fore end is slid rearward by hand and the expended cartridge ejected. It is then reloaded by manually moving the fore end to the front.[37]

The pump action is used in both rifles and shotguns. The term pump-action can also be applied to various airsoft guns and air guns, which use a similar mechanism to both load a pellet and compress a spring piston for power, or pneumatic guns where a pump is used to compress the air used for power.

A pump action is much faster than a bolt-action and somewhat faster than a lever-action, as it does not require

---

[36] https://commons.wikimedia.org/w/index.php?curid=16306231
[37] https://en.wikipedia.org/wiki/Pump_action

the trigger hand to be removed from the trigger while reloading.

The first slide (pump) action patent was issued to Alexander Bain of Britain in 1854 and pump action rifles have been commercially available for over a century. Colt manufactured the Colt Lightning Carbine from 1884 to 1904 chambered in .44-40 calibre.

Like most lever-action rifles, most pump-action shotguns and rifles use a fixed tubular magazine. This makes for slow reloading, as the cartridges have to be inserted individually into the magazine.

Like all manual action guns, pump-action guns are inherently more reliable than semi-automatic guns under adverse conditions, such as exposure to dirt, sand or climatic extremes. Thus, until recently, military combat shotguns were almost exclusively pump-action designs.

With shotguns, the pump-action also offers greater flexibility in selection of shotshells, allowing the shooter to mix different types of loads and to use low-power or specialty loads. Semi-automatic shotguns must use some of the energy of each round fired to cycle their actions, meaning that they must be loaded with shells powerful enough to reliably cycle. The pump-action avoids this limitation.

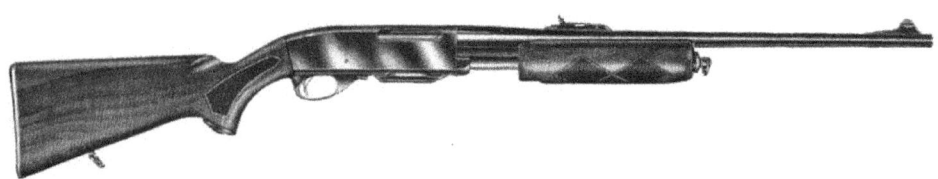

A Remington Model 760 Springfield pump-action rifle in .30-06 calibre.[38]

---

[38] https://commons.wikimedia.org/w/index.php?curid=67973268

Mossberg 590 pump action shotgun in 12g.

Break action

Break action is a type of firearm action in which the barrel or barrels are hinged and rotate perpendicularly to the bore axis to expose the breech and allow loading and unloading of cartridges. A separate operation may be required for the cocking of a hammer to fire the new round.[39]

Break actions are universal in double-barrelled shotguns, double rifles and combination guns, and are also common in single shot rifles, pistols (especially derringers) and shotguns, and can also be found in flare guns, grenade launchers, air guns and some older revolver designs.

While most firearms are designed for right-handed shooters, break action guns operate identically when fired from either shoulder.

Break actions are ideal for interchangeable barrel firearms, such as the popular Thompson/Center Arms Contender, which permit the user to change the calibre of the firearm simply by changing the barrel.

Break action firearms do not have a magazine and must be reloaded manually between each shot (or two shots if double-barrelled).

---

[39] https://en.wikipedia.org/wiki/Break_action

Break action of a double-barrelled shotgun with the action open and extractor visible. The opening lever and safety catch can also be seen.[40]

Falling block

A falling-block action (also known as a sliding-block or dropping-block action) is a single-shot firearm action in which a solid metal breechblock slides vertically in grooves cut into the breech, actuated by a lever.[41]

It is a very strong action; when the breech is closed, the receiver essentially becomes a single piece of steel (as opposed to other actions which rely on lugs to lock the

---

[40] https://commons.wikimedia.org/w/index.php?curid=3162586
[41] https://en.wikipedia.org/wiki/Falling-block_action

breech). This type of action is used in heavy artillery as well as small arms.

Falling-block action military rifles were common in the 19th century. They were replaced for military use by the faster bolt-action rifles, most of which are reloaded from a magazine holding several cartridges.

Falling-block action rifles are still manufactured and used for hunting and target shooting. Like break action firearms, they are slow to reload.

Ruger No. 1 single-shot falling-block rifle in .243 Winchester with custom barrel with action open.[42]

---

[42] https://commons.wikimedia.org/w/index.php?curid=2717765

THE AUSTRALIAN FIREARMS CATEGORIES

Category A

Air rifles

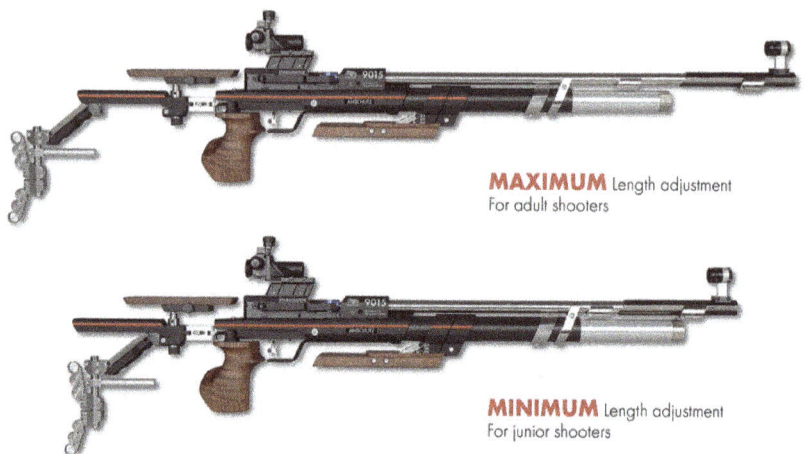

Anschutz air rifles for high level competition.[43]

A collection of air rifles fitted with telescopic sights.[44]

---

[43] http://jga.anschuetz-sport.com/index.php5?menu=325&sprache=1&newsID=980&newsAlle=1

[44] https://commons.wikimedia.org/w/index.php?curid=82098452

Rimfire rifles

.22 bolt-action rifles: 1922 Springfield2. Winchester M52 Sporter3. Kimber M824. Remington 541-T5. Ruger American Rimfire6. Kleinguenther K-227. Remington M5048. Ruger 77/22s.[45]

Remington Fieldmaster pump action .22 rifle.

Henry lever action .22 rifles.[46]

---

[45] https://content.osgnetworks.tv/shootingtimes/content/photos/22-Bolt-Action-Beauties-1.jpg
[46] https://www.henryusa.com/rifles/henry-small-game-carbine-rifle/

Shotguns

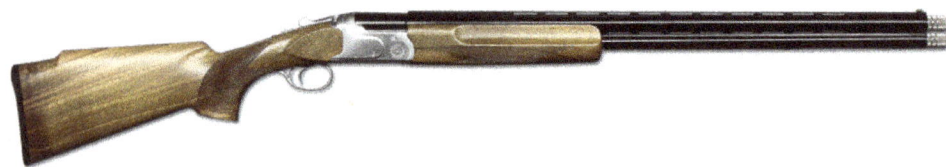

CZ Redhead Target 12g break action under/over double barrel shotgun.[47]

Category B
Lever action shotguns

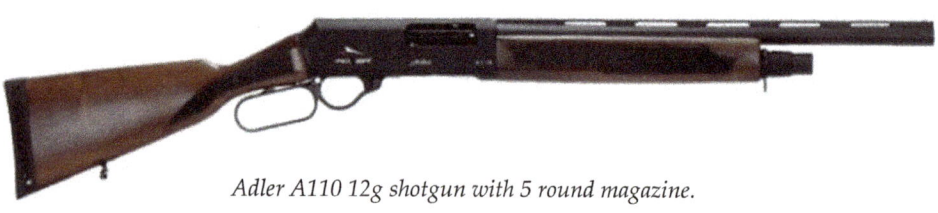

Adler A110 12g shotgun with 5 round magazine.
The 7 round version (Cat D) has a longer magazine under the barrel.

Bolt action centrefire rifles

Short Magazine Lee Enfield Mk I (1903) .303.[48]

---

[47] https://cdn.cz-usa.com/hammer/wp-content/uploads/2014/04/cz-usa-redhead-target.png
[48] https://commons.wikimedia.org/w/index.php?curid=17812143

Steyr Tactical Elite .223.

Winchester Model 70 Featherweight .223.

Lever action centrefire rifles

Henry lever-action .30-30 rifles.[49]

Pump action rifles

Remington 7600 pump action rifle (centrefire).

---

[49] https://www.henryusa.com/rifles/the-henry-3030/

GUN CONTROL

Category C

Ruger 10/22 .22 semi-auto.

12g pump action shotgun.

Shotguns 12g semi-auto.

Category D
Semi-automatic rifles

Ruger Mini 14 .223 semi-auto.

From top: Colt AR-15; US M1 Garand; Ljungmann AG-m42b.

Norinco SKK 7.62x39 with no magazine (top), 5 rd and 30 rd magazines.

Category H: Pistols/Handguns

Benelli Kite pneumatic compressed air pistol, as used in 10 metre air pistol ISSF shooting events.[50]

Daisy BB Pistol with CO2 cartridges and BBs. The cover on the grip is removed to show the CO2 powerlet in the handle. The groove along the barrel is the magazine, which holds 15 BBs.[51]

---

[50] https://commons.wikimedia.org/w/index.php?curid=13494178
[51] https://commons.wikimedia.org/w/index.php?curid=3172653

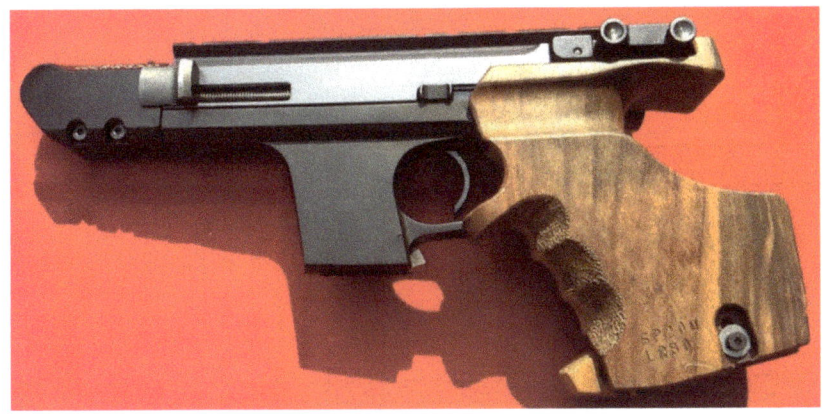

Hammerli SP20 target pistol .22 calibre.

Smith and Wesson Model 686 in .38 Special/.357 Magnum.

Glock G19 9mm.

Prohibited

AK-47 assault rifle 7.62x39 calibre.[52]

M16 assault rifle 5.56mm NATO (.223) calibre
Current rifle of numerous military forces.

SA80 assault rifle 5.56mm NATO (.223) calibre
Current rifle of British army.

---

[52] https://commons.wikimedia.org/w/index.php?curid=17048180

Steyr Aug A1 5.56mm NATO (.223) calibre[53]
F88 Austeyr version currently used by Australian army.

Heckler and Koch G3 in 7.62×51mm NATO (.308)[54]
Used by the armed forces of over 40 countries.

Belgian FN FAL in 7.62x51mm NATO (.308)[55]
Used by more than 90 countries including Australia.

SIG SG 550 in 5.56 NATO (.223)[56]
Used by the Swiss military.

---

[53] https://commons.wikimedia.org/w/index.php?curid=1079723
[54] https://commons.wikimedia.org/w/index.php?curid=78136714
[55] https://commons.wikimedia.org/w/index.php?curid=32207441
[56] https://commons.wikimedia.org/w/index.php?curid=257111

6

HOW TO LEGALLY OWN A GUN IN AUSTRALIA

The following information is mostly based on NSW. However, the process of obtaining a firearms licence and acquiring a firearm, plus the rules determining the types of firearms and the conditions for retaining the licence, are essentially the same in all States and Territories.

1. OBTAIN A LICENCE

Anyone seeking to possess and use a firearm must be authorised by way of a licence or permit. Apart from the military and police, it is an offence to possess or use a firearm without such authorisation.

To obtain a licence or permit, an applicant must be at least 18 years old. Juniors cannot obtain a licence but those 12 and above may be issued a permit to use firearms under the direct supervision of an adult.

To qualify for a licence or permit, a genuine reason is required. Licence or permit holders are only authorised to possess and use the category of firearm for which the licence has been issued, and the firearm may only be used for the purpose established as being the genuine reason.

Genuine reasons are:

Sport/recreation/hobby

>Target shooting
>Recreational hunting / vermin control
>Firearms collection

Occupational

>Primary production
>Vertebrate pest animal control
>Business or employment
>Rural occupation
>Animal welfare

An application for a licence must be supported by evidence of the genuine reason. For target shooters and collectors, this means proof of membership of an appropriate club. For hunters, evidence may be either proof of membership of a hunting club or proof of access to a rural property of sufficient size.

For target shooting, the club must be authorised to conduct competitions or activities involving the type of firearm authorised by the category of licence for which an application is made. For example, if the club is approved for target shooting activities using category A and B firearms, then membership of this club would only support an application for an A and B category firearms licence.

Those who have never previously held a licence are required to complete a firearms safety training course and provide confirmation of successful completion. There are separate courses for pistols and long arms, with the safety training program for pistol licences run by clubs over a six to twelve-month period.

Those who have previously held a firearms licence, either in

NSW or interstate for the same category of licence for which they are applying, may not need to complete the course again. A firearms licence can be issued for 1 or 5 years and there may be fee exemptions or concessions for primary producers and pensioners in some states.

For each occupational category, relevant evidence must be provided.

2. OBTAIN A PERMIT

A firearms licensee must obtain a permit for each firearm owned. A permit to acquire a firearm will only be approved within the category covered by the licence.

All firearms are registered (including air rifles and air pistols) and firearm transactions must occur via a licensed firearms dealer.

3. STORE AND TRANSPORT THE FIREARMS LEGALLY

Anyone who possesses a firearm must take all reasonable precautions to ensure that it is kept safe, not lost or stolen, and does not come into the possession of an unauthorised person.

There are rules for the safekeeping and storage of firearms. For example, storage cupboards and safes must meet certain standards, and bolts and ammunition must be stored separately. Pistols require a more robust safe than rifles and shotguns.

A monitored alarm may be required if there are more than a certain number of firearms (eg 15 or so pistols).

Only those with an appropriate licence may have access to

the storage cupboards and safes. This can have significant implications for the non-shooting members of a household in which there is a licensed firearm owner.

The police can and do inspect firearms and storage facilities, sometimes by arrangement but also without notice.

The rules for transport of firearms vary according to their category.

Category C and D firearms (semi-automatic rifles and shotguns) and category H firearms (pistols) must be conveyed unloaded with the ammunition kept in a separate locked container. They must be rendered temporarily incapable of being fired (eg by removal of the bolt/firing mechanism or the use of trigger locks) or kept in a locked container that is properly secured to or is within the vehicle.

Category A & B firearms (ie non semi-automatic rifles and shotguns) must also be carried unloaded and the firearm not visible from outside the vehicle. Ammunition must be carried in a separate container.

Firearms must not be left unattended in a motor vehicle unless in accordance with the requirements of category C, D & H firearms and no other alternative safe storage is available.

Some people are exempt from the requirements for the transportation of firearms if there is a reasonable likelihood that the firearm will be required to kill vermin or stock. This includes primary producers or employees of primary producers, and certain public servants.

Those involved in commercial transportation of firearms must ensure transport is concealed in a locked container which is secured to the vehicle or in a locked compartment within the vehicle, and that all reasonable precautions have been taken to ensure that firearms are not lost or stolen whilst in transit.

Reasonable precautions to prevent loss or theft includes the security of the vehicle in general; security of the vehicle when left unattended; how long the vehicle is left unattended; the length of time the firearms were in transit; and whether arrangements are made to expedite the delivery of firearms over the other items being transported.

Leaving the firearms unattended overnight or for extended periods of time without added security or locking the vehicle in a secure compound would not be considered to be reasonable precautions to prevent loss or theft.

4. MEET PARTICIPATION OBLIGATIONS

Firearms licence holders are required to comply with a range of general obligations as well as specific obligations applicable to each licence category and genuine reason.

Most firearms licence categories entail annual attendance obligations to demonstrate that the licensee is maintaining the genuine reason.

Those who own pistols are required to shoot pistol matches a minimum of six times a year. They must also shoot at least four matches for each type of pistol - air, rimfire and centrefire.

Those who nominate rifle or shotgun target shooting must shoot a relevant match at least four times a year.

Those who nominate collecting must attend a relevant collectors' club meeting at least once a year.

Those who nominate hunting must either attend two hunting club meetings a year or participate in two club authorised hunting or range safety events. However, this does not apply to those whose genuine reason is based on access to rural property.

5. **AVOID CONFLICT**[57]

A criminal history may prevent a person from obtaining a firearms licence or permit in NSW or from having their existing licence or permit re-issued. A firearms licence or permit will be refused if

1. The applicant is not considered to be fit and proper to possess firearms without danger to public safety or the peace.
2. Has not completed the required firearms safety training course.
3. Does not have a genuine reason/legitimate reason for obtaining the licence or permit.
4. Is subject to an Apprehended Violence Order (AVO) or an Interim Apprehended Violence Order, or has been subject to an AVO within the last 10 years.
5. Is subject to a good behaviour bond for a prescribed offence.
6. Is subject to a firearms or weapons prohibition order.
7. Is a registrable person or corresponding registrable person under the Child Protection (Offenders Registration) Act 2000.
8. Has been convicted within the last 10 years of an offence prescribed by the regulations.

---

[57] https://www.police.nsw.gov.au/online_services/firearms/licences/suspension_refusal_revocation_of_a_licence_or_permit/frequently_asked_questions_-_suspension_refusal_and_revocation#Hed1

The prescribed offences include those:

1. Relating to firearms or weapons
2. Relating to prohibited drugs/plants
3. Relating to prescribed restricted substances
4. Involving violence, public order, riot, affray
5. Involving assaults against law enforcement officers
6. Of a sexual nature
7. Involving fraud, dishonesty or stealing
8. Involving robbery
9. Relating to terrorism
10. Involving organised criminal groups and recruitment.

An existing firearms licence or permit must be suspended if a person is charged with a domestic violence offence or there is reasonable cause to believe that the licensee has committed or has threatened to commit a domestic violence offence.

A firearms licence or prohibited weapon permit is automatically suspended if the licence or permit holder becomes subject to an Interim Apprehended Violence Order.

Once a licence or permit has been suspended the person must not possess or use firearms unless the term of the suspension has expired or the suspension has been lifted by the Firearms Registry.

Police may seize any firearms in possession of a person who has been served with a suspension notice and also seize the licence or permit. Licensees are also obliged to surrender any firearm and the licence/permit upon suspension.

7

DID THE HOWARD GUN LAWS WORK?

Australians frequently congratulate themselves on having implemented "tough gun laws". Indeed, it is common to hear criticism of other countries for failing to learn from our experience and to be genuinely mystified that they have not followed Australia's example.

Whether the gun laws achieved any worthwhile purpose should be a matter of facts rather than feelings. It is not sufficient to argue the laws feel right, or that they have the support of a majority of the population.

Given the gun laws were adopted in response to a mass shooting, one measure of success would be whether mass shootings still occurred. If mass shootings were present prior to implementation of the gun laws but did not occur subsequently, this might be viewed as a success.

Perhaps a better measure is whether the overall rate of firearms deaths changed. If mass shootings declined but overall gun deaths did not, it could hardly be argued that this was a useful change.

Even then, a decline in the rates of murders and suicides attributable to firearms would be meaningless if overall rates of murders remained unchanged or increased. Whether a murder is committed with a firearm or another method, the outcome is the same. Thus the only true measure of success is the overall rate of violence including murder.

Of course, some claim they feel safer if there are fewer guns "in the community" or "on the streets", and that the Howard gun laws contributed to this. Such people never mention the number of guns in the hands of the police and security industry (both of which are obviously in the community and on the streets); their discomfort is limited to guns in the hands of those who do not wear a uniform.

This is emotional nonsense. Moreover, it is profoundly authoritarian to restrict the liberty of a group of people based on feelings. If it was applied more broadly, who knows how many things and people might be prohibited or restricted because it made some people feel safer?

OVERALL FIREARM DEATHS

The best assessment of the impact of the Howard gun laws is its effect on overall deaths (murders and suicides) attributable to firearms. However, murders and suicides should also be considered without regard to the method, to allow for the possibility that just as many people are being killed or taking their own lives, but fewer due to shooting.

Since 1999 there have been a number of published studies of the impact of the Howard gun laws. In 2015 a review of these studies was undertaken by Dr Samara McPhedran, of Griffith University.[58]

Papers for inclusion in the review were identified based

---

[58] S. McPhedran (2016) A systematic review of quantitative evidence about the impacts of Australian legislative reform on firearm homicide. *Aggression and Violent Behavior* 28, 64–72.

on a systematic search of English-language peer-reviewed published articles, plus supplementary searches of the Cochrane Collaboration library and peer-reviewed 'grey literature' (eg, government reports which are subject to peer review but published through government outlets rather than traditional academic outlets).

Papers were required to contain original quantitative data analysis, focus specifically on firearm homicide in Australia, include time series data, and use formal statistical methods to detect legislative impacts/change over time. Five such papers were identified.

All used the same dependent variable (firearm homicide and suicide rates) and the same, publicly available, data source (Australian Bureau of Statistics 'Causes of Death' data, which consists of annual data about all Australian deaths from the Registrar of Births, Deaths and Marriages and the National Coronial Information System).

The review found that NONE of the papers confirmed a statistically significant impact of the legislative intervention on firearm death rates. Nor did any of the values reported in each paper approach the 0.05 level of statistical significance that was adopted across all studies.

Despite the fact that the data came from the same source, there were widely divergent opinions and no consensus on whether the gun laws had an impact on firearm homicides.

The only rational conclusion is that the data does not support the conclusion that the Howard gun laws resulted in a reduction in the overall number of deaths.

Reuter and Mouzos (2003)[59] used data from 1980 to 1999 to

---

[59] Reuter, P., & Mouzos, J. (2003). Australia: A massive buyback of low-risk guns. In J. Ludwig, & P. J. Cook (Eds.), Evaluating gun policy: Effects on crime and violence. Washington, DC: Brookings Institution Press.

conclude that the Australian buyback may have had a modest effect on homicides. They note, however, that the absence of another mass shooting in the five years following the gun laws can be viewed as a slightly more promising outcome.

Chapman et al. (2006)[60] used data from 1979 to 2003 to compare the trends in firearm deaths pre- and post-gun laws. They concluded that, post-gun laws, there were accelerated declines in annual total gun deaths and firearm suicides and a non-significant accelerated decline in firearm homicides.

They also make the point that swings in the data by the year 2003 are so obvious that if one were given the data and asked to guess the date of a major firearm intervention, it would be clear that it happened between 1996 and 1998. However, their claim of a reduction in the post 1997 rate was not supported by their own analysis, which found no significant difference.

They also highlighted the absence of mass shootings during the period without providing data.

Baker and McPhedran (2006)[61], based on a slightly longer time series of data from 1979 to 2004, found that an examination of the long-term trends indicated the only category of sudden death that may have been influenced by the introduction of the gun laws was firearm suicide. Homicide patterns (firearm and non firearm) were not influenced. They therefore concluded that the gun buy-back and restrictive legislative changes had no influence on firearm homicide in Australia.

Baker and McPhedran (2007)[62] critique the conclusions

---

[60] Chapman, S., Alpers, P., Agho, K., & Jones, M. (2006). Australia's 1996 gun law reforms: Faster falls in firearm deaths, firearm suicides, and a decade without mass shootings.*Injury Prevention*, 12, 365–372.

[61] Baker, J. and S. McPhedran. (2006). "Gun Laws and Sudden Death: Did the Australian Firearms Legislation of 1996 Make a Difference?" *British Journal of Criminology*, Advance Access published on October 18, 2006.

[62] Baker, J. and S. McPhedran. (2007). "Review and Critique of Chapman, S., P. Alpers, K. Agho and M. Jones. (2006)." Manuscript.

reached by Chapman et al. (2006) on the basis that the conclusions reached in Chapman et al were contrary to the results of the statistical tests undertaken.

Neill and Leigh (2007)[63] re-analyzed the results of Baker and McPhedran (2006). They found that using either a longer time series or the log of the death rate strengthens the evidence against the claim that the gun laws had no effect on firearm suicides or homicides. In particular, they found a statistically significant reduction in deaths due to both firearm homicides and suicides. This is the only study of the five that reaches such a conclusion based on the data.

Leigh and Neill (2010)[64] undertook detailed econometric modeling looking at individual jurisdictions rather than Australia as an aggregated whole. It uses the shortest amount of pre-1996 data (1990–1995), making it most likely to be affected by short-term fluctuations.

Unlike other papers, it did not focus on impacts of legislative reform as such, but examined associations between numbers of firearms handed in to state authorities during the 1996–1997 'buyback' program (which represented one component of the overall changes) and firearm homicide rates. The study relies on assumptions that the number of firearms surrendered equates proportionally to changes in firearm ownership levels (that is, it is assumed that higher numbers of firearms handed in equals a greater reduction in total levels of ownership in a given jurisdiction).

Testing that assumption necessarily requires knowledge about pre- and post-1996 levels of ownership. However, reliable administrative data concerning pre-1996 firearm ownership levels are not used in the study, with data instead

---

[63] Neill, C. and A. Leigh. (2007). "Weak Tests and Strong Conclusions: A Re-Analysis of Gun Deaths and the Australian Firearms Buyback." Australian National University, Discussion Paper No. 555.
[64] IZA Discussion Paper No. 4995

drawn from point-in-time self-report survey data from the International Crime Victimization Survey, as provided in Reuter and Mouzos (2003) for the years 1989 and 1992 (this may reflect an absence of pre-1996 record keeping by state authorities).

Hence, the analyses lack information about what the raw number of firearms handed in translates to, in terms of actual percentage ownership reduction. Consequently, the study is unable to control for differences between jurisdictions in terms of the percentage reduction in firearm ownership following the legislative changes.

Ozanne-Smith et al (2004)[65] adopts a novel and useful approach - taking advantage of some pre-1996 legislative changes in Victoria in order to use three time periods rather than two as most other studies did, and attempting through this to approximate a case–control approach. However, the lack of detail provided about firearm homicide trends within each of the three time periods poses a significant challenge for interpretation of the results.

While examining a single state rather than Australia as a whole provides more geographically-specific detail than most other studies included in this review, the absence of comparative data from other individual jurisdictions means that any effects that may have been unique to Victoria during its first period of legislative change cannot be reliably identified.

The aggregation of all other Australian jurisdictions into one group provides not only a far greater total number of firearm homicides than that obtained for Victoria (ie very unequal sample sizes), but also draws on assumptions about the homogeneity of each other jurisdiction in regards

---

[65] Ozanne-Smith, J., Ashby, K., Newstead, S., Stathakis, V. Z., & Clapperton, A. (2004). Firearm related deaths: The impact of regulatory reform. *Injury Prevention*, 10, 280–286.

to historical firearm homicide trends. It is therefore open to question whether comparing Victoria with the 'rest of Australia' provides an appropriate comparative approach for examining legislative impacts on firearm homicide.

Lee and Suardi (2010)[66] used the longest time series of all studies (1915 to 2004) and applied a battery of different statistical tests of aggregated Australian firearm homicide trends in an attempt to identify any structural breaks in those trends, rather than presupposing that impacts would occur at any particular time point.

This allowed identification of impacts that may have occurred as a possible result of the gun laws but which may not have been apparent if that point was arbitrarily imposed as a break in the data. This is arguably the most detailed and exhaustive analysis of firearm homicide rates in Australia over time.

Based on an exhaustive series of statistical tests on homicide and suicide data the authors concluded:

> ... there is little evidence to suggest that [the National Firearms Agreement] had any significant effects on firearm homicides and suicides. In addition, there also does not appear to be any substitution effects – that reduced access to firearms may have led those bent on committing homicide or suicide to use alternative methods.

The McPhedran review showed that a relatively small number of studies have examined the impacts of Australia's legislative change on firearm homicide, using time series analyses that lend themselves to good quality policy evaluation. It also showed that, irrespective of the differences in methodology, time periods examined and level of geographical disaggregation, none found evidence for a

---

[66] Lee, W. -S., & Suardi, S. (2010). The Australian firearms buyback and its effect on gun deaths. *Contemporary Economic Policy* 28, 65–79.

statistically significant impact of Australia's 1996 legislative changes on firearm homicide rates.

Notwithstanding suggestions made in popular debate that legislative reforms in Australia have been very effective in reducing firearm misuse, empirical studies do not validate those assertions.

It may be reasonable to suggest that policy changes have been 'effectively achieved', in the sense of implementing changes around regulating firearm ownership, but it is not accurate to equate the process of legislative and policy change with outcomes resulting from that process.

Others have agreed with this conclusion. Based on the paper by Baker and McPhedran, the head of the NSW Bureau of Crime Statistics and Research, Dr Don Weatherburn, said:

> *I too strongly supported the introduction of tougher gun laws after the Port Arthur massacre.*
>
> *The fact is, however, that the introduction of those laws did not result in any acceleration of the downward trend in gun homicide. They may have reduced the risk of mass shootings but we cannot be sure because no one has done the rigorous statistical work required to verify this possibility.*
>
> *It is always unpleasant to acknowledge facts that are inconsistent with your own point of view. But I thought that was what distinguished science from popular prejudice.*

Quite simply, the evidence does not show that the Howard gun laws had any significant impact on firearm homicides and suicides.

MASS SHOOTINGS

According to popular legend Hitler's master of propaganda, Joseph Goebbels, said: "A lie told once is still a lie, but a lie told a thousand times becomes the truth."

The claim that there have been no mass shootings since the introduction of John Howard's 1996 gun laws has probably been repeated far more than 1000 times, which is perhaps why so many view it as the truth. It is not true.

There is no universally accepted definition of either a mass shooting or a massacre. Some argue that a mass murder can be described as a massacre only if undertaken by groups, not individuals, with a political motivation. Some historians claim that describing small-scale mass murders as massacres diminishes the large-scale mass murders that unquestionably fall within the definition.

Yet others insist a massacre is defined by the number of victims. As of November 2017, the US Federal Bureau of Investigation defined a mass shooting as an incident involving "four or more people shot at once."

The United States' Congressional Research Service acknowledges that there is no broadly accepted definition, and defines a "public mass shooting" as one in which four or more people selected indiscriminately, not including the perpetrator, are killed.

According to the US Investigative Assistance for Violent Crimes Act of 2012, a mass shooting is defined as a killing with at least three deaths excluding the perpetrator.

Some of those responsible for the claim that there have been no mass shootings in Australia since 1996 insist there must be at least five victims. Following the 2014 Hunt family murder-suicide in which there were five victims, they then suggested the minimum should be six, or that only public shootings should count.

Since then there has been a murder suicide in WA in 2018, with six victims plus the perpetrator, and a public shooting in Darwin in 2019, with four victims shot at random.

Most of those who believe there have been no mass shootings since 1996 have probably not thought much about it. They have simply been told that mass shootings occurred before the gun laws, but not after. It sounds compelling, as if it ought to be true.

Wikipedia has a list of Australian massacres including shootings.[67] The author is not identified but the list appears to be accurate, at least for the last half century. Those from the beginning of the twentieth century are reproduced on the following pages.

---

[67] Based on https://en.wikipedia.org/wiki/List_of_massacres_in_Australia

Name	Date	Location	Deaths	Non-fatal injuries	Notes
June 2019 Darwin Shooting	June 4 2019	Darwin, NT	4	1	Four people were killed and one person critically injured in a mass shooting carried out with a prohibited pump-action (Cat C) shotgun. The shooter, 45-year-old Benjamin Glenn Hoffman, had been released from prison on parole in January 2019 and was wearing a GPS-tracked electronic monitoring bracelet as a condition of his parole.
Sept 2018 Bedford massacre	Sept 9 2018	Bedford, WA	5	0	Five people were fatally stabbed or bashed in a house in the suburb of Bedford near Perth. The victims were two women, one girl aged 3, and two girls aged 18 months. In April 2019, 25-year-old Anthony Harvey pleaded guilty to murdering his 5 family members.
Ellenbrook murders	July 15 2018	Ellenbrook, WA	3		Stabbing murder of a mother, son and daughter by Teancum Vernon Petersen-Crofts.
Osmington shooting	May 11 2018	Osmington, WA	7	0	A grandfather shot his four grandchildren, his daughter, his wife, and then himself.
2017 Footscray arson attack	March 2017	Footscray, Vic	3		Darren Patrick Glover murdered three people by setting fire to a disused factory in Footscray. He killed his former partner Tanya Burmeister, 32, her boyfriend David Griffiths, 39, and Ms Burmeister's 15-year-old daughter Zoe, who were squatting in the old Kinnears rope factory in March 2017.
Northern Sydney gassing	Oct 17 2016	Davidson, NSW	4		Fernando Manrique used carbon monoxide gas to kill himself, his wife and their two children.

GUN CONTROL

Event	Date	Location	Deaths	Injuries	Description
Cairns child killings	Dec 19 2014	Cairns, Qld	8	1 (self-inflicted by perpetrator)	Stabbing attack and familicide. Eight children aged 18 months to 15 years killed. A thirty-seven-year-old woman was also found injured. The woman, Raina Mersane Ina Thaiday, was later charged with the murder of the children, seven of whom were hers, plus her niece.
Jan 2017 Melbourne car attack	20 Jan 2017	Melbourne, Vic	6	30	Vehicular attack. Dimitrious Gargasoulas drove a Holden Commodore into Bourke St Mall, resulting in the deaths of six people and injuring 30+ others.
2014 Sydney hostage crisis	15 - 16 Dec 2014	Sydney, NSW	3	1	Siege. A lone gunman, Man Haron Monis, held hostage twenty customers and eight employees of the Lindt café at Martin Place for 16 hours. The NSW Police Tactical Operations Unit shot Monis dead, after he executed a hostage. In the exchange, one person was killed by police bullet fragments.
Wedderburn shooting	23 Oct 2014	Wedderburn, Vic	3	0	A mass shooting and siege by Ian Francis Jamieson who shot a husband and wife, after stabbing their son to death.
Hunt family murders	9 Sep 2014	Lockhart, NSW	5	0	A mass shooting and familicide by Geoff Hunt who killed his wife and three children before turning the gun on himself.
Rozelle fire murders	4 Sep 2014	Rozelle, NSW	3	2	Arson murder by Adeel Khan which killed three and injured another two.
Quakers Hill nursing home fire	18 Nov 2011	Sydney, NSW	11		Arson attack by Roger Kingsley Dean, a nurse, which killed 11 people.
2011 Hectorville siege	29 Apr 2011	Hectorville, SA	3	3	Siege attack where Anthony Carbo murdered three people and injured three more including two police officers.
Lin family murders	18 Jul 2009	North Epping, NSW	5	unknown	Blunt instrument attack that killed five members of the Lin family.

DID THE HOWARD GUN LAWS WORK?

Churchill Fire	7 Feb 2009	Churchill, Vic	10	unknown	Arson attack by Brendan Sokaluk that killed ten people, during the Black Saturday bushfires period.
Annerley arson	Feb 2006	Annerley, Qld.	3		Errol Graham Hayes set fire to the Annerley home shared by former lawyer Theresa Marchetti, their son Joshua and her then partner Mark Christensen killing all three.
Winchelsea drowning	4 Sep 2005	Winchelsea, Vic	3		Robert Farquharson deliberately drove his car into a dam drowning his three sons.
Poulson family murders	15 Sep 2003	Wilberforce, NSW	4		Four-year-old Marilyn, one-year-old Sebastian and their grandfather Peter were murdered by Phitack Kongsom, who then killed himself.
Oakhampton Heights Shooting	20 Mar 2005	Hunter Valley, NSW	4		Mass shooting attack and familicide. Sally Winter uses a firearm to kill her husband, two children, and herself.
Singh family murders	22 Apr 2003	Brisbane, Qld	3		Triple homicide of Singh siblings by the eldest sisters boyfriend, Max Sica.
Monash University shooting	21 Oct 2002	Melbourne, Vic	2	5	Mass shooting attack by Huan Yun "Allen" Xiang.
North Ryde, NSW triple murder.	10 Jul 2001	North Ryde, NSW	3		Sef Gonzales killed both parents and sister by bashing, strangling and stabbing.
Childers Palace Backpackers Hostel fire	23 Jun 2000	Childers, Qld	15	unknown	Arson attack by Robert Paul Long, which killed 15 international backpackers.
Wright St Bikie murders	8 Oct 1999	Adelaide, SA	3	2	Hell's Angels feud (mass shooting).
Murder suicide	28 Jun 1997	Richmond, Tas	5		Peter Shoobridge cut the throats of his four daughters whilst they slept then took his own life with a rifle after cutting off one of his hands with an axe.
Port Arthur massacre	28 Apr 1996	Port Arthur, Tas	35	24	A spree shooting by Martin Bryant.

99

Hillcrest murders	25 Jan 1996	Hillcrest, Qld	6	0	Rampage killing by Peter May, who shot dead six members of his family before killing himself.
1993 Cangai siege	Mar 1993	Cangai, NSW	5	0	Leonard Leabeater, Robert Steele and Raymond Bassett went on a nine-day rampage resulting in their taking hostages in a siege in a farmhouse at Hanging Rock Station in Cangai.
Greenough Family Massacre	21 Feb 1993	Greenough, WA	4	0	William Patrick Mitchell (Bill Mitchell) murdered Karen MacKenzie and her three children with an axe at their remote rural property in Greenough, Western Australia.
Central Coast massacre	27 Oct 1992	Terrigal, NSW	6	1	A spree shooting by Malcolm George Baker.
Strathfield massacre	17 Aug 1991	Strathfield, NSW	7	6	A spree shooting/murder – suicide by Wade Frankum.
Surry Hills shootings	30 Aug 1990	Surry Hills, NSW	5	7	A spree shooting by Paul Anthony Evers who killed five people and injured seven with a 12 gauge pump-action shotgun at a public housing precinct in Surry Hills before surrendering to police.
Oenpelli shootings	25 Sep 1988	Oenpelli, NT	5	0	Rampage killing by Dennis Rostron, shooting six members of his family at a remote Arnhem Land outstation in Oenpelli.
Queen Street massacre	8 Dec 1987	Melbourne, Vic	8	5	A spree shooting/murder – suicide by Frank Vitkovic.
Canley Vale Huynh family murders	10 Oct 1987	Canley Vale, NSW	5		Rampage killing by John Tran, who shot dead five members of a family.
Hoddle Street massacre	9 Aug 1987	Clifton Hill, Victoria	7	19	A spree shooting by Julian Knight.
Top End Shootings	Jun 1987	Top End, Northern Territory	5		Spree killing by Joseph Schwab over a five-day period. Shot dead by police.

DID THE HOWARD GUN LAWS WORK?

Event	Date	Location	Killed	Injured	Description
Pymble shooting	23 Jan 1987	Pymble, NSW	4		Richard Maddrell went to the family home of his former girlfriend, shot her and 3 others.
Milperra massacre	2 Sep 1984	Milperra, NSW	7	28	Shootout between two rival motorcycle gangs. One bystander was among those killed in the incident.
Wahroonga murders	1 Jun 1984	Wahroonga, NSW	5	0	Rampage killing by John Brandon, who shot dead five members of his family before killing himself.
Inland Motel murders	18 Aug 1983	Uluru, NT	5	16	Vehicular attack by Douglas Crabbe, who drove a truck into the bar of the Inland Motel after being refused service.
Party Shooting Spree	18 Apr 1982	Canley Heights, NSW	2	8	Peter Sinfield, his brother Derek Sinfield along with friend Adrian John Mills, armed variously but Peter Sinfield with a rifle, gatecrashed a party and fired several shots that killed two people and severely wounded eight others.
Campsie murders	24 Sep 1981	Campsie, NSW	5	0	Rampage killing by Fouad Daoud, who shot dead five members of his family before killing himself.
Sydney Hilton Hotel bombing	13 Feb 1978	Sydney, NSW	5	11	Terrorism, bomb attack on hotel where world leaders were staying. 2 garbage collectors and 1 police officer died.
Whiskey Au Go Go fire	8 Mar 1973	Fortitude Valley, Qld	15	Unknown	Arson attack that killed 15 people and injured many more at a nightclub.
Hope Forest massacre	6 Sep 1971	Hope Forest, SA	10	0	Rampage killing by Clifford Bartholomew, who shot dead ten members of his family.
Boulder & Kalgoorlie bombings	1 Feb 1942	Kalgoorlie-Boulder, WA	14	15	Bombing of a boarding house containing 30 people in Boulder, Western Australia.
Coniston massacre	14 Aug – 18 Oct 1928	Coniston, NT	60–170	Unknown	Probably the last known massacre of Indigenous Australians.

Forrest River massacre	May–Jul 1926	Kimberley Region, WA	11	Unknown	Massacre of Indigenous Australians by law enforcement.
Mowla Bluff massacre	1916	Kimberley, WA	Up to 12	0	Massacre of Indigenous Australians. Aboriginal Men, women and children were rounded up and subsequently shot and their bodies burned.
Battle of Broken Hill	1 Jan 1915	Broken Hill, NSW	4	7	Spree shooting by two Ghans gunmen. Terror attack by modern definition.
Ching family murders	16 Nov 1911	Alligator Creek, Mackay, Qld	6	0	George David Silva murdered six members of the Ching family by shooting and bashing. Silva was hanged at Boggo Road Gaol in Brisbane on 10 June 1912.

There have also been several attacks causing many injuries but few deaths. These include:

- Sydney Yugoslav General Trade and Tourist Agency bombing in 1972: 16 people were wounded by a bomb planted at Yugoslav tourism agencies. Nobody was killed.

- Sydney Hilton Hotel bombing in 1978: a bomb exploded outside the Hilton Hotel in Sydney, injuring 11 people and killing 3.

- Russell Street bombing in 1986: 23 people were wounded when a car bomb ignited outside Police Headquarters. One of the wounded, a female police officer, died later of injuries from the explosion.

- 2007 Melbourne CBD shootings in 2007: a Hell's Angels member shot 3 people, 1 of whom died.

- December 2017 Melbourne car attack: a man drove a car into pedestrians, injuring 18 people (including himself) and killing 1.

The list shows no massacres in the period 1942 to 1971. This obviously ignores deaths attributable to the war, particularly the bombing of Darwin and Broome. However, it is not clear whether there were in fact no other massacres or the data are incomplete.

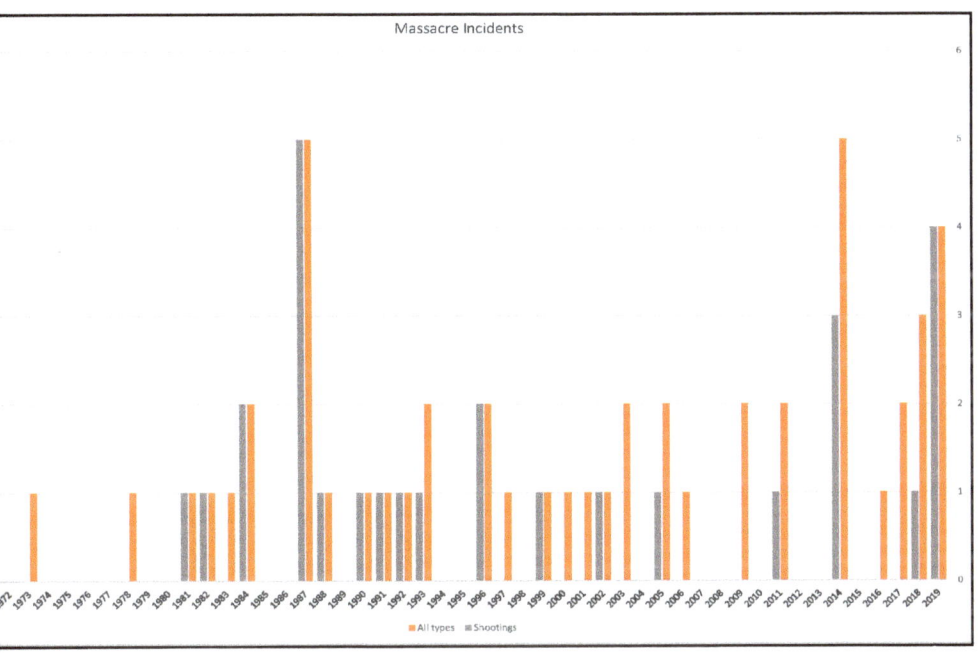

In order to avoid confusion and to facilitate analysis, the period commencing 1971 is used in the following calculations. The graph above shows the number of massacre events, both firearm and non-firearm, over the period 1971 to 2019.

The following graph shows the total number of deaths attributable to massacres, by both firearm and non-firearm methods, in the period 1971 to 2018. Note that the Port Arthur massacre occurred in 1996 and the Howard gun laws were introduced in 1997.

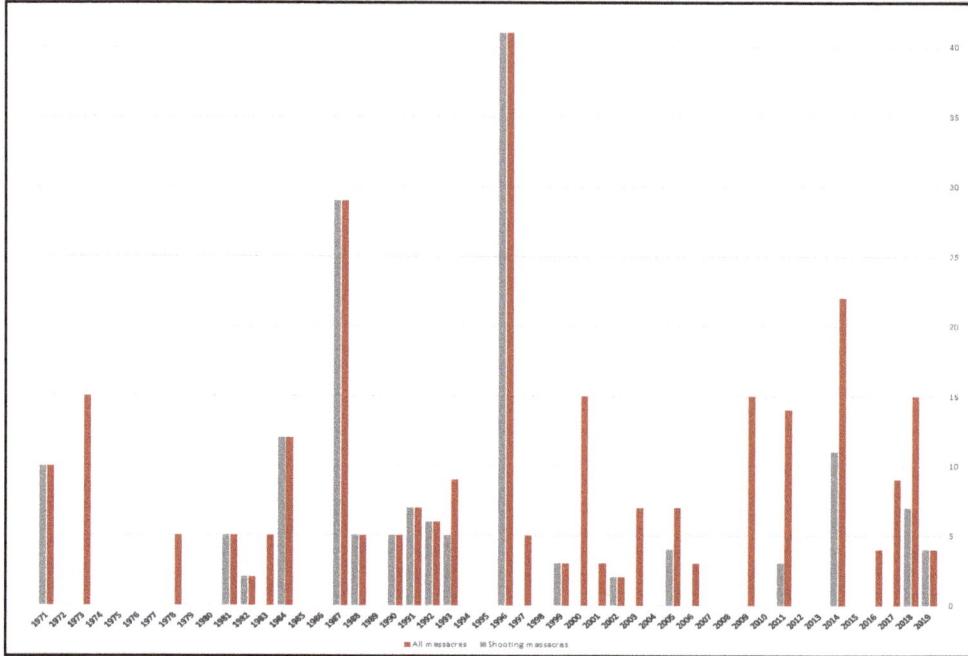

Dividing the period 1971 to 2018 into two periods, pre and post the introduction of the Howard gun laws, enables the following analysis.

	All massacres		Shooting massacres	
	Mean deaths	Mean incidents	Mean deaths	Mean incidents
1971-1996 (24 years)	4.60	0.76	3.44	0.60
1997-2019 (22 years)	5.82	1.32	1.55	0.55

From this it can be seen that, since the gun laws were introduced, there has been a slight reduction in the number of shooting massacres (0.55 versus 0.60 per year) but an increase in the number of massacres of all kinds (1.32 versus 0.76 per year).

It also shows that the mean number of deaths due to shooting massacres has fallen (1.55 versus 3.44 per year), but the mean number of deaths due to all massacres has risen (5.82 versus 4.60).

Thus, while it is technically accurate to claim that both the number of shooting massacres and the number of victims of such massacres have declined (although they continue to occur), the number of massacres of all kinds has increased along with the number of victims.

Whether the victims of massacres and their families would regard death by shooting as materially different to death by burning, stabbing, bludgeoning or any of the other non-firearm methods is obviously doubtful.

It is clear that the gun laws have not saved any lives by preventing massacres.

FEWER GUNS IN THE COMMUNITY

It is common to hear it said that fewer legally owned guns in the community contributes to lower levels of gun violence. There is no evidence for this, and no reason that it ought to be true, but it is nonetheless a popular perception.

As a consequence the media periodically report on the number of registered guns or firearms licensees by postcode or suburb, accompanied by an assumption that a lower number is better. We also see sensational stories about individuals (typically collectors) who own a large number of firearms, as if this is indicative of some kind of risk factor.

There was no logical reason for the number of legally owned firearms to have permanently fallen as a result of the 1996 gun laws. While around 700,000 prohibited firearms were surrendered, their owners received full compensation. Many owners used this money to buy new, legal firearms. This might have caused a temporary drop in legally owned guns as those surrendering several guns initially bought fewer replacements, but eventually they acquired more.

In fact, the number of legally owned guns has been higher than the number owned prior to the introduction of the 1996 gun laws for many years.

There were some people who decided that compliance with the new gun laws was not worth the trouble and decided to get rid of everything. This was a more significant factor in 2002, when the 'buyback' of pistols included an offer to surrender everything including equipment, in exchange for an undertaking not to resume pistol shooting for a period of ten years. However, the number of people who chose that option was insufficient to have had a material impact on the number of guns owned.

The shooting sports and recreational hunting have also continued to attract new participants at a significant rate.

The Australian Criminal Intelligence Commission reports that in the 20 years to 2016 more than 1.16 million firearms were imported under federally administered laws and regulations, although this includes imports by federal and state police and other authorities upgrading their weaponry.

Clearly the increase in legally owned firearms has not been accompanied by a surge in gun violence. There is an obvious reason for this - licensed firearm owners with legally owned firearms are not responsible for gun violence.

FEWER ILLEGAL GUNS

It is widely assumed that because all legally owned firearms have been registered since the introduction of the 1996 gun laws, the number of illegally owned firearms must be minor.

In fact, nobody knows how many illegal firearms there are. Estimates range from a few hundred thousand to several million.

The Australian Criminal Intelligence Commission has estimated there are more than 260,000 unregistered or prohibited firearms (250,000 long arms and 10,000 handguns), including fully automatic and semi-automatic rifles. This estimate is not based on reliable data (obviously rather difficult to obtain) but is an extrapolation based on firearms seizures. The commission acknowledges it is little more than a guess.

The Commission notes:

> *The United Nations Office on Drugs and Crime (UNODC) estimates the global illicit market contains the equivalent of approximately 10 to 20 per cent of the number of firearms in the licit market.1 If this ratio is applied to Australia's illicit firearm market, it would contain somewhere between 300,000 and 600,000 firearms.*

There are several sources of illegal guns. One is smuggled imports, which is thought to be the main means by which criminals acquire them (particularly pistols). Another is theft of locally owned guns. The rate of thefts is actually quite small, although occasionally there are high profile thefts including some from the police.

Yet another is the reactivation of legally imported inactivated guns, specifically pistols. The Australian Crime Intelligence Commission writes in relation to these:

> *A substantial number of handguns entered the illicit firearms pool through regulatory loopholes in the legislation around deactivated firearms, some of which still exist. It is estimated more than 5,000 handguns have entered the illicit market in this way. Issues around deactivation are not limited to a single jurisdiction. The ACIC's FTP has identified a number of previously deactivated firearms that have been reactivated. The most significant loophole relating to deactivation was in Queensland's firearms legislation, which was subsequently changed in 2000.*

Probably the largest pool of illegal firearms is those owned legally prior to 1996 but not surrendered, in defiance of the gun laws. The Australian Crime Intelligence Commission describes this as the "grey market" and discusses it as follows:

> Most grey-market firearms are unlikely to be held for the purpose of committing violent offences; however, these firearms are unlikely to be reported as stolen if theft occurs by criminals. Motivated criminals are more likely to be interested in using unregistered firearms, as they are unlikely to be traceable by law enforcement agencies. Many members of the community still possess grey-market firearms because they did not surrender these during the 1996–97 gun buyback. Many firearm owners chose at that time to maintain possession (albeit illegally) during the implementation of the National Firearms Agreement. The ACIC has received reports of thefts where both registered and unregistered firearms were stolen; to avoid adverse police attention, the victim reported only the theft of the registered firearms. It was during the recovery of the registered firearms that police discovered the existence of the unregistered and unreported stolen firearms.

The Commission has no idea how many firearms are present in the grey market and no means of finding out.

An article published in 1998[68], which sought to calculate the number of firearms never surrendered in the 'buy-back', suggests the Commission's estimate of the number of illegal guns is wildly inaccurate.

Using data on gun imports plus informed sources, it concludes there may be three million illegally owned firearms in Australia. The article is reproduced below, edited for brevity and clarity but with no verification of the data.

---

[68] https://www.foaa.com.au/buy-back-statistics-and-australia-stock-of-firearms-compiled-in-1998/

BUY BACK STATISTICS AND AUSTRALIA STOCK OF FIREARMS COMPILED IN 1998

The best official figures available were from the State of Victoria. Although there were no final figures (and they won't be forthcoming!), the State gave a breakdown up until three weeks before the end of the "buy-back". The State also handed in a third of the firearms in Australia, so it is a pretty good sample to draw from.

Here is what it shows.

Table 1: The Great Australian Gun "Buyback"
by SSAA Research Team December 1997

Automatic	204	0.1%
Semi-auto centrefire	6,216	3.2%
Pump-action shotguns	29,084	15.1%
Semi-auto shotguns	63,012	32.7%
Semi-auto rimfires (Pea Rifle)	91,612	47.5%
Other	2,812	1.5%
Total Prohibited (Vic)	192,940	100.0%

The automatics came primarily from museums and RSL Clubs and were therefore a non-event. However, the "Center-fire self-loading" firearms were the primary target of the buy-back.

The 3.2% are not broken down between military and civilian rifles, but note this: Victoria had registration prior to the "buy-back"; without registration the level of compliance would have been lower.

So what do the figures show us? It shows that almost half of the firearms turned in were lousy .22 pea rifles, a rifle that not one nation in the world issues to its soldiers because of its anaemic power. The figures also show that 47.8% of the firearms surrendered were shotguns, a firearm that Hitler allowed the occupied

French to keep.

".....Whilst the Attorney-General's Department crows about the success of the "buyback", others are not so sure. The Northern Territory News reports that "police remain convinced there could be millions of prohibited firearms still on the streets".

Even the gun prohibitionists acknowledge that the so-called buyback was a failure. Gun Control Australia's John Crook says, "It may be that we have to start this buy-back again because it is estimated there are still approximately 300,000 prohibited weapons to be brought in".[2]

....

As so much of the necessary data is unavailable, it is impossible to conclude that the "buyback" achieved anything other than the collection of 640,381 firearms at a huge and unwarranted cost.

ABS firearm import statistics for 1996-97 indicate that 125,594 of these firearms have been replaced already.

....

Imports

Concerning the import of firearms, the only official statistics available from the Australian Bureau of Statistics (ABS) are for the period 1934 to 1997. The collection classifications have changed every few decades, making analysis difficult.

ABS import records indicate that for the 63-year period from 1934 till June 1997, a total of approximately 5,005,060 firearms made up of 4,569,664 rifles and shotguns and 435,396 handguns were imported into Australia.

The ABS statistics contain gaps, inconsistencies

and likely errors. Also, because of the groupings of classifications that occurred prior to 1958 and during 1985-87, it is not possible to separate the numbers of rifles from shotguns. There are no statistics before 1934, nor are figures concerning Australia's internal production available.

Out of 209 years of European settlement, import statistics are only available for the last 63 years. That leaves 146 years unaccounted for, in the latter part of which semi-automatic and pump action firearms were freely imported. Many of such firearms imported from the late 1880s to 1934 are still serviceable, perhaps adding another two million to the overall tally. There is no way of ever knowing.

Interestingly, records concerning the import of shotguns only commenced in 1958. If 863,700 are on import records in that 40-year period till now, then it is fair to estimate that at least a further 500,000 shotguns would have been imported in the more than seventy years between the 1880s and 1957. Shotguns have routinely been owned in numbers by farmers and rural dwellers.

In addition, consideration must be given to unknown numbers of firearms, especially pistols, brought back to Australia by returned servicemen and women from all conflicts in which Australia has participated in over the last century.

Overseas amnesties and surrender patterns show that because guns do not deteriorate quickly and are stored indoors. It can be assumed that a large proportion of these older arms still exist in firing condition.

Also to be considered is the smuggling of illegal firearms into Australia. Obviously numbers can never be known, but a single shipping container could contain thousands of firearms and it has even recently been alleged that our own Navy has been involved in gun-running.

Roughly a million containers come into Australia on 10,000 vessels annually and according to a news report in 1996, under 3,000 of them, less than one third of one per cent, "are even looked at."[4]

Exports

Some would suggest that our exports have reduced the overall firearm numbers.

Prior to 1966, no export records of firearms were kept. For the 31-year period from 1966 when record keeping commenced, to June 1997, Australia recorded 536,288 firearms exports. Again, classifications are non-specific and details few.

It is recorded, however, that for the 15-year period 1970-85 a total of 186,959 firearms were exported, 42,054 being from internal production, 66,802 being re-exports and 78,103 being unknown military. While a significant number of Australian-manufactured firearms were being exported overseas (an example is Sportco rifles to Great Britain), re-exports of imported firearms do not appear to have had a major impact upon the lowering of overall firearm numbers in Australia.

Local manufacture

Many firearms have been manufactured here. Apart from the military .303 there are also the well known Lithgow .22 bolt-actions.

Some statistics concerning internal production are available. Lithgow's .303 production from 1912-1956 was 640,000. While many .303s were lost in war service, British and allied forces also replaced many rifles which eventually returned to Australia.

280,000 L1A1 SLRs were manufactured by Lithgow; many were sold overseas, some were sold to the public, and many others were either destroyed or placed in storage. 76,000 of the new Austeyr rifles were produced.

Australian-made .22 rifles comprise Slazenger (Lithgow), with 120,000 bolt action single shot rifles and 84,918 bolt action repeating rifles. The production figures for Sportco and Fieldman are unknown.

Centrefire rifles included Lithgow's .303s and SLRs enumerated above, but Slazenger .22 Hornets and Sportco Model 33 .222s and .303 conversions were also produced in unknown numbers; Australian Automatic Arms (AAA) Tasmania, Omark and Small Arms Factory (SAF) had unknown production figures.

All shotguns from Sportco (exported in numbers to Britain and sold by Parker Hale) and Lithgow, this latter being a .410 shotgun on the SMLE action, had unknown totals.

ABS Statistics regarding internal firearm production by private companies are classified as 'Commercial-in-Confidence' and are not available for publication as they may identify the manufacturer. They are unable to be released to anybody, even the government, so accurate figures are impossible to collect.

Some amazing arithmetic is thus required for the Attorney-General's Department's Newspoll figure of only 2.5 million firearms in the country to be correct.

According to the Government's own ABS import statistics, more than five million firearms have been imported from 1934-97. For the Attorney-General's figures to be correct, at least half of these must have gone missing because re-export figures do not account for them. Then there must have been no such thing as any internal production in Australia, no wartime souvenirs by returning soldiers and, of course, no illegal imports.

The Department of Attorney-General Daryl Williams expects us to believe this, even though the entire concept is patently absurd and at odds with the facts.

Guestimates by those who should know

Firearm dealers are understandably reluctant to disclose the actual figures of their own imports. Many figures circulating publicly may not be entirely accurate.

In addition, the collection of customs statistics as forwarded to the ABS may not be accurate. For example, irregularities may occur in the completion of the "Nature 10" Customs Form, used to record gun imports. An incoming case of firearms may be recorded as a unit, rather than as the actual number of individual firearms in that case. The number of firearms recorded as imported may read, for example, as six cases, when in fact each case may contain ten firearms. Thus official statistics regarding the actual numbers of firearms imported into Australia might have been under-reported.

Fuller Firearms in Sydney estimate that 150,000 SKS self-loading centrefire rifles were imported in the late 1980s, along with up to 500,000 ex-US military M1 Carbines and up to a million semi-automatic and pump-action shotguns.

Other reliable sources within the firearms importation industry indicate that at least 350,000 SKS and SKK rifles were imported into Australia up until the early 1990s.

In addition, the sources estimate that during the 1960s and '70s at least 10,000 Stirling and Squibman .22 rifles were imported into Australia annually with a total of at least 300,000 for these two brands of .22 alone. ABS statistics suggest that this view is correct.

Bob Green, President of SSAA Queensland, noted: "There's 400,000 of one model of firearm, a semi-automatic, that have been brought into this State over the past 25 years".[7] Other authorities estimate the number of Ruger 10/22 self-loading .22 rifles imported into Australia since the late 1960s as being in excess of 55,000.

The Coalition for Gun Control's Rebecca Peters also disagrees with the Attorney-General's Department as she believes that there are four million guns in Australia.[8] She also is incorrect.

The Police Ministers were told at the May 10th, 1996 meeting that "No reliable figures of total numbers of firearms in Australia are available. Estimates for all firearms vary from 3.5 million… to over 10 million. Best estimates of the numbers of military-style semi-automatics suggest around 350,000 throughout Australia. Best estimates for other semi-automatic, self-loading (sic) or pump action longarms suggest around 3,000,000."[9]

Even the Attorney-General's Department itself estimated that 3.35 million firearms would become prohibited.

Some of the above estimates may appear high and others low, yet they total in excess of 1.2 million self-loading rifles alone, without even mention of self-loading and pump-action shotguns which greatly outnumber centrefire rifles.

NSW Shooters Party MLC John Tingle estimates the number of banned firearms in Australia at between two and five million.[10]

The Attorney-General's Department listed 334 models of firearms as now prohibited and to be "bought back" by the Government.[11] Some of the listed models were imported in very small numbers, perhaps only hundreds or a few thousand. Others were imported in the tens or even hundreds of thousands. Even if there were only, for example, 10,000 of each model in the country, that alone adds up to 3.34 million now-illegal firearms, which is very close to the Attorney-General's Department's original estimate of 3.35 million.

Clearly many people involved in the firearms industry, and some of them for generations, are fully aware that the Attorney-General's Department's figure of 2.5 million firearms is ridiculous, and we can only wonder what the motivation is for such an under-estimation.

Table 2: Estimated Actual Number of Firearms in Australia – 1997

Considerations	Number	Balance
Opening balance of recorded imports 1934-97	5,005,060	5,005,060
Gaps in recorded import statistics 1934-97	750,000	5,755,060
Other imports prior to 1934 and back to 1895	2,000,000	7,755,060
.303 production balanced against loss & replacement	640,000	8,395,060
Internal production, non-military types only	450,000	8,845,060
Illegal, covert and undeclared imports	200,000 (could be a lot more)	9,045,060
Less total recorded exports 1996-1997	536,288	8,508,772
Less natural attrition by age or loss	1,500,000	7,008,772
Less "Buyback" total	640,381	6,368,391

The estimated number of pre-"buyback" firearms in Australia

is approximately 7 million. The estimated number of post-"buyback" firearms in Australia is approximately 6.4 million.

Note 1: Figures indicate a best estimate. The actual figure is likely to be higher.
Note 2: Figures do not include 76,000 F88 Austeyr rifles in the Australian Defence Forces
Note 3: Figures include 125,594 firearms imported into Australia during the buyback.
Sources: ABS, Firearms Industry, Independent Researchers, Museums & Manufacturers.

Summary

Table Two suggests that, pre-"buyback", it can be estimated that there were about seven million firearms in Australia. It can also be estimated that probably about 40% were prohibited under the Howard-Beazley bi-partisan confiscation. Using the estimated pre-"buyback" figure of seven million firearms, 40% equates to about 2.8 million prohibited firearms of which the "buyback" collected 640,000, or about 23%.

That is hardly a success. If Daryl Williams's advice given to the Police Ministers on May 10th of 3.35 million prohibited firearms is correct, how then can his office claim an 80% compliance rate when, by its original figures, the compliance rate is only 19%?

Again, using the seven-million figure and incorporating the number of new firearms already imported to replace those handed in, post-confiscation there are now probably about 6.4 million firearms of all sorts on this continent, well over twice the figure quoted by the Attorney-General's Department. It is likely that there are still two million now-prohibited firearms in Australia, and this says nothing of those which will doubtless continue to be imported by criminals for their illegal purposes.

The Attorney-General's Department has criticised both pro- and anti-firearm groups for inflating the figures, yet Williams's office is clearly on the weaker ground, having based the new figures on self-reported telephone polls.[13]

The "buyback" has failed utterly in the stated aim of removing all the now-prohibited firearms from the community. It has been rejected by many firearm owners of Australia as unjust and not to be taken seriously. It is bad law, contributing to the undermining of people's already eroded confidence in their elected representatives.

Notes:

1. Attorney-General's Department, Fax to Coordination Group, 26 August, 1997.

2. *Northern Territory News*, Editorial, 'Fewer guns on the streets', 6 October, 1997.

3. *Brisbane Courier Mail*, 'Call to lift secrecy over gun payouts', 9 October, 1997.

4. *Brisbane Courier Mail*, 'Navy under fire over gun running', 9 October, 1997.

5. Channel Nine, "A Current Affair", 26 August, 1996.

6. *Sydney Morning Herald*, 'Gun buy-back blasted as costly failure', 22 August, 1997.

7. *Brisbane Courier Mail*, 'Most illegal guns "not surrendered"', 27 September, 1997, p10.

8. *The Canberra Times*, 'Setting the safety catch', 26 July, 1997.

9. Daryl Williams, Attorney-General and Minister for Justice, Australasian Police Ministers' Council Special Meeting: 'A Proposal For Effective Nationwide Control Of Firearms', 10 May, 1996.

10. Sydney Radio 2UE, 30 September, 1997.

11. *Tasmanian Country*, 'What You Will Get For Your Guns', 2 August, 1996.

12. Attorney-General's Department, 'Thanks to Participants in the Firearms Buyback', 26 August, 1997.
13. *Australian Shooters Journal* ILA Report, 'Too Good to Be True Or Too Absurd to Believe?', November, 1997, p12.
14. *The Courier Mail*, '130,000 guns handed over in Queensland by deadline', 1 October, 1997.
15. *Sydney Sun Herald* 'Gun crime up despite buyback', 26 October, 1997.
16. *Geelong Advertiser*, 'Shooting murders on the rise', 11 September, 1997.
17. ABS Statistics, 1996.
18. ABS Statistics, 19 March, 1997.
19. *The Weekend Australian*, 'Black market threatens guns buyback', 29 September, 1997.
20. *Geelong Advertiser*, 'Shooting murders on the rise', 11 September, 1997.
21. ABS Statistics, 1996.
22. The Royal Australian and New Zealand College of Psychiatrists, Position Statement #25 Firearm Legislation in Australia, October, 1996.

A PERSONAL REFLECTION ON AUSTRALIA'S GUN LAWS

Peter Whelan
Shooters Union NSW Pty. Ltd.

Growing up on a farm in East Gippsland, Victoria, it was natural that I was exposed to firearms from a young age. My father would sometimes take his old Hollis 12 gauge shotgun to a nearby lagoon and bring back a couple of plump wild ducks for my mother to roast.

That Hollis was handed down to him by his father and I can still recall stories of how that old gun had kept their family of seven alive during the Great Depression of the 1930s, not only harvesting wild ducks, but rabbits and an occasional wallaby, all of which were in plentiful supply.

I inherited that Hollis upon my father's death and I still fire it sometimes, as it reminds me of my forebears and their hard life and traditions.

At the age of about 10 or 11 I was given an air rifle and a packet of slugs, with orders from my dad to "Keep those birds off the cherry trees". Many hours were spent after school, plinking birds, to ensure a good harvest and the cherries were free of bird pecks.

My reward was to have first pick of the ripe fruit, before the main harvest. I would pack the early season cherries in small paper bags and sell them at school for one shilling each!

Good lessons, not only in responsible firearms ownership and marksmanship, but also generating income, as a reward for effort.

REGISTRATION BEGINS

The Victorian Government introduced compulsory firearm registration in the early 1980s and all our firearms were dutifully registered. We were assured that this was for "community safety" but there were protests in Melbourne, by farmers, hunters and other sporting shooters, who saw it as an invasion of privacy and an unnecessary bureaucratic intrusion into their lives.

Ted Drane, then President of the SSAA (Sporting Shooters Association of Australia) was often quoted as claiming that "Registration is the first step to confiscation".

Sure enough, in 1996 Prime Minister John Howard forced all States and Territories to make semi-automatic rifles and shotguns and slide (pump) action shotguns illegal. It was incorrectly labelled a "buy back" as the Government had never owned those firearms in the first place. It should have been more correctly named "compulsory acquisition for destruction", with penalties of massive fines or gaol terms for failure to comply.

Yet again, sporting shooters, farmers and their friends and families held anti-government protest rallies in capital cities; the largest protest marches seen since those against the Vietnam war.

Some friends and I joined the march in Sydney, from Hyde Park to Parliament House in Macquarie St. We carried signs which read, "We are not criminals" and "My guns are not the government's property". Some compared John Howard to Adolph Hitler, who had introduced gun control in Germany in the 1930s, depriving the Jewish citizens of any means of defence.

At the time I had been involved in some complex commercial legal issues, involving a barrister. Knowing I was a firearm owner involved in sporting shooting, in addition to having firearms as a farmer, we began discussing the new gun laws. Without much prompting, he boasted that he had "ordered another Bentley" as from his experience and observations, in most countries after "gun bans" were introduced, crime goes up, so the demand for his services would increase!

He was happy to provide me with crime data from countries that had "tough gun laws", like Mexico and Jamaica, which had very high levels of crime. Similarly, certain cities in the USA such as Chicago and Washington had gun bans but very high rates of crime.

His theory was that such an increase in crime may come from two areas. Many otherwise law-abiding citizens may decide to keep their firearms, for a variety of reasons such as family heirlooms, hunting, etc. They would then be arrested for having an "illegal" firearm and so those "criminals" would be pursued through the courts and face heavy financial penalties or prison.

His other theory was that police, whose main purpose was to protect society by apprehending criminals, would be too busy monitoring otherwise law-abiding citizens, for breaches of the firearms laws and regulations, allowing real criminals to be free to go about their business. Police would be going after the easy targets, while organised criminals would be considered too much like hard work.

My barrister friend even compared such "gun bans" to the prohibition era, where alcohol bans fueled a surge in criminal activity, controlling the black market for alcohol. He also explained that Australia's ban on drugs had not stopped the flow or use of drugs; it had simply driven it underground, to be controlled by well-organised crime syndicates.

The "Buy Back"

The "buy back" should never have been called that. The Government never owned those newly-illegal firearms and the owners had never committed any crimes with them. It was a forced hand-over, or confiscation, with extreme penalties for non-compliance.

Since Victoria already had a long-established registration scheme, the government knew who owned which firearms, so the process began fairly quickly. I had to hand over two old semi-automatic .22 rifles which had been used around the farm for years.

However, since I had now moved to NSW, the licensing system there allowed me to obtain a Category C licence as a Primary Producer, so I was able to buy a brand new .22 calibre semi-automatic rifle.

It was the same for many firearms owners; they used the payment for a handed-in firearm to purchase a brand new (often superior) firearm. It became a "cash for clunkers" scheme, in which old guns were replaced with new guns.

Because the Victorian system of registration was already in place, figures from that State were most accurate as to what type of firearms had been handed in. Most were rabbit rifles (.22 calibre) and 12 gauge fox/duck shotguns. There were very few firearms handed in of the type used by Martin Bryant to kill 35 people at Port Arthur!

Sadly, for history buffs, the most notable among those handed in for crushing were the semi-automatic rifles and machine guns which had been safely displayed at RSL clubs and museums.

The Brookings Institution, after studying the data, would later refer to it as a "massive buyback of low-risk guns".

The anti-gun fever which John Howard had whipped up manifested itself in ANZAC memorials, showing statues of soldiers holding rifles, being vandalised in many parts of the country.

One of my relatives had to register a Brno rifle. Soon after the registration process had concluded, he received a visit from members of the Australian Defence Force, grilling him as to how he had possibly been able to obtain and register a Bren gun! In entering the data, someone had mistakenly read Brno (a city in Czech Republic) for a Bren gun, used by the military in several campaigns.

That may be the best example of how a typographical error can create a "dangerous criminal" with an "illegal military style" firearm. Just one of the many "paper" crimes!

In my own case, one of my rifles has a serial number ending in "B" which is the manufacturer's designation for bolt action. However, the registration certificate, issued by NSW Police Firearms Registry shows it as an "8". On several occasions, when I have had an inspection from those highly qualified members of the NSW police force, they have had a good look at the (slightly blurred) number, queried whether it was in fact a B or an 8, mumbled something about "a paperwork mix up" and moved on.

Strictly, in accordance with the law, I had an "illegal, unregistered firearm" because of that "paperwork mix up".

One of my staff decided to hand in a pump action shotgun belonging to his father. It had been custom-made with beautiful walnut stock and fore-end with intricate gold engravings. It was truly a family heirloom. He attended the temporary buyback station, set up at Castle Hill (NSW) three months before the buy-back ended. Because the make and model of this special shotgun did not appear on the standard list of firearms, he did not receive an instant cheque, but instead was given a receipt and told that it would have to be "sent away to be valued".

Several weeks passed and he heard nothing. He was getting worried, so he decided to phone the newly established Firearms Registry. Imagine his shock when he was told that "Oh, we've received hundreds of these sorts of queries. You people must be trying to deceive us, because those receipts don't exist."

From their comments, it seems that police in many parts of NSW had been issuing "false" receipts, claiming that firearms had to be sent away for valuation.

The situation was very distressing for my employee, which prompted him to contact both the NSW Minister for Police (Paul Whelan) and Shooters Party MP John Tingle. Neither could offer any explanation, but it is assumed that hundreds, possibly thousands, of firearms handed in to police, during the buyback, were not crushed but kept by police or on-sold to others.

My employee eventually received a "form" letter from Police Minister Whelan, with a cheque for $10,000.00, which was much more than he had imagined! No explanation was received as to what had happened to the vanishing shotgun.

Later (April 28th 2004) an article in The Daily Telegraph headed "Weapons found on property" described how police had found more than 45 high powered weapons in a container, on a property owned by a former police officer.

Anecdotally, there have been several cases of deceased estate firearms being handed in to police, paid $200, but on-sold for thousands of dollars.

Political Consequences

According to the Constitution, laws relating to firearms are a State matter. In 1996, when the Howard gun laws (National Firearms Agreement) were forced on the States and Territories, all were Liberal (Coalition with Nationals) or Nationals (Qld) apart from NSW (Labor).

John Howard realised there was a lot of opposition to his gun laws (eg Sale Victoria rally where Howard wore a flak jacket) so he said "If people don't agree with these gun laws, they can show their opposition at the ballot box".

So, what happened?

At each subsequent State/Territory election, as each State implemented those gun laws through 1997/98, those Liberal/National governments were voted out.

At the next Federal election in 1998, Howard lost one million votes and the popular vote, barely holding on to government despite the massive win in 1996. At that stage it was estimated that those one million votes equalled the number of gun owners in Australia.

The hatred towards John Howard by gun owners manifested itself during the Sydney 2000 Olympics when he decided to attend the final of the Men's Trap Shooting, where Michael Diamond was a hot favourite to take out the gold medal. I was in attendance that afternoon. Immediately Howard appeared, the crowd spontaneously erupted in loud boos and chants of "get out of here" and "you're not welcome". When I arrived home that evening, I described the scene to my wife, who informed me that she had recorded the whole event so we could watch it together. Imagine my surprise when, as Howard walked into the venue, the only sound that could be heard was the "Olympic Fanfare"!

State by State Elections

Most significant was the election in Victoria in September 1999, where the government led by Jeff Kennett (Liberals) held a comfortable majority. The "belting from the bush" they called it, as Kennett lost power when three Country Independent MPs took seats from the National Party, aligning with Labor to give power to Steve Bracks Labor party. The National Party leader resigned soon after.

In Queensland in 1998, the National Party was defeated after holding government for most of the previous 20 years. The Liberals were wiped out, losing their political party status and later being forced to merge with the Nationals to become LNP (Liberal National Party). One Nation won 11 seats after Pauline Hanson campaigned at shooting clubs and farming groups and wrote a detailed criticism of the gun laws in the SSAA Shooters Journal.

Later, ex-Police Minister Russell Cooper was interviewed by ABC radio and said, "The Nationals should never have agreed with John Howard's gun laws. It wiped the Nationals out in Queensland".

In NSW in 1999, Labor actually increased its majority. The Liberal party fell into disarray and had about a dozen leaders over the next few years until Labor scandals and mismanagement eventually enabled the Liberals to return to power.

As their election cycles came around, Liberal governments in WA and SA also fell to Labor. (The National Party is either not present or not in coalition with the Liberals in these states.)

The Liberal Party continues to stubbornly persist with an anti-gun platform. The National Party maintains an embarrassed silence for much of the time, although it has made clear to the Liberal Party that it will not countenance anything similar in future.

Pro-shooting parties have proliferated, with several parties now represented in parliament that have policies opposed to the status quo on firearms regulation.

Currently (2019) in NSW, the Shooters Fishers and Farmers Party has two members in the Legislative Council (upper house) and three in the Legislative Assembly (lower house).

In Queensland, Katter's Australia Party has three members and One Nation one member in the Legislative Assembly. (Queensland does not have an upper house.)

In Victoria, the pro-freedom (and pro-gun) Liberal Democrats have two members and the Shooters, Fishers and Farmers Party has one member in the Legislative Council.

In WA, the Liberal Democrats have one member, the Shooters, Fishers and Farmers Party has one member and One Nation has three members in the Legislative Council.

In the federal parliament the Liberal Democrats had one member in the Senate for five years (David Leyonhjelm). Currently One Nation has two members in the Senate while Katters Australia Party has one member in the House of Representatives .

Scientific and Educational Corruption

Following the introduction of the Howard gun laws, there were many academic and semi-academic papers written about their impact.

Many of these exposed the poor standard of academic rigour among Australia's universities. A good example was Monash University's Accident Research Bureau. Its "Quackademics" produced a report which "proved" that the gun laws had saved lives. While pointing to the downward trend in gun deaths since 1996, they failed to note many other factors during that time which may have helped reduce those gun deaths. They also minimised the fact that that gun deaths had halved in the 15 years prior to 1996, and that the subsequent downward trend merely maintained that trend.

In any true scientific experiment, so as to eliminate other factors, it is critical that a "control group" is included where such gun control and gun bans had NOT been implemented. Such a "control group" is seen in New Zealand, which has similar social and economic structures to Australia.

New Zealand had a firearms mass murder pre-1996 but did not introduce gun bans and gun crushing, nor long arms registration. It also did not have a single firearm mass murder until 2019. Semi-automatic rifles and shotguns and pump action shotguns are readily available (and popular) among sporting shooters, farmers and hunters, simply by holding a police approved licence. NZ also has a homicide rate lower than Australia's.

Others have similarly used "junk science" to try and prove that Australia's gun laws stopped suicides, referencing the decline in gun suicides. What they failed to mention is that suicides by other methods also declined. Furthermore, none of those studies relating to firearm suicides was able to explain why suicide by gun, which takes just one single shot, had been influenced by the reduction in the number of semi-automatic, rapid-fire rifles and shotguns.

Perhaps those "quack-ademics" can point to exactly how many pre-1996 gun suicides, had been carried out using multiple shots!

In an effort to justify his gun bans, John Howard addressed a Youth Suicide Prevention Conference in Canberra in February 1997, claiming that "...easy access to firearms has made it easier for some people in a desperate state of mind, to take their own lives". (reported in Daily Telegraph 1st March 1997).

He had obviously never heard of "method substitution". In the Daily Telegraph 11th July 2000, it was reported that "Male suicide rate rising" based on a report from James Harrison from the Australian Institute of Health and Welfare, which explained that "hanging and death from motor vehicle exhaust have overtaken firearms as the most used methods of suicide since the early 1990s."

Surely the efforts of suicide prevention groups such as Beyond Blue, Black Dog Institute and Life Line had had some influence on declining suicides? Maybe it was nothing to do with "Tough Gun Laws" after all.

Community Reactions

In the years after the gun laws were introduced, crime actually increased. The Australian Institute of Criminology reported that murder was up 16% in one year, 1998-99. From 2000-2001 to 2001-2002 murder increased a massive 20%.

The Australian Institute of Criminology report no 46 "Facts and Figures" highlighted the fact that serious assaults had increased by 5 times the population increase!

The National Homicide Monitoring Program 2001-2002 Summary even explained that murders may have been much higher if it wasn't for advances in emergency medical care, so that victims of serious assaults were saved who might otherwise have died.

So, with crime increasing, what was community reaction? The headlines in Sydney newspapers and other media at the time summed it up.

The Sunday Telegraph September 2, 2001. "How Ryan failed

to reduce crime" (NSW Police Commissioner Peter Ryan was to resign soon after)

The Bulletin February 4, 2003. "Crook Land. Forget what your local police force tells you: Australia's crime rate is rising and out of step with the rest of the western world."

Sydney Morning Herald October 29-30, 2005. "Gun laws fall short in war on crime. There is no definitive evidence that a decade of restrictive firearms laws has done anything to reduce weapon-related crime, according to NSW's top criminal statistician, Don Weatherburn."

Sydney Morning Herald March 29, 2006. "Australians top the world when it comes to crime"

The Sunday Telegraph May 6th, 2007. "Explosion of gun crime across city" covered the 40 gun-related crimes across Sydney in the previous month.

What resulted was a big increase in police numbers on a "Law and Order" push. The NSW Police Force is now one of the largest in the Western world. Police in NSW (and other states) are now equipped with military style M4 semi-automatic rifles.

Many in the community are now concerned about the "militarisation" of our police, although those same firearms, or variations of them, are readily available to sporting shooters and hunters in New Zealand, Canada and Switzerland, without concern.

Opportunity Cost

The cost to taxpayers of the two buybacks (long arms in 1996/97 and handguns in 2003) has been estimated at around $1 billion (in 2003), comprising direct payments to gun owners plus payouts to firearms dealers.

Further costs of running the Firearms Registries in each State and Territory, including gun registration, safe storage inspections, etc has been estimated at $100 million per annum.

So, what if Australia had done nothing, like New Zealand? Or, if the States and Territories had chosen to shut down their firearms registries, given they have never solved or prevented a crime? Canada shut down its long arms registry in 2012 (April 5th Bill C-19), as it was costing too much and had been shown to have had no effect on gun crime.

What could have been achieved with that $3 billion? (Initial $1 billion plus $100 million p.a. for 20 years)

How many hospital beds and nurses?

How much for mental health and suicide prevention programs?

How many lives saved?

8

GUN CONTROL IN OTHER COUNTRIES

Many people assume Australia's gun laws are typical of most other countries, the only exception being America. That is not the case – while only four countries have a right to bear arms in their constitution, very few have gun control laws as strict as Australia's.

Mexico, Haiti, and Guatemala all provide for the right to carry in their constitutions. Guatemala's Article 38 is the only one as broad as the American Second Amendment (it guarantees "the right of possession of arms for personal use").

Article 10 of the Mexican constitution and Article 268-1 of Haiti's constitution limit the right to the confines of the home and allow the government to pass laws significantly restricting ownership. Mexicans, for example, are supposed to get a permit from the military, renewable every year, and all firearms must be registered. (The law is widely ignored and only 4,300 licenses have been issued for Mexico's 105 million people.) Handguns must be .38 calibre or less, shotguns cannot be greater than 12 gauge, and rifles must be .30 calibre or smaller. Privately owned guns may only be sold to the government. Mexico's murder rate is almost six times that of the United States.

A majority of countries allow the ownership of guns for self-defence in the home. Some, like America, also allow carrying of guns for self-defence outside the home, either on a permission basis or as a right.

This chapter discusses the gun laws of a number of countries of interest.

NEW ZEALAND

CHAZ FORSYTH

New Zealand is a parliamentary democracy in the Westminster tradition, with a single chamber parliament.

Its population is about 4.9 million people with at least 1.5 million legally owned firearms. More than 10,000 firearms are imported annually, of which about half are non-cartridge-firing (ie powered by gas, air or spring).

New Zealand is also a very safe country. In a 1997 study[69] New Zealand was reported to be second only to Finland in numbers of firearms per 1,000 persons, at 308.90. In the same study Canada had 241.48 and Australia 195.90. The study also noted that the observed homicide rate for New Zealand was 0.22 per 100,000 persons; for Australia, 0.56; and Canada, 0.60; while the accidental death rates were 0.29, 0.11 and 0.13 respectively.

New Zealand was first discovered by Polynesian explorers in the 13th century. It was later rediscovered by European

---

[69] Thorp, T.M. (1997) *Review of Firearms Control in New Zealand – Report of an Independent Inquiry Commissioned by the Minister of Police.* Wellington, New Zealand: GP Print.

explorers, which gradually led to casual settlement by itinerants and the establishment of whaling outposts early in the 19th century.

Firearms have been a part of its history since at least the early 19th century. In 1792, sealers from Australia formed communities in Fiordland in the southwest of the South Island, and a trade in timber developed after the seal population was reduced as a result of unsustainable hunting pressure. Other early exports were timber and flax.

This soon led to imports of muskets as their utility as weapons became apparent to Maori tribes in the early 1830s. An arms race developed between tribes with muskets and those without, resulting in the 'musket wars'. By the signing of the Treaty of Waitangi in 1840 these wars were over as all tribes had muskets. One estimate of the total deaths in this fighting was 20,000.[70]

Early New Zealand firearm legislation

New Zealand firearm laws at first strongly reflected those of Britain, controlling who might deal in firearms, who could import them, and general restrictions on their possession.

The first legislation (Arms Importation Ordinance 1845) was primarily enacted to keep firearms out of the hands of 'natives'. This arose in the context of the Land Wars of 1845 to 1872, originally a result of cultural misunderstandings about property ownership but later more about the loyalty of the indigenous people to the Crown.

In the 20th century many governments around the world became uncomfortably aware that millions of men experienced in the use of firearms had returned from the four years of the First World War. There was also alarm

---

[70] Sinclair, K. (2000), *A History of New Zealand*. London, England: Pelican.

at the rising tide of Bolshevism in the immediate post-war period following the 'Russian Revolution'.

Controls on the private ownership of firearms had been enacted in many countries by 1920. The Arms Act (1920) set the scene in New Zealand for the next 63 years, requiring firearm registration, prohibiting the carriage and possession of handguns, and tighter controls on the import and export of all firearms.

Some of these measures were discarded after the police found the workload of full firearm registration proved impossible, but other provisions endured until 1983.

An upsurge in interest in handgun shooting led to revolvers being allowed for competitive pistol shooting, and in 1969 semi-automatic pistols were permitted. Anomalous measures such as the 'permit to retain an unlawful weapon' and 'permit to retain unlawful ammunition' (defined as ammunition for unlawful weapons) were introduced to work around the law.

All handguns were registered, with the New Zealand Pistol Association (now Pistol New Zealand) negotiating modifications to allow licensed owners to store and transport them to and from approved ranges.

The firearm registration system was reviewed during the late 1960s when it was accepted that not only had it never solved a major crime, it was not keeping up with many failures to advise of changes of address.

In 1982 the New Zealand Police concluded that:

> There is no evidence to suggest there is any relationship between the registration of firearms and their control. Education will reduce misuse more than registration... .
> It is unlikely that firearm registration controls firearm use in domestic violence... . The present system for shotguns,

which amounts to licensing the owner without registering the firearm, has existed since 1968 without difficulty.

After considerable liaison between police, user groups and the community, a new Arms Act was introduced.

Arms Act (1983)

The New Zealand Arms Act (1983) was ground-breaking because it switched from registration of rifles to user-licensing (with vetting for suitability).

(Shotguns were initially registered under the 1920 Act but this was soon dropped when the police understood the enormity of the task. In 1969, under the 1958 Arms Act, a permit was introduced to buy a shotgun but there was no need to register them and the permit to procure entitled the purchaser to obtain as many shotguns as they wished).

The abolition of registration was described as streamlining because the police argued that they knew where firearm owners lived. Registration continued for handguns and restricted (collectors) firearms.

Possibly one of the few laws to provide an indication of its philosophical thrust, the new Act was:

> An Act to consolidate and amend the law relating to firearms and to promote both the safe use and the control of firearms and other weapons.

The effect of these changes was considered by the Commissioner of Police to:

> "...provide frontline police with rapid access to data on firearms which will increase the safety factor for these members....The Act provides the police with additional powers to deal with persons who commit offences with

firearms but at the same time will enable licensed persons to pursue their chosen sport without undue interference. The Act will also substantially reduce the amount of work that is currently undertaken administering arms records."

Severe penalties for infringement were retained to promote compliance among the law-abiding. However, with its focus on the user and not the firearm, the legislation gained a high level of compliance.

Conditions of ownership included the need to provide two referees for establishing the 'fit and proper' nature of the licensee, an understanding of the fundamentals of firearm safety, gauged by the passing of a formal test, and the provision of approved (secure) storage for the firearm.

These requirements were increased by requiring two more referees should the owner wish to gain an endorsed licence, necessary for the keeping and/or use of handguns or the collection of firearms (all of which had to be registered), in addition to meeting higher levels of security.

Despite social upheavals later in that decade (massive unemployment resulting from structural reforms to the New Zealand economy), violent offending with firearms remained largely static with criminal misuse of firearms as a proportion of overall criminal offending generally unchanged.

However, there was a two-thirds reduction in unintentional shooting incidents while rates for intentional self-harm (suicide) approximately halved during the same period. In contrast, the overall suicide rate rose sharply before declining as other social measures took effect.

Changes 1990 to 2019

Public calls for changes to firearm legislation followed a mass shooting in 1990 at Aramoana (a small seaside settlement in the south of New Zealand approximately 20 km from Dunedin) in which 13 people died.[71]

The outcome was the Arms Amendment Act (1992), which took effect in 1994. This abolished lifetime licences and licence holders became subject to periodic review. A complete relicensing programme was undertaken and a new licence issued containing a digitised image of the licence holder. This was required for purchases of ammunition as well as firearms.

It also created a new class of firearm known as a Military Style Semi-Automatic (MSSA). This was defined as a semi-automatic firearm which had any of the following features:

> (a) A folding or telescopic butt.
>
> (b) A magazine that is capable of holding, or that,
> by its appearance, indicates that it is capable of holding,-
>> (i) In the case of a magazine designed to hold .22 inch rimfire cartridges, more than 15 cartridges; or
>>
>> (ii) In any other case, more than 7 cartridges.
>
> (c) Bayonet lugs.
>
> (d) A military pattern free-standing pistol grip.
>
> (e) A flash suppressor.

These firearms could only be lawfully owned on an "endorsed licence" known as an 'E Category endorsement' and were subject to more strict storage requirements, further vetting involving two more referees, and the firearm was registered.

After further shooting incidents (two of which took place overseas, five of them featuring mental abnormalities or behavioural disorder by the perpetrator), a review of the

---

[71] https://en.wikipedia.org/wiki/Aramoana_massacre

law relating to firearms was undertaken by retired Appeal Court Judge Sir Thomas Thorp. His review included an examination of the history of firearm controls and made 59 recommendations.

Among the recommendations was eventual full firearm registration, although noting that unless "...a compliance rate of not less than 90 per cent can be achieved, the benefits derived from registration would be significantly reduced", and "...there is insufficient evidence to conclude that the assistance which registration would provide to crime prevention and detection would in itself support the costs involved in establishing it."

The argument that police need to be aware of the presence of firearms at a property by consulting their records before deployment relies on an assumption of absolute precision in the registration system. Recent checks have revealed error rates of 10% to 15%.

Thorp also called for tighter controls on semi-automatic firearms and for permanent deactivation of registered firearms held by collectors at the time in an inoperable condition. None of the recommendations he made were implemented.

Later changes in policy, focussing on the cosmetic aspects of Military Style Semi-automatics (MSSAs), were unilaterally introduced by the police in 2009. This was followed by an Amendment in 2012 which again attempted to address anomalies and difficulties of definition with the MSSA category, which were based on cosmetic features of these firearms rather than the concept of the 'fit and proper' person. It also introduced interpretive challenges, both for the courts and the bureaucrats. Import provisions were also tightened.

Further consideration of firearm control was undertaken

by a Select Committee in 2016, convened for the purpose of inquiring into "...issues relating to the illegal possession of firearms in New Zealand". The inquiry resulted in 20 recommendations, some of which repeated or closely followed those made by Sir Thomas Thorp in 1997. Many dwelt on licensed firearm owners and none led to law changes.

2019 Amendments

The mass shooting of 51 people in Christchurch in 2019 prompted near immediate changes to the private ownership of firearms, including hastily contrived regulations and an Arms Legislation Bill rushed through parliament so quickly it precluded most public debate or considerations. This became known as the 'first amendment'.

A second bout of amending legislation has since appeared. This seeks a return to individual registration of all firearms, further controls on clubs relating to firearms and shooting ranges, and removes the right to silence of an accused person.

This 'second amendment' also provides for a reduced licence term of five years with more rigorous checking of referees. Medical professionals are likely to become involved and may be required to liaise with the police should any of their patients seem likely to cause harm to themselves or others.

Opportunities for data sharing between the police and other central government services have been proposed. A 'buy-back' concluded at the end of 2019, but prohibitions on certain ammunition came into force on 30 September 2019 with little fanfare. There are reports the buy-back accounted for less than a third of the intended firearms.[72]

---

[72] https://thebfd.co.nz/2019/12/total-failure-gun-confiscation-reached-13-compliance/

An indication of the haste and lack of understanding of those bringing forward the legislation can be seen from the fact that a ban on steel shot was imposed despite steel shot being required by game regulations for use over Crown waterways. This was subsequently rectified by an equally hasty amendment, and there are sure to be many more errors like it.

As of November 2019, the firearms which may be owned are as follows:

Pistols – no change to the present legislation

Licence endorsement ('B' – category for pistol shooters, 'C' – category for collectors, who are not permitted to fire them, and a subset of the 'C' category endorsement for producers of theatrical entertainment, who are permitted to fire blank ammunition).

There are no calibre limits or limits on magazine capacity

Semi-automatic centrefire rifles.

May only be held under 'P' category endorsement, which is limited to approved pest controllers. Collectors may hold such firearms but are not permitted to fire them.

Theatrical armourers may have a 'P' category endorsement which permits the firing of blank ammunition.

Magazines for semi-automatic centrefire rifles are to be serially numbered to the firearm, with sequential numbering for each magazine.

Semi-automatic rimfire rifles

Permitted provided magazine capacity does not exceed 10 cartridges and the rifle is not capable of having a centrefire 'upper' attached to it (to prevent anyone from owning anything that looks like an AR style rifle).

Semi-automatic shotguns

Permitted provided their non-detachable magazines hold no more than five cartridges

Other types of rifles

Permitted provided their magazine capacity does not exceed 10 cartridges

Other types of shotguns

Permitted provided their non-detachable magazines hold no more than five cartridges.

Suppressors (known as silencers in the media) are legal and widely used to reduce hearing damage and avoid alarming neighbours, particularly during pest control operations.

New Zealand firearm owners

Research into New Zealand firearm ownership patterns is sparse. Licensed firearm owners represent about 5.2% of the population.

Approximately 10,000 applicants are granted arms licences each year, while approximately 5,500 licences are cancelled either as a result of the death of the licence holder or because of non-renewal, creating a net annual gain of approximately 4,500.

Between 5% and 10% of New Zealand recreational firearm users choose to belong to clubs relevant to their involvement with firearms.

There is no reliable estimate of the number of unlicensed arms users, nor the number of firearms in their possession.

The number of firearms in New Zealand

Quantifying the number of firearms in New Zealand began with a registration index check which started in the late 1960s.[73] This resulted in: "...approximately 460,000 registered rifles which belong to 280,000 individuals recorded in the

---

[73] New Zealand Police (1982), Firearms Registration in New Zealand. Wellington, New Zealand: Support Services Directorate, Police National Headquarters. (34 pp. + Appendices).

index".

In addition, 96,500 permits to procure a shotgun were contained in the index (these had been required since 1969, entitling the holder to obtain any number of shotguns).

Results from surveys of the early 1980s and late 1990s were extrapolated to between 350,000 and 400,000 lawful firearm users, suggesting a national total of approximately 2 million firearms. Nugent (1989)[74] found from a survey of nearly 5,000 licence holders an average of 2.7 firearms per owner, equating to a total of 777,000 shoulder firearms (ie rifles and shotguns).

Thorp (1997)[75] attempted an estimate of the firearm 'pool' in New Zealand by obtaining the number of firearms imported, the accumulated total exceeding 1.2 million at the end of 2008 (1.47 million to end of fiscal year 2017). However, no reliable record is available for the number of firearms exported, destroyed or physically lost. Thorp estimated firearm 'survival' to be "...30% for all firearms manufactured before 1950, and 10% for all later importations...", these estimates being derived from interviews and some survey data.

Forsyth and Berg undertook further survey work in mid-2019, deriving a conservative average value of 5.88 firearms per licensed owner and user, which with more than 248,000 license holders suggested a holding of between 1.2 and 1.9 million firearms currently in lawful ownership.

How long do firearms last?

Studies on the working life of firearms are rare, although

---

[74] Nugent, G, (1989), *Hunting in New Zealand in 1988: Survey Results*. Christchurch, New Zealand: Forest Animal Ecology Section, Forest & Wildland Ecosystems Division, Forest Research Institute. (26 pp + App.).

[75] Thorp, T.M. (1997) *Review of Firearms Control in New Zealand – Report of an Independent Inquiry Commissioned by the Minister of Police*. Wellington, New Zealand: GP Print. (281 pp.).

defence forces project the operating life of certain components of their firearms when determining future costs for their budgets.

The life of civilian firearms, intended for much less arduous use, is almost certain to be longer than for service firearms. Civilian firearms rarely wear out and can last for decades when properly maintained.

It is thought that there are two broad classes of firearms in New Zealand: firearms in normal recreational and sporting use, and heirlooms handed down from generation to generation, which are cherished, given more care and last longer.

New Zealand firearm ownership patterns

Firearm ownership is high in New Zealand in comparison to other countries. However, a mail-out survey in 1988 found approximately 9% of firearm licence holders do not own firearms.

A breakdown by firearm type is provided in Figure 1. Most of the 'rifles' are .22 rimfire, a relatively low-powered calibre commonly used for small pest destruction. Such firearms have a working life of at least 50 years.

Non-cartridge firing 'airguns' include 'Airsoft' guns, which fire plastic pellets approximately 6 mm (0.24") in diameter, and those firing lead pellets, usually of 4.5 mm (0.177") or 5.5 mm (0.22") calibre. Both use compressed gas, spring-compressed air or pre-charged gas ('PCP') as their propelling agent.

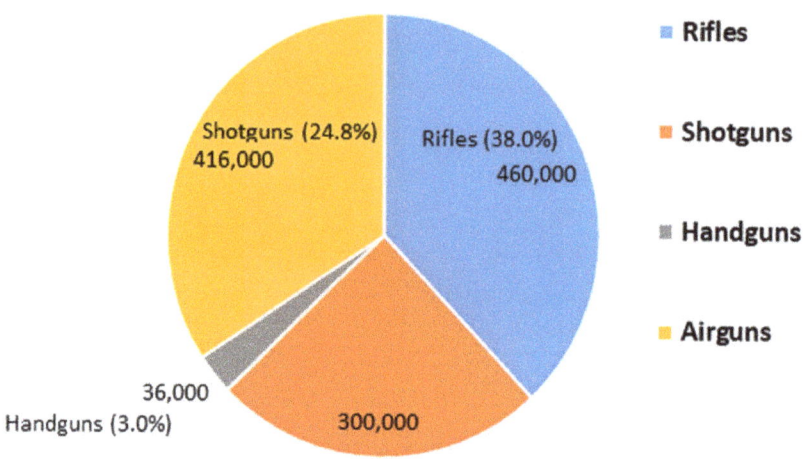

Figure 2: A breakdown of the basic firearm types lawfully held by New Zealanders. (After Alpers and Wilson, 2018).

New Zealand firearm ownership displays regional differences (Figure 2, next page) with a higher density of firearms in rural areas. The percentage of the population holding arms licences is higher in largely rural Police Districts such as Tasman, Southern and Central for example (10.6%, 10.4% and 8.1% respectively), with much lower figures for the Police Districts of Auckland, Counties/Manukau and Waitemata (1.4%, 2.4% and 2.3% respectively).

The Police Districts of Tasman, Southern and Central contain populations of approximately 180,000 to 350,000 and are of largely rural character. Those of Auckland, Counties/Manukau are almost entirely urban, and Waitemata is urban but to a lesser extent. These three areas contain populations of between 540,000 and 570,000.

It might be expected that with a far higher firearm-owning proportion of the population in the Tasman, Southern and

Central Police Districts, that higher rates of crime would be found in these districts. This is not so; in fact, for the premeditated offences related to robbery, blackmail and extortion, the highest rates for these offences (by an order of magnitude) are found to be Auckland Central and Counties/Manukau, while the lowest rates for such offending are to be found in the Waitemata and Southern Police Districts.

Factors other than levels of firearm ownership appear to determine the incidence of these crimes.

It is similar with aggravated robbery, which involves an accomplice or any weapon, or the actual use of physical force in the offence (or any combination of these factors) as per the darker colour in the following graphic below. Robbery is an offence of interest because of its implied premeditation, and aggravation becomes of special interest because the decision to use weapons is a further indication of the planned aspect of a robbery. Notably, it is often when a robbery does not proceed to plan that a firearm, if involved, is discharged (Figure 2, next page).

GUN CONTROL

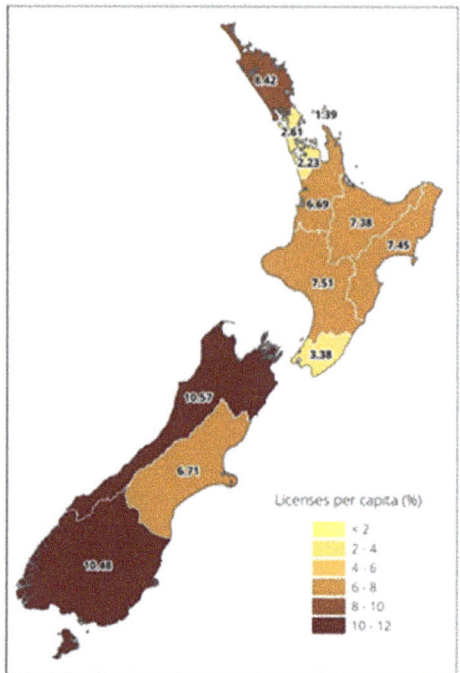

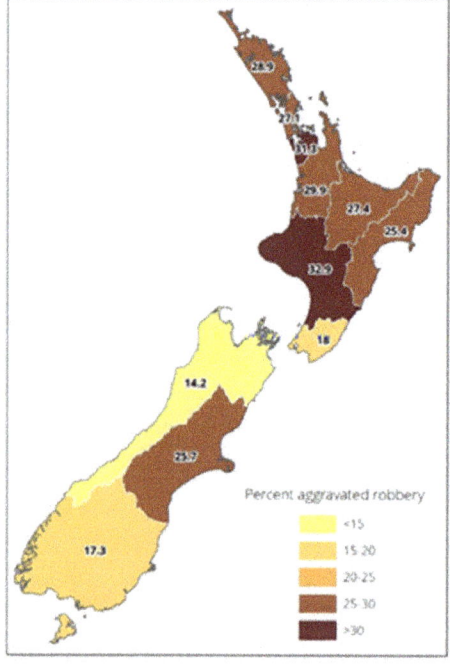

Figure 2, firearm licenses held per capita; percentage of robberies that are 'aggravated' (i.e. perpetrator is accompanied by another, or is armed with any weapon, or actually uses force when offending, or any combination of these factors is involved). Darker colours indicate higher percentages in both charts.)

In fact, the relationship between the percentage of the population licenced for firearm ownership and the incidence of aggravated robbery is somewhat inverse, particularly in the South Island, although this ignores the mobility of putative offenders who have shown a willingness to drive more than 500 kilometres before offending.

Firearm misuse

The level of firearm misuse in criminal offending is low. If all firearm-armed offending is considered be violent (either implied or actual), then the incidence of firearm involvement, including remotely peripheral firearm involvement (where a firearm might be found hidden on the premises after an incident, but was not used in the assault or threats) is less than 2%.

In his review of New Zealand firearms, Thorp indicated that, "For non-shooters (an increasingly large section of the New Zealand public), firearms are now generally associated with crime or violence and only slightly with any legitimate use".

He went on to state that:

> In overall terms firearms are not by any means a dominant feature of violence in New Zealand...in the region of 1.7 percent..." and there is, "... no evidence of the widespread illegal use of restricted weapons in crime in New Zealand...

This situation has remained to the present.

Casualties from New Zealand misuse

Victims of firearm misuse in New Zealand may be classified into two groups – those who survive, and those who do not. Most fatal outcomes are due to intentional self-harm, largely a consequence of proximity to the firearm muzzle. The fatality rate from intentional self-harm is over 70%.

For intentional shootings by another person, almost all 'criminal' in nature, the fatality rate of slightly over 20% reflects the greater distance from the shooter and the reduced likelihood of a vital body part being hit, although of course the timeliness of medical assistance is also a factor.

In the case of unintentional shootings, the fatality rate of just over 3% is attributable to the preponderance of long arms. Of a total of 109 unintentional shooting incidents for which data were collected over the calendar years 2004 to 2015, 43 (39.4%) were self-inflicted and 66 (60.5%) were inflicted by another. This suggests that it is almost twice as likely that a companion will unintentionally shoot another than s/he will do it to themselves.

Intent behind shootings plays a major part in whether survival is an outcome (Figures 3(a) and (b)):

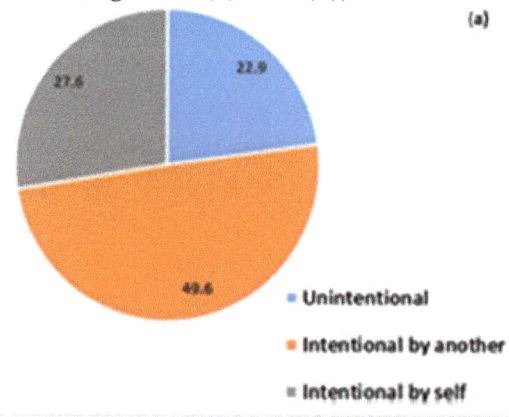

Figure 3: (a), Percentage of annual shooting casualties in New Zealand by intent, 2000 – 2006 (n = 273);

Non-fatal shooting injuries typically occurred in the limbs when inflicted by a solitary individual. When unintentionally inflicted by another shooter due to firearm mis-handling, injuries tended to involve the trunk of the victim although some injuries were to the limbs.

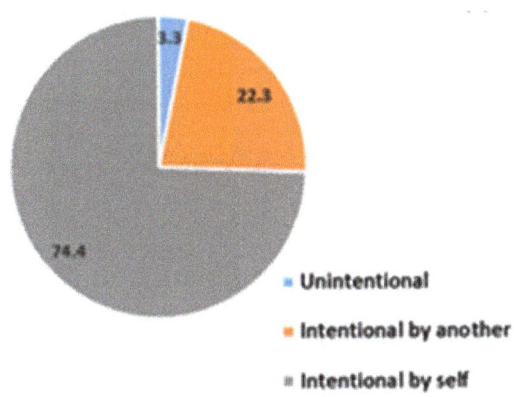

Figure 3: (b), Percentage of annual shooting fatalities, by intent 2000 – 2006 (n = 68).

Long arms generally develop twice the kinetic energy of handguns, so shootings from rifles and shotguns are typically more destructive and injurious to health than those from handguns, resulting in lower survival rates when they occur.[76]

Casualties arising from intentional self-harm

Suicide remains one of the major causes of death in New Zealand, ranked second behind transport accidents for the period 2002 – 2004 and ahead of deaths by accidental falling, and is a major source of concern with a rate of approximately 11 per 100,000 population.

Casualties arising from intentional self-harm by firearm have undergone a sharp decline in number and rates, particularly since the early 1990s (Figure 4) although suicide by firearm remains the major cause of death by firearm, amounting to 74% of the total annual casualties by firearm (Figure 3(b)). Yet suicide rates by firearm remain at less than 1.0 per 100,000 for the most recent decade for which data are available.

---

[76] Wilber, C.G. (1977), *Ballistic Science for the Law Enforcement Officer*. Illinois, USA: Charles C Thomas.

The reduction in such firearm misuse appears to have been accompanied by an increase in the rate of suicides involving other means such as hanging, strangulation and suffocation.

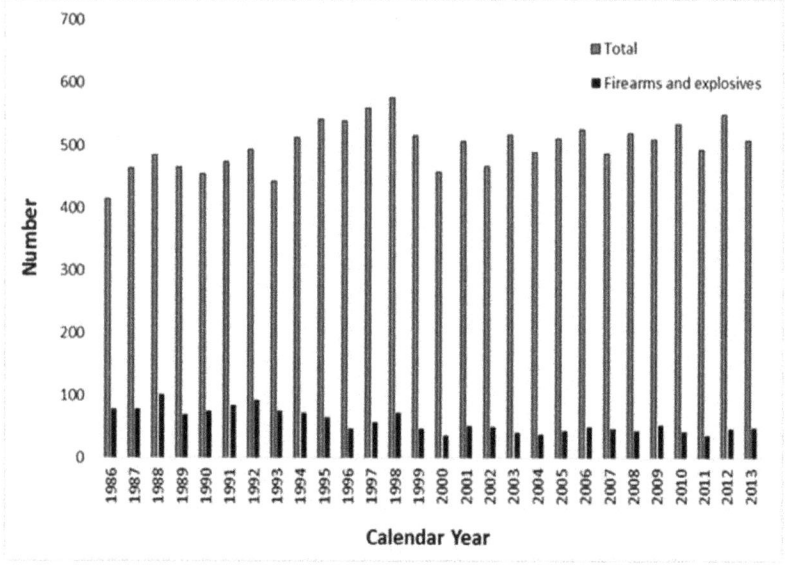

Figure 4: Total New Zealand suicides and suicides involving 'firearms and explosives', 1986-2013. Data for attempts with non-fatal outcomes are much harder to obtain, and are not so recent.

New Zealand crime statistics

Statistics on criminal offending in New Zealand are not always of much use in research. Data providers warn that the compilation of long-term historical series is, at best, inadvisable, because of changes in data compilation methodology, changes in the law, changes in practice, changes in international data collection, in police procedures, and in technology.

Although fraught with discontinuities, the available data can serve to identify trends. The data for homicides, for example, although showing wide annual variations, indicates that firearm involvement in such offending is miniscule (Figure 5).

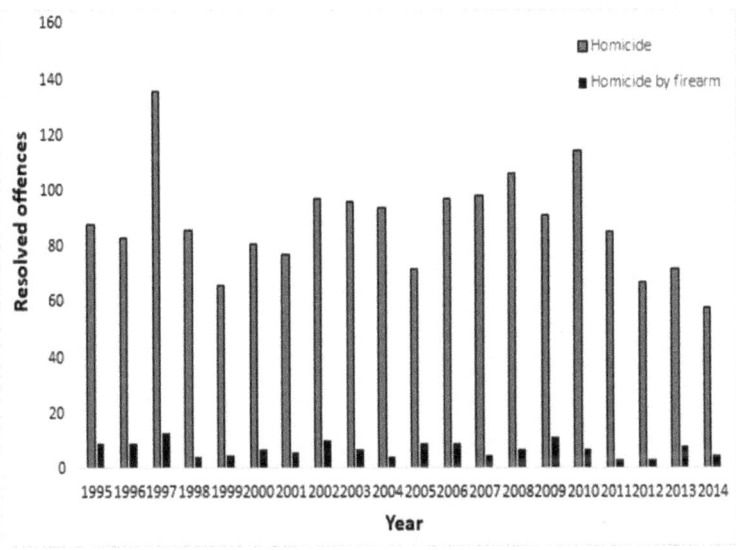

Figure 5: Total homicides resolved in New Zealand (perpetrator identified), and resolved homicide by firearm, 1995-2014.

For every offence against the person involving a firearm in New Zealand, approximately twice as many involve knives and cutting instruments, and more than two and a half times feature blunt instruments (such as kicking, helmets, fists and bottles).

Data on casualties arising from unintentional shootings have been collected since the 1930s in New Zealand and show a steady decline since then. The average annual casualty rate from unintentional shootings for the five years 1935 - 1939 was 3.2 per 100,000. For the decade beginning in 1960 it was 2.0 per 100,000. For the most recently available decade, 2015, the rate was 0.22.

As the overall casualty rates for unintentional shootings have declined, so has the average annual fatality rate. For the period 1960 – 1969, the rate was 0.44 per 100,000, which declined to 0.06 per 100,000 for the decade ended 2015.

Efficacy of New Zealand firearm controls

Gauging firearms legislation to ascertain its 'effectiveness' is difficult because of obvious difficulties in defining what is meant by "effectiveness". For example, did the legislation prevent a crime from taking place?

Statistical data and annual reports provided by the police to Parliament offer an opportunity to see if offending rates have changed, but such reviews ignore social and other changes which may have influenced offending. Reviews of the administration of the Arms Act and of firearm ownership have taken place, sometimes in conjunction with inquiries into violent offending (1978, 1987, 1996/97, 2016/17), and their findings often provide a springboard for amending or even introducing new legislation.

However, the monitoring of annual levels of recorded offences merely provides insights after the fact, hardly a useful indicator of the level of compliance to be found in a population in light of the numerous other variables which affect offending. Additionally, Thorp found that of 453 police files examined for his review and which featured in the offence statistics, 29% (131 of them) were found to be "miscodes or non-offence situations".

A recent inquiry into the sources and possession of illegal firearms in New Zealand perhaps predictably uncovered very little that was new, and demonstrated that very little research into the topic had been undertaken. Furthermore, previously published investigations into illegal firearms seem not to have been considered, including one where 51 prison inmates convicted of illegal possession of a firearm had been surveyed on methods of acquisition, deployment in crime, and the street value of such illicit firearms.[77]

---

[77] Newbold, G. (1999), The Criminal use of firearms in New Zealand. *The Australian and New Zealand Journal of Criminology*, 32 (1).

The findings and recommendations of the inquiry were headlined by the news media and, as a result, served to heighten public concern about the existence of illegally held firearms. The president of a police officers' association repeated earlier calls for the full registration of firearms, arguing that such a measure would diminish thefts of firearms. The distinct absence of information about the topic was obvious.[78]

It is thought that most of the 'grey' firearms, when they become 'black', are taken primarily as ornaments for impressing criminal peers. Only a few firearms would suffice, even if only used once, for all firearm-armed violent offending in New Zealand. The number of homicides, attempted homicides and aggravated robberies involving firearms recorded annually totals less than 300.

Overseas researchers suggest that firearms for violent offending are passed around via underground trading circles, often with the proviso they are used only once and if fired, are destroyed because their anonymity after discharge becomes compromised.[79]

Suggestions from the Law and Order Committee (2017) included recording of all ammunition sales, upgrading of the security measures required for the storage of lawfully-held firearms, and changes in regulations relating to the type of firearm available for purchase. It also called for an arms amnesty, where unwanted firearms may be handed in for disposal by the authorities with no questions asked.

In fact, nine amnesties have been held since 1972 and even now, more than 25 years since the Arms Act (1983) was signed into law, a permanent amnesty in effect exists,

---

[78] Law and Order Committee (2017), *Inquiry into issues relating to the illegal possession of firearms in New Zealand – Report of the Law and Order Committee* I.8A, Wellington, New Zealand: New Zealand Government Printing Office.

[79] Greenwood, C. (1972), *Firearms Control*. London, England: Routledge and Kegan Paul.

allowing the holders of the appropriately endorsed firearm licence to register hitherto unregistered ('off-ticket') firearms against their licence.

Very few of the measures appeared to address the issues for which the Law and Order Committee had been established, which was to enquire into the source(s) of illegal firearms and of those who had them. Most of the measures recommended would have applied to licensed arms owners on the premise that most illegally held firearms had been stolen from lawfully held sources, despite this not being established.

Greenwood (1972) found that criminals in England and Wales found it less risky to buy their firearms on the 'black' market (from the pool of illegally held firearms in circulation) than to break into a private dwelling on the off-chance of finding firearms.

Perceptions and reality of the hazard from firearms

Perceptions that the more firearms there are in a community, the more 'problems' in the form of firearm misuse and crime to be encountered by and in that community, are found throughout many of the reviews and analyses.

The question of whether the presence of firearms is a causal factor in community violence, or is merely coincidental, is rarely explored. Other studies argue that issues relating to social inequality, social disorganisation and illicit drug control are more likely to be contributing factors.

Furthermore, if the controls placed on those willing to comply with the law become too onerous, they may be tempted to obtain firearms without bothering with a firearm licence, so depriving themselves of access to even basic training in firearm safety. Worse, they may be tempted to manufacture a firearm for themselves, and improvised uncertainty will greatly increase the risk to life and limb of the user and of any people who may be nearby.

New Zealand data shows that approximately 9% of all offending involves violence, and that of all violent offending, firearms are involved in less than 2%. The suggestion that firearms feature prominently in violent offending, at times vigorously promoted by the news media, is obviously false.

Changes in public attitude

Public attitudes towards the private ownership of firearms are rarely surveyed. In New Zealand, anecdotal perceptions of firearm owners are available only to a limited extent.

Support for stricter firearm controls arises from a desire unrelated to a fear of firearms, but is instead based on misperceptions of the actual hazard of firearms to others in a community. Calls for greater restrictions on ownership also sometimes arise from a wish to stigmatise groups identified as owning firearms, having firearms for sport, or for other purposes such as collecting. Oddly, many who sought a ban on privately owned firearms also indicated support for the building of approved firearm shooting ranges!

Interestingly, many calls for 'gun control' are made even though it is widely accepted that such controls have little or no impact upon firearm-armed violence. Indeed, many proponents of control have little idea of the current legislative controls placed upon firearm ownership.

Abhorrence of mass homicide has also aroused concern at the types of firearms used in such incidents. These are sometimes the firearms which are uniquely described in New Zealand as MSSAs. However, amok (multiple) killings had been known since Viking times, when killing frenzies took place as a result of ergot poisoning. It is well known that such massacres have occurred throughout the world, throughout history, involving different weapons and all ethnic and social groups.

Concluding commentary

The topic of firearms in any society involves two major groups: those who own them, and those who do not. A large subgroup within the second group includes people who have no interest in them and so are unlikely ever to be firearm owners. A far smaller subgroup of owners is those who have firearms but are not licensed, so in the eyes of the law they have them illegally or for illegal purposes.

The two major groups, those that have and who don't have firearms, often co-exist in ignorance of each other. However, on firearm ownership matters, a dichotomy arises whenever a discussion on firearm control arises, usually following news reports of offending or violence involving firearms. This arises from tensions between licensed firearm owners, who believe they have in every way complied with the law and see no reason for more laws which will affect them; and those who, not licensed for firearm ownership and not directly affected by firearm laws, are happy for 'the others' to be so affected. Some of this group may also feel threatened by knowing that there are firearms in the community.

The trend for modern firearm control legislation has changed from general controls upon access based on race or religious affiliation, to specific regulation focussing upon particular firearm types.

An emphasis on 'fit and proper' people having lawful access to firearms, with provision for further vetting to ensure conditions are met for 'higher risk' firearms and their owners, requires monitoring to ensure that unsuitable individuals remain unlicensed and do not gain access to firearms.

Material for this chapter has been derived largely from material gathered for a PhD thesis which is currently under preparation by the author.

SWITZERLAND
GRANT BAYLEY

Firearm ownership in Switzerland falls into two main categories: the militia and civilian owners.

Military

The first of these refers to firearm possession (not ownership) in the context of conscripted military service of able-bodied males in the Swiss Army, consisting generally of Swiss-made SIG SG550 (*'Sturmgewehr* 90') rifles and Glock 17 or 19 pistols.

During their years of service with the Swiss Army, conscripts keep and store these firearms at home, normally with an operative part (eg the bolt or bolt carrier) removed but no other storage obligations. Their service is rendered in formal operations with the Army plus *Obligatorisch* ('obligatory') shooting qualifications run on local shooting ranges at 300m for rifles and 25m for pistols between spring and autumn.

Prior to 2008 these citizen soldiers were issued 50 rounds of ammunition to be stored at their house, but since then ammunition has been issued and controlled by the ranges during qualification matches, with any unfired rounds being returned. However, they are not prevented from buying additional ammunition at their own expense at private gun shops.

A somewhat unique characteristic of the Swiss system of military conscription is that at the end of military service (at age 34 or higher depending on rank), service members are given the opportunity to purchase their service firearms for private use at a heavily discounted price. This has led to many civilian target shooting competitions at local ranges (with subsidised ammunition) including matches for former Swiss

Army service firearms dating back as far as the *Karabiner* 11 (K11), *Karabiner* 31 (K31), the *Sturmgewehr* 57 (SIG SG 510) and the *Pistole* 49 (SIG P210-1), all of which are very popular.

Most of the rifles are permitted modest upgrades to their sighting systems to adapt them for target shooting competition.

During the 20th Century it was considered a form of military preparedness to sell these firearms to ex-service members but not to further record or register the firearms, denying a potential enemy information on the extent to which the country was armed.

Foreign reporting of Swiss gun possession and culture frequently confuses and conflates civilian ownership of firearms with the possession and use of firearms supplied by the Swiss Army during military service. Misreporting the details of their possession and ownership, storage conditions, supply of ammunition and transport to and from obligatory shooting events and other military exercises is quite common.

It is worth noting that these firearms are frequently transported openly (slung over the shoulder, typically), including on public transport, without any sense of alarm on the part of members of the public.

Civilian

The other main (and larger) group of firearm owners in Switzerland is civilian owners. Their modes of ownership have historical roots in regional Arms Acts, often with wide differences in the permits necessary (if any) for firearms up to and including fully automatic firearms.

In the late 1990s a Federal *Waffengesetz* ('Arms Act') was passed with subsequent amendments arising from the

Swiss accession to the EU Schengen Agreement. The most recent amendments came into force on 15th August 2019 following amendments in 2018 and an unsuccessful popular referendum to overturn them in May 2019.

The current situation is as follows.

Firearms (and some related items) in Switzerland are classified into three main categories:

Category A:
- Fully automatic firearms
- Fully automatic firearms converted to semi-automatic operation
- Semi-automatic rifles able to be shortened to less than 60cm overall length without loss of function (eg via folding/telescoping stocks)
- Semi-automatic centrefire rifles with an attached magazine capacity over 10 rounds
- Pistols with an attached magazine capacity over 20 rounds
- Firearm suppressors (moderators/silencers)
- Night vision sighting devices
- Laser sighting devices

Category B:
- Revolvers
- Pistols with attached magazine capacity up to and including 20 rounds
- Semi-automatic rimfire rifles (provided they cannot be shortened to less than 60cm)
- Semi-automatic centrefire rifles with attached magazine capacity up to and including 10 rounds
- Pump-action repeating firearms with magazine capacity up to and including 10 rounds
- Lever action firearms
- Foreign bolt-action military rifles not adapted or used for hunting

Category C:
- Bolt-action hunting rifles (incl combination shotgun/rifles)
- Bolt-action Swiss military rifles (eg K11, K31)
- Bolt-action firearms
- Single-round firearms
- Double-barrel (break action) shotguns
- Other air rifles, air pistols etc

Notes:
- A permit is required for the purchase of key components such as barrels, bolts (ie bolt face, bolt carrier), 'upper receivers' and as of August 2019, for revolver cylinders and 'lower receivers' for semi-automatic firearms.
- The shooting of fully automatic firearms is subject to the issuance of a permit (typically a day permit) by Cantonal Police; they cannot just be taken to a range and shot. Such permits normally require a range invitation and current personal liability insurance.

Category A and B firearms require a purchase permit. Category C firearms only require a simple sale contract between the buyer and seller, with the 'third copy' sent to the buyer's local Police as a post-sale notification. This also applies to firearms directly acquired from the military authorities by ex-soldiers.

Foreigners residing in Switzerland on a "B" temporary residence permit (usually renewed yearly) are able to apply for purchase permits where they supply evidence of permission given in their home country (eg a firearms licence or permit from their home country; this can cause problems for citizens of countries that do not issue permits, eg United States).

Permits for purchase/possession of firearms are handled by the Canton (State) Police forces, though in some areas local councils are delegated the authority to issue firearms permits in consultation with Cantonal Police (for example, Bezirk Affoltern in the rural southern area of Canton Zurich).

For all firearms purchases (and ammunition purchases by new purchasers) a *Strafregisterauszug* ("Criminal Records Extract") is required. This is available for 20 CHF (approximately 30 AUD) from the Federal Office of Justice (EJPD) and normally takes several days to process, resulting in either a printed document verifiable at the EJPD website or a cryptographically-signed PDF file. The Extract is attached to the relevant permit application form along with a copy of the applicant's identification, or shown to the seller in the case of ammunition or Category C firearm sales.

The type of permit needed varies by the type of firearm.

As noted, Category C firearms (for Swiss citizens and permanent residents) only have a post-sale notification requirement.

Category B firearms require a *Waffenerwerbsschein* ("Weapon Purchase Licence") that costs 50 CHF (approximately 75 AUD) and can include up to three firearms (or essential components, spare barrels etc) on a single permit.

Until August 2019, Category A firearms (and related devices) required either an *Ausnahmebewilligung* ("Exception Permit") costing 100 CHF (approximately 150 AUD) for suppressors, etc, or a similarly named permit (sometimes referred to as a *Sonderbewilligung* ("Special Permit") for fully-automatic firearms. After August 2019, when additional EU/Schengen-mandated changes to the Federal Arms Act came into effect, two additional *Ausnahmebewilligung Klein* ("AB Klein" or "Exception Permit Small") permit types were created, costing 50 CHF each, having been tailored for Collectors and Sports Shooters and the firearm types recently moved into Category A.

The politics surrounding these firearm category changes arising from Switzerland's membership in Schengen (but not the EU) were highly controversial, as Switzerland was required to fully implement the letter of the changes despite widespread domestic opposition. It resulted in the 'compromise' of a new exception permit type ('AB Klein') for which essentially *everyone* would qualify with little effort (5 shooting matches in 5 years to qualify as a 'sports shooter', for example), but with some restrictions on the configuration of the firearms available with the permit.

Firearms ownership is essentially guaranteed in the Swiss Constitution, although not as clearly and symbolically as the American Second Amendment. It essentially guarantees relatively free ownership of Category C firearms and 'shall issue' permits for Category B firearms (unless there are reasons to deny, such as mental incapacity, criminal record etc). The only firearms that are Forbidden Weapons (*"Verbotener Waffen"*) are those in Category A.

However, unlike the situation in Australia where firearms are euphemistically 'reclassified' and almost no permits issued for the 'higher' classifications, in Switzerland permits for 'forbidden weapons' for collectors (in operational condition, not ruined by deactivation modifications) are linked to sane, objective criteria: things like safe ownership of firearms for over 5 years, possession of a collection of more than 10 firearms, implementation of increased storage security and demonstrated interest in collecting via membership of a collecting society.

The legal situation has another dimension, too. As Switzerland is a Confederation, with the exception of imports and exports Swiss gun laws are administered at the Canton (State) level. Since the early 2000s these have included a separate firearms registry in each Canton, although the long history of no-registry, no-permit ownership until relatively recently means that only new imports, transfers and sales since 2008 are entered into it.

These Cantonal firearm registries are not part of a national firearm registry, with a proposal for such a registry defeated by referendum after being characterised as a 'criminal shopping list' in 2011. However, as technology often does, the Cantonal Registries were later linked into a single search platform that simply searches each of the registries in parallel, conveniently circumventing the prohibition on a national registry.

Other Aspects:

Ownership of firearms for self-defence in Switzerland is exceedingly rare, as are permits for carriage of firearms for self defence (*"Waffentragschein"*). Though the requirements (including a shooting qualification) are published, in practice the occupational requirements and/or discretionary aspects of assessing threats against the applicant mean they are relatively rarely approved. However, 'defence sprays' (sometimes advertised as 'animal defence sprays') are freely available to people over 18.

Swiss Gun Laws in Practice (My Experience)

As a former Australian target/sports shooter, I began shooting in Switzerland with the purchase of a *Sturmgewehr* 90 (SIG SG 550) and a SIG P210 pistol, joining a local club for both rifle and pistol matches (each having a 12 month club probationary period after which time, if they didn't like me, they could have rejected my membership).

As a foreigner on a "B" temporary residence permit, I initially had to seek the permission of the Cantonal-level military authorities to take part in the club's competitions (whose format and firearm classifications are dictated by the Swiss Army) and to purchase the subsidised ammunition.

I later branched out into IPSC competition (joining an additional club that has a private indoor 25m range built underneath a sawmill facility) and began a collection of (non-Swiss) military rifles, shooting at a private range with both an indoor 100m underground tunnel range and an outdoor sighting-in range.

As my collection grew, I later applied for and received collectors permits for suppressors (both rifle and pistol, and for firearms with integral suppressors), buying some as off-the-shelf items from local manufacturers and others (including one with no serial number) via local auctions. I also bought some firearms at auction that were Category A, but of the 'fully-automatic converted to semi-automatic' type, which can be shot without the permit necessary for shooting fully-automatic firearms.

Under normal circumstances, Swiss Police would not have grounds to visit your residence (or storage location) for any sort of check of your firearms and their storage. The main exception is firearms collectors with permits for fully-automatic firearms - the Police will visit (sometimes without pre-notification) to check serial numbers and verify that one necessary component (usually the bolt and/or bolt carrier) is stored separately (in a separately locked safe is fine).

For a number of years, I shared the reservation that most Swiss shooters express about inviting such a visit. However, around the time David was beginning this book, I became aware of some invitation-only, full-auto shooting events that sounded fun (they're in a purpose-modified underground granite mine). As I was already voluntarily storing my firearms like most Australian firearm owners are forced to, a visit from the police seemed like a reasonable price to pay to get to enjoy such events.

I then applied for and obtained permits for a WWII Sten gun (and then added a suppressor, also with permit) and a WWII US M3 Grease Gun. The fun appeared complete until the other full-auto day participants showed up with guns like a Soviet-made PKM, a Swiss LMG25 (which uses a Luger-like toggle lock action), an Israeli Uzi, a domestic Swiss copy of an M249 SAW, an MG34, an MG42 and a Singaporean Ultimax 100. And some belts of tracer ammunition. We all had our day permits, shot in the granite mine until early evening, then everything went back into the safe, waiting for the next event.

In researching the 'outer edges' of Swiss firearm ownership for this book, I even tested the necessary procedures for import of a Category A firearm part (a fully-automatic-capable Heckler & Koch HK416 lower receiver with all parts). After receiving the necessary purchase/possession permit from the Cantonal Police, I sent my application to the *Zentralstelle Waffen* ("Central Weapons Office") in Bern, which sent back the necessary import permit about a week and a half later. For me to use the part on a full-auto shooting day, I simply need to list it along with the other firearms I wish to shoot that day.

As a customer of the Cantonal Police (in Canton Zug and later Canton Zurich) for firearms permits, I have found them to be highly professional, interested to know what your intentions are (your first purchase of a Category B firearm normally results in an interview) and also often interested to see what firearms are coming 'on the books' after spending most of the 20th Century 'off the books' with a prior owner.

Once they 'know you', permits are issued without any real delay and they're as friendly in person as you'd want them to be (one of them even brings her AK-47 to the full-auto shoots and installs her MG42 on an anti-aircraft mount to her Dodge Ram Ute).

In other regions (notably Geneva), friends tell me things are not always so jovial but permits are eventually issued. They have been known to refuse permits which involve more than one firearm and to seek information not explicitly defined in the Arms Act.

Another article on Swiss gun ownership[80] is available online at the link shown in the footnote.

UNITED KINGDOM
RICHARD LAW

The United Kingdom comprises six legislative administrations with differing firearms laws.

Westminster's laws sometimes include Northern Ireland. Northern Ireland's Stormont Assembly is sometimes functional, often dysfunctional, and at the time of writing has just recommenced meeting. Local authority-type powers have been devolved to a Welsh Assembly and a Scottish Parliament. The latter has some powers relating to firearms, while the main controls are the same as in England and Wales.

The Isle of Man and the Channel Islands are not part of the United Kingdom and thus outside the European Union. As Crown Dependencies they have their own Parliamentary administrations but are 'controlled' through the Home Office on behalf of the Crown.

The Isle of Man's Parliament is the Tynwald; Jersey has the

---

[80] https://www.reddit.com/user/Zorthianator_V2/comments/7zm6rm/swiss_gun_laws_for_dummies/

States Assembly and Guernsey, which includes the islands of Alderney, Sark and Herm, has the States of Deliberation. These control their own firearms legislation.

In the beginning

There are two distinct threads to any governmental approach to its public having firearms: one is 'defence', and the other is 'sport'.

For over a thousand years, the possession of arms for personal defence and defence of the realm was an obligation for all able-bodied residents of the kingdom.

The United States Supreme Court told us in 2008 (Heller v District of Columbia) that the right to keep and bear arms is an individual right. Its judgment was based on the fact that King Alfred the Great required the public to turn out as militia to defend the realm without his government having made any provision to either arm or train them.

The reference to 'militia' indicates that they were expected to come out of the box ready for the fight and, since the enemy of the day was Vikings, turning up well armed and trained was a really good idea.

Men have long possessed weapons: swords were a badge of rank or office that also proved useful on social occasions – in court cases (trial by combat), out-of-court settlements (duels), and for sporting purposes (jousts and tournaments) – as well as the preparation for war. Other weapons (eg bows and spears) served the dual purposes of hunting and war.

The earliest legislative controls on weapons were directed at hunting – variations of the legend of Robin Hood poaching the king's deer originate with the Norman kings declaring some areas as hunting grounds (forests) for their own use and the game within those areas restricted to the king's gift.

Plantagenet laws (1154–85) made practicing with the longbow obligatory – but don't shoot the deer – while in the 1660s King Charles II restricted possession of crossbows to landed gentry in an attempt to make poaching more complicated.

Prior to the Civil War (1642-48) every town had a militia: the able-bodied armed themselves and practised, although longbows gave way to muskets during the 16th century.

Much of the Civil War was fought by these militias, called out by either Crown or Parliament. With both sides calling, individual towns had to decide who to support. Part of the Restoration settlement – Parliament made peace with the Royal family by allowing King Charles II back in 1660 – was that a standing army was funded from taxation. That let local volunteers off the hook somewhat.

In the following century the Hanoverian kings George II and III built roads to assist troop movements and trade, not to mention the King wanting to get to the races at Newmarket or to the seaside at Brighton. A by-product was that gentlemen who were wealthy enough could ride in carriages on the better roads instead of on horseback.

As a consequence, gentlemen stopped wearing swords and consigned them to the luggage rack. This badge of rank or office, so important that it rates a mention in the 1689 Bill of Rights, dropped out of sight. Swords are *de rigeur* in portraits painted before 1745 and have just about vanished from the civilian wardrobe thirty years later. Only the military wore them as a badge of rank for officers, continuing into the Great War (1914-18).

Being seen well-dressed in public without a sword became a mark of wealth, indicating ownership of a carriage. Lesser mortals then aped the wealthy around town. Gentlemen discovered pistols as a convenient alternative for defence, carried discreetly in overcoat pockets.

After nearly two hundred years of relying on the standing army to defend the realm, in 1859 the possibility of the French invading Britain was real enough to galvanise the public into resurrecting their common law rights and privileges to defend the realm.

Britain in 1859 was a different society: the industrial revolution had spawned a new middle class. These men could afford to kit themselves out and weapons were entering an evolutionary phase that the spontaneous formation of volunteer rifle regiments did much to fund and accelerate.

The proto P51 rifle musket made its debut at the Great Exhibition in 1851, where Sam Colt was also an exhibitor, and the resultant trans-Atlantic cross-fertilisation of ideas set off a rapid development of small arms and manufacturing capacity.

By the end of the American Civil War in 1865, breech-loaders, repeating rifles and machine guns had made their appearance on the battlefield, while in Britain the volunteer rifle regiments' competitions had become a fixture of the social calendar.

Demand for 'modern' rifles from well-heeled volunteer soldiers fuelled development, from the Snider breech-loading conversion of Enfield muskets through the Martini Henry of the Zulu wars to the Lee Metford/Enfield repeating rifles of the early 20th century.

In 1870 the government introduced the gun licence – a ten-shilling tax – required to carry any firearm beyond the confines of one's home. There were multiple exemptions from the tax – game shooting, target practice, defence of the realm or in the course of one's duties: bank officers, police officers, night watchmen and Post Office staff routinely carried concealed sidearms (only the military used holsters) – so the only people who needed this licence were the ladies and gents who discreetly carried pistols and revolvers to keep themselves and Britain's streets safe. It was a dip into their pockets.

In 1899 the British army found that their skill at arms with Lee Enfield rifles didn't measure up well to the Boers in South Africa, who had Mauser rifles and better long-range skills. The experience caused further interest in shooting, with working men's clubs and places of work developing miniature rifle ranges to use .22 rifles. What was actually miniaturised was the targets: a postcard size kneeling figure at 25 yards simulates a real enemy at 300. Prime Minister Lord Salisbury is quoted as saying that he would laud the day when there was a rifle in every cottage in England.

After the Boer War came the Pistols Act 1903. Another ten-shilling licence, but this time one needed it to buy a pistol. Another wealth tax – the price of a hundred cartridges and anyone who had a game or gun licence was exempted. You only needed one of the three up to 1920.

In 1908 the government formed the Territorial army for volunteers from the industrial working class who did not have the money to join a part time rifle regiment and kit themselves out, so by 1914 Britain had a considerable number of men in the regular, volunteer and territorial armies trained and ready for war.

Meet Sir Ernley Blackwell

This chap was a lawyer and senior civil servant in the Home Office prior to the Great War. His concern was the availability of handguns; safe in his ivory tower, he probably never felt the need to have one but what other people did with theirs intruded on his thinking.

In January 1909 an armed robbery attempt by Latvian immigrants turned into a street chase in which 1,000 shots were fired. History remembers this as the 'Tottenham Outrage'.

Two years later another couple of Latvians were cornered in 'the siege of Sidney Street' after killing three London policemen. Blackwell's boss – Home Secretary Winston Churchill – can be seen in newsreel footage of the incident visiting the action.

Blackwell was in a flap about anarchists with guns and felt no better about private gun ownership when the Irish rising took place over Easter 1916.

Blackwell chaired a committee of his choice convened to decide what to do about bankrupt European governments selling off war surplus to potential third-world hotspots. His (never published) 'Blackwell Report' didn't address his brief and was largely a rant about the availability of firearms, particularly in Ireland.

What he recommended was *"stringent regulation"* of rifles and small arms as *"the number of persons who can urge any reasonable ground for possession of a revolver or pistol is extremely small...the danger attending the indiscriminate possession of such weapons is obvious"*.

The danger to whom is unsaid. Ten police officers on the British mainland had been shot dead in the preceding two decades; four of them by the Latvians mentioned above.

In a country at war, whose government had been giving away captured German rifles, machine guns and even field artillery to the public as inducements to buy war bonds, in which nearly every town, village, factory and mine had a rifle range and every commissioned officer, bank officer, nightwatchman and most citizens had a sidearm, he couldn't think his way past the problems caused by a few Latvians a decade earlier to see why Britain was such a safe place – a well-armed, polite society.

Now the Actual Gun Laws

Influenced by Sir Ernley Blackwell's report, firearms legislation was introduced in 1920. The government presented it as an anti-crime measure – London had an average of four armed robberies a year during the war – but its actual objective was to restrict firearms ownership to 'friends of the government'. Who might or might not be the government's friends is a matter of perspective – the government of 1920 was fearful of a revolution as had occurred in Russia.

The Firearms Act is silent about common law rights, neither referring to them nor repealing them. It refers to exemptions from the need to have a firearm certificate within itself, including preparation for defence of the realm, but makes no mention of the defence of life and property. To this day, police officers rely on these common law rights for their possession of arms.

In a brief exchange in the House of Commons, the Home Secretary told Commander Kenworthy (Liberal MP for Hull Central) that the firearms bill would make no difference to his right to defend himself.

In fact, the Firearms Act 1920 made no difference to the country. Working men had .22 rifle clubs as a result of Lord Salisbury's aspiration, with numerous workplaces having practice ranges. Full bore (centrefire) target rifle shooting was a university thing, students being recruited to the clubs formed at Bisley and elsewhere when the Territorial Army superseded the volunteer rifle regiments. Every surviving officer of the Great War came home with his revolver or pistol to shoot the rust out of at summer events, numerous servicemen brought souvenirs home, and millions of citizens had a pocket revolver or pistol 'just in case'.

The British Government was far from stable between the wars but prevailed as a democratic government, one of just eleven on the planet in the 1930s. Public opinion divided into two camps: those who expected a further war and sought to be prepared for it, and those for whom the last war should have been just that.

Home Office policy, as articulated by Sir Ernley Blackwell, was against the private possession of arms, handguns in particular. There were three amnesties in the 1930s for the organised surrender of arms to the police that netted 38,878 guns, three-quarters of which were pistols and revolvers.

The rifle clubs continued to be prepared. Carrying concealed sidearms remained the practice of those professions and citizens who had been doing it before the war and, while legislation may not have prevented owners keeping their guns, the Firearms Act 1920 did prevent the sale of ammunition to anyone other than certificate holders. That sparked amnesty surrenders of guns people had no use for.

The under-current was the Home Office squeezing the public into disposing of guns, a marked reluctance by chief constables to issue certificates, and difficulties placed in the way of people trying to remain prepared for defending the realm.

There were a few amendments to the law in the 1930s plus one decided case in the Court of Appeal and then came the Second World War, in which every armed forces' commission came with a free revolver.

1945 and after

While post-Great War concerns had been about revolution, the issue after the second war was feral youth running amok. Growing up in wartime with less adult supervision than any other generation of the 20th century, the likes of Derek Bentley, Christopher Craig, Ruth Ellis, Reggie and Ronnie Kray, Charlie Richardson and Harry Roberts (all born 1926-36) didn't do well in the national service finishing school. Once let loose on society, this lot and their contemporaries worried Home Office civil servants and led, first, to the Prevention of Crime Act 1953.

This introduced the concept of 'offensive weapons'. To this point carrying any weapon was regarded as a right to personal protection, but this Act treated the possession of certain weapons in public as offensive per se (e.g. flick knives, coshes and some legitimate items carried dubiously in public, such as a motorbike chain or lead pipe).

The Act was silent about firearms and didn't declare them 'offensive' or identify any weapon as 'defensive', so at this point an anecdote. A firearm certificate holder in Wiltshire had a 1st model Ladysmith revolver for his personal protection. After the 1953 Act, local police told him it was no longer policy to permit firearm certificates for this purpose, so they changed his 'good reason' for having the revolver to 'pest control' as that, they said, amounted to the same thing. The revolver and the documentation entered the gun trade from his estate in the 1990s.

This was a shift of policy, not law, so what didn't change was the common law right to arms. The common law can only be amended by a statute that says it's doing so on its face, and none such exists. The Wiltshire anecdote shows that at least some firearms owned for protection were put onto certificates, while other anecdotal evidence suggests many were simply kept 'in case'.

Such as in 1940: Winston Churchill's wartime bodyguard borrowed an automatic pistol and holster from a constabulary and persuaded them to write him a certificate for it before returning Churchill's Colt .45 automatic to him. Churchill put it in his overcoat pocket and then they went off to meet the French government for the last time in the spring of 1940. Whether Churchill ever held a certificate for any of the firearms he possessed or not is a matter for further research.

Another policy shift following the Second World War was when the government decided all firearms issued to or captured by British forces were government property, so souveniring was discouraged.

Then we had the step-change in thinking caused by atomic weapons. While the Swiss government opted to build adequate bomb shelters for all, the British government could not afford to do so. Instead it opted for strategic nuclear bunkers – for government and local government officials — from which to ride out the catastrophe.

All the scenarios played out in war games in the cold war envisaged having to defend these facilities against bands of heavily armed men roving the streets and countryside; i.e. rifle clubs pissed off at being left out in the cold. It was this thinking and planning that led to the change of policy regarding the public having arms for their defence. The Home Office didn't trust the public it purported to serve because its policy was to abandon them to the fallout.

Above ground the sport shooting scene gradually recovered, but our society had evolved. The 'you've never had it so good' generation of skilled working-class men had increased mobility – they could afford cars and motorbikes — and were buying shotguns, for which one needed a gun licence from the Post Office. A firearm certificate was only required for those shotguns that had barrels less than 20 inches long.

What the skilled working classes got up to with their shotguns was clay pigeon shooting, as landowners realised the profits to be made from facilitating the sport; it occupies less real estate than a golf course, involves far less maintenance and you get your money quicker. But there was no crime or public order issue with this increase in gun ownership.

Nor was there any legislation. A 1947 Court of Appeal case considered whether a flare pistol converted to fire shotgun cartridges needed a firearm certificate or not, and the thorny issue of whether an air gun should be classed as a toy or a weapon reached the Court of Appeal (again) in 1960 – the case of Moore v Gooderham. The issue was that a youth had bought the gun: legal if a toy, but he'd be under-age to buy a weapon.

The court concluded 'weapon', which brought low-powered air guns into scope as firearms, albeit firearms not requiring a certificate. This kicked off a statistical rise in 'firearms offences' as prosecutors locked onto air weapons as 'firearms' in cases of broken windows and such.

Departmental policies tend to drive change when a weak or distracted government is in charge, and new Ministers are easily led by the nose to whatever policies the department has waiting. In October 1964, Harold Wilson's Labour Party won election to form a government with a majority of four seats. This opened the door to a five-year trial abolition of the death penalty in 1965.

Then in August 1966 Harry Roberts – one of the feral youths mentioned earlier — was one of the gunmen who shot three policemen in London. He would have been for the drop but for hanging having been abolished, as would the other famous murderers that year: Ian Brady, Myra Hindley, Reggie and Ron Kray — all made famous by newspaper campaigns to restore the death penalty. But instead of bowing to media pressure, the Home Secretary introduced shotgun certificate legislation as a diversionary tactic.

The Cold War 1968 - 88

The 1968 Act – still in force — was an act of consolidation – bringing all the firearms laws together in one chapter. The requirement to obtain a shotgun certificate was announced on noticeboards in Post Offices – the place where law-abiding citizens had gone to buy their gun licences and still had to go for a game licence.

Some 600,000 people applied for the new certificates out of a population of 55 million. That attracted the concern of the chief inspector of constabularies (Sir) John McKay, who formed a committee to 'do something' about the number of guns in the hands of the public. His conclusion was that reducing that number to an absolute minimum was a desirable end in itself.

As with Sir Ernley Blackwell fifty years earlier, his was a committee of his clones. Neither committee had any counterbalance, and both were only concerned with firearms in the context of crime and public disorder.

His 1972 report was never formally published but a green paper (Cmnd 5297) containing some of his suggested provisions was. It had the effect of creating a gun lobby in Britain — the British Shooting Sports Council.

Parliament voted against the proposals; its members lobbied by gun owners alert to the blinkered attitude presented in the green paper. The Home Office put the plans onto the backburner to await a 'suitable legislative opportunity' and the police adopted many of McKay's proposals as practice.

The organisations that came together to form B.S.S.C., such as the National Rifle Association, were governing bodies of aspects of the shooting sports — the rule-makers and competition organisers. None of them knew at the time that they had become a public order problem that police were trying to solve by eroding their membership.

Getting a firearm certificate prior to 1972 was a matter of joining a shooting club and passing social muster with its committee, for the very good reason that they didn't want to be in the same room or range as someone they could not trust with loaded firearms. Once through the social – almost masonic — test, probationary members could begin to learn from the club's masters and once they thought the beginner ready, apply for a firearm certificate.

The result was that nobody who wasn't ready for a certificate applied, so nobody was refused one. That 'anomaly' led to policing 'taking over' the decision as to who was fit and ready in the early 1970s.

Police involvement from 1920 amounted to checking an applicant's history and antecedents against the answers given on the application form. The minutiae of what firearms the applicant wanted was sorted out with club trainers and firearms dealers. The step-change in 1973 was that policing created application failures by intervening in this process: there were refusals for centrefire pistols because a policeman said beginners should start with a .22 and such. 'Collecting' ceased (administratively) to be recognised as a 'good reason' and many other little tricks were tried to reduce the number of certificates. Parliament hadn't provided policing with any means to restrict the number, so they were winging it.

In addition to the 1968 Firearms Act, the Home Office also

took over the management of prohibited weapons from the Defence Council. It had long been a thorn in policing's side that people and businesses requiring this authority could not be refused the necessary firearm certificate or dealer's registration. It was introduced in 1937 to prevent the police interfering in defence of the realm matters and now they were getting the opportunity back. 'Section 5' controls at that time only covered machineguns, explosive shells and poison gas.

The Home Office drafted a 'memorandum of guidance for the police' in 1969 and circulated it to chief constables. It was a 'restricted' document, never published, but served for the next twenty years as the bible for firearms administrators.

Firearm certificate holders gradually felt the changes as they came up for the three-yearly certificate renewal. Target shooters found new conditions on their certificates; machinegun ownership and collecting ended and section 5 authorities were restricted to businesses involved in manufacturing and export.

The problem with the Home Office being in charge is that it has nothing to do with any aspect of the gun subculture: manufacturing is a Department of Trade and Industry matter and firearms exports concern the Foreign Office and Ministry of Defence. Sport comes under the Department for Culture, Media and Sport, while pest control and game shooting are the province of the Department for Environment, Food and Rural Affairs. The Home Office is only concerned with public order, disorder, crime, immigration and such.

Legitimate gun owners were targeted by police investigations, sparking a massive wave of prosecutions in which more firearms cases reached the Court of Appeal after 1968 than in the half century before that. And all the defendants were registered firearms dealers – or had been until charged – followed by a stream of erstwhile certificate holders.

Despite this – or possibly because of it raising the profile of the shooting sports in the media — shooting was on the up with four national shooting organisations launched in the 1970s.

Another contemporary gun-user trend was re-enactment. The Sealed Knot Society started it in 1968 – dressing for the English Civil War. Other organisations formed around specific periods, all requiring the correct weapons. The law counts replica muzzle-loaders as firearms, so Sealed Knot members needed shotgun certificates for their matchlocks. The WW2 types also went for shotguns - smooth-bored Lee Enfields became popular. Policing's attempt to block these downgrades failed at the Court of Appeal in 1980 (Attorney General's Reference No 3). Every sport and leisure pursuit was on the up in this period, as were the court cases directed at preventing the public enjoying guns.

Another way of reducing certificate numbers was to deny certificates for antiques. That led to various prosecutions and a Court of Appeal decision in 1977 (Richards v Curwen) that became legal guidance – but was ignored by the Home Office. Since then, numerous antiques cases have gone to court because of the chasm between police guidance and the Court of Appeal guidance. So many lives disrupted by a policy anomaly.

It was very clear in the mid 1980s that the Home Office was uncomfortable with the increasing popularity of sports and pastimes that involved the public owning firearms. Almost every aspect of what was on sale and in use had been attacked by prosecution or legislation, from Noel Corry's Spanish replica flintlocks to Kavanagh's shotgun action, from Hucklebridge's smooth-bored Lee Enfield via Curwen's antique revolvers to Fred Clarke's machinegun parts.

The problem was, and remains, that the Home Office was still worried about roving bands of heavily armed men trying to get into their nuclear bunker. Police concerns about gun crime ranged from concerns for their own safety as a result of the death penalty being abolished, to frantic trawls through certificate holders in search of prosecutions in order to generate higher conviction rates to justify their own ever-increasing arsenals.

The 1988 knee-jerk

In August 1987 a spree killer shot twenty-nine people in Hungerford, Berkshire after committing a kidnap and murder in Wiltshire. Just over a month later, Home Secretary Douglas Hurd announced – at the Police Superintendents' conference – a ban on semiautomatic machine guns, whatever they are.

'New' legislation (actually Sir John McKay's work, rejected in the 1970s and dusted off) banned all pump-action and semi-automatic centrefire rifles, most other military surplus, and some shotguns that the police wanted to be 'police-only'. The main casualties of this reversal of so many Court of Appeal decisions were service rifle competitors and 20th century re-enactment groups.

New Home Office guidance to the police published in 1989 green-lit the Forensic Science Service's aim to catch more firearms in the prohibition net than Parliament had intended, thus setting the scene for court battles involving law-abiding firearm owners as defendants over the next few years.

New administrative restrictions on what rifle clubs could use and do, along with increased micromanagement by police of who could join, progressively separated the clubs from their constitutional defence of the realm objectives, with this separation becoming complete in the mid-1990s.

And then another knee-jerk – Dunblane

Hungerford murderer Michael Ryan had used a Norinco type 56 rifle, an M1 carbine and a Beretta 92F pistol to fire 119 shots in his 1987 killing spree: half his victims fell to his pistol.

On 13 March 1996, Thomas Hamilton walked into a Dunblane primary school carrying two Browning GP35 pistols and two Smith and Wesson model 19 revolvers. Firing about 100 rounds he shot 32 staff and pupils, of whom half died.

Conspiracy theories abound and won't go away, but what should be made clear is that both men had firearm certificates *issued by the police* for the weapons and ammunition they used in their crimes.

That is what officialdom focussed on: that they'd obtained firearms legally and used them in crimes, which led to the official view that Britain's firearms controls were inadequate.

Our view is that it's how the law is administered that counts. When policing took over deciding who could have what in the 1970s – taking all that social control away from the gun subculture of clubs and dealers – they were also taking responsibility for the outcomes. Michael Ryan would not have stayed the course through probation and training at his second club and would not have had the murder weapons had the police not approved those acquisitions without him going through probation and the training phase of club membership first.

Thomas Hamilton's club had closed in the mid 90s and he was in the process of trying to get into another one (which didn't want him because he failed the social test) when his certificate was renewed; so it appears to us that his certificate was renewed contrary to Home Office rules. Both cases show signs of having fallen through the police controls and might not have occurred had those controls been used fully and properly – or just left to the clubs as pre-1973.

The same can also be said of the more recent spree killings by men who didn't belong to the shooting subculture at all – Derrick Bird and Mike Atherton. Only the police knew they had guns *and had approved them having them.*

After each spree killing, certificate holders became scapegoats, as the Home Office added ever more firearms types to the prohibited list.

The post-Dunblane legislation banned handguns. Legislation after that banned air cartridge revolvers and air soft 'firearms' with some savings, and then in 2010 we got a really weak government and a sleep-walker for a Home Secretary. The result has been a drip, drip, drip of some new initiative for its own sake each year. Statutory Instruments in 2010, 2011, 2014, 2015, 2018 and 2019 and some primary legislation in 2014 and 2017 made up new crimes and restrictions.

Explosives regulations were revised in 2014, creating limits on the amount of propellent powder and primers that can be kept without an explosives licence. Black gunpowder is subject to explosive licence controls while propellent powders can only be sold to reloaders who have a firearm or shotgun certificate.

Hefty fees were introduced for 'section 5' authorities which now embrace more than 40 subdivisions ranging from machine guns through automatic rifles to pistols, mortars, rocket launchers, some air guns, some shotguns; expanding ammunition and most military spec cartridges. It also includes tranquiliser darts and gas munitions. Anything that projects a 'noxious' thing is also caught by section 5, such as a water pistol loaded with ammonia.

Acquiring a section 5 authority involves, apart from the fee, meeting Home Office criteria for possession. This is defined as 'need', thus vets can get authority for tranquiliser darts. Authority for any of the weapons or ammunition requires a business purpose with foreign buyers holding an end-user certificate who are acceptable to our government.

In 2017 the Policing and Crime Act rendered all deactivated firearms as 'defectively deactivated', meaning they could not be sold – a parting gift from Europe. A whole collectors' market vanished at a stroke. In 2019 a statutory instrument created a register for the transfer of deactivated firearms and a few other nasties from Europe that may lapse once Britain leaves the EU, such as repeating a firearm's serial number on all its parts including the firing pin.

Another SI was drafted to make a medical compulsory for all. This disappeared in the confusion of the general election but the police have taken the law into their own hands, relying on a SI to contact every applicant's doctor to confirm there are no grounds for concern about the applicant possessing firearms.

The law currently requires all applicants to be registered with a general practitioner and to declare *any relevant medical condition*. Home Office guidance suggests what's relevant, ranging from depression/anxiety through drug abuse to dementia.

It is relevant that none of the killers on whom the Home Office have relied for their knee-jerks – from the Latvians in the 1900s to spree killers a hundred years later - was diagnosed as having any of these things. It's purely a device for trying to reduce certificate numbers.

Some doctors are refusing to take part and, since the SI is not on the statute books, its instruction to police to refuse certificates where doctors refuse to cooperate has no judicial authority. Despite potentially acting unlawfully, the police persevere.

What's left?

Clubs that meet Home Office criteria are approved for rifles and loose ammunition (i.e. cap and ball or muzzle-loaded reproduction) pistols. Club members can then use club guns – and each other's – without holding a certificate.

Anybody other than a prohibited person can possess any antique firearm as a curiosity or ornament. What meets that definition is a movable feast and may be targeted for additional controls in the near future, but currently anything with an obsolete ignition system or that takes an obsolete cartridge, or loose ammunition and was made before 1939 is fairly safe.

Air rifles that generate less than 12-foot pounds and pistols less than 6-foot pounds at the muzzle are currently exempted from firearm certificate controls in England and Wales. There is no definition of a pistol to distinguish it from a rifle in this context, but any 'pistol' that exceeds 6-foot pounds at the muzzle is a section 5 prohibited weapon.

Airsoft guns are now exempted from Firearms Act controls, but owners can run afoul of public order legislation if seen with them in a public place.

Who can own guns?

For legally available products, one has to be over 18, not 'prohibited', and legally resident in the country. There is no bar on foreign nationals applying for certificates, but references will be sought from UK residents who have known the applicant for more than two years and criminal checks are made in the country of origin.

The main conditions of ownership are 'good reason' and secure storage, requiring a gun cabinet or safe.

'Good reason', in general, means proving that one has an accepted reason plus somewhere safe and legal to use the gun.

For target shooting, that means membership of a suitable club. For vermin control, owning or having provable permission to shoot over land on which there is a problem (rabbits, foxes, etc) is required. The applicant also needs an open licence from DEFRA. For deer stalking, owning or having provable permission to shoot over land where there are deer.

Collecting is recognised for possession on certificate of non-prohibited weapons without ammunition.

Examples of 'good reasons' that have not been accepted include 'retention of family heirlooms' and 'investment'.

The gun also has to be of an acceptable type (to the Home Office) for the intended purpose. For deer, a minimum calibre of .240 and muzzle energy of 1,700 foot pounds is required and you can't have a big game rifle for deer stalking or an air weapon for fox control.

Firearms and shotguns held on certificates must be stored securely when not in use to prevent access by unauthorised persons, which includes other members of the household who aren't certificate holders. Air weapons have to be kept securely to prevent access by under 18s.

Regional Variations

Scotland has the same firearm and shotgun certificate arrangements as England and Wales, with an additional air weapon certificate for owners of low-powered air rifles and pistols. The Scottish Parliament is lobbying for more devolution of powers to add further restrictions on firearm ownership for Scottish residents and visitors.

The Isle of Man has similar controls to the UK but hasn't banned handguns, walking stick shotguns or air cartridge revolvers. They have a separate 'regulated weapons certificate' for owning air guns and crossbows, subject only to being over-18.

The States of Guernsey also haven't banned handguns yet but have more controls over access to ammunition and regular lobbying by their police for more powers to restrict gun ownership further. The Guernsey police website relating to firearm certificates starts with the sentence: "Firearms are dangerous weapons."

Jersey likewise has no handgun ban, but as with Guernsey the private ownership of firearms has been continually reviewed and lobbied about for the past three decades, and that trend seems set to continue.

These islands are not in the EU and have thus not adopted any of the EU regulations relating to firearms.

Northern Ireland laws differ from the rest of the UK in many respects. They don't have a handgun ban or shotgun certificates – everything goes on the firearm certificate including air weapons. Pistol magazines are included on the certificate and personal protection is a good reason for having a handgun although only ball ammunition can be used for defence – courtesy of an EU directive in 1993.

Gun Crime

Gun crime in the UK takes some dismantling. The problem is a conviction for 'possession without a certificate' could relate to a drugs gang member left holding the baby or his squeeze having it in her handbag. Just as easily, it could relate to a firearm certificate holder who was late handing in his renewal application.

I have dealt with cases (as an expert witness) where 'possession without a certificate' included a guy who had authority to acquire a gun. He'd made the piece but hadn't finished it when busted. Similarly, the police have been putting conditions on humane killer handguns, restricting them to two shots. One chap, with the gun on his certificate, was convicted of possessing his gun without a certificate because someone on the police side deemed the blanking materials used to reduce the cylinder's capacity from six to two as inadequate.

Firearms homicides averaged about 50 a year after WW2 and stayed pretty level while the population increased. As a proportion of the homicide rate it's never been more than 10% of the death total in any year. Current murder rates show knife killings as the most numerous (285 in 2018 – 39% of the total) with beatings (with or without a blunt instrument) lying second with 106 deaths. That's the norm: sharp instruments always seem to top the list.

The most recent annual figure for gun deaths in the year to March 2018 was 29 and the year before was 32 – the highest number for six years. The lowest in that period was 21. In the preceding decade (which included the Cumbria spree killings and the Mike Atherton murders, ranged from 39 to 60 a year.

As to whether firearms legislation has any impact on crime prevention, I think the facts speak for themselves. The four spree killers who held weapons on police-issued certificates killed 48 people. (In the same period -1987-2019 - terrorists killed 1,111 people with explosives being the commonest method.) Pinning down what guns were used in other murders, where they came from and how the killers got hold of them is not easily done; so much of the information being anecdotal.

Practically every firearm in existence started out 'legal', either because there weren't any rules where and when it was made or because it and its first owner complied with the rules of the day. The Latvians who shot four policemen dead in the first decade of the 20th century did so with 'legal' guns; we don't know if they'd bought pistol licenses in the UK or brought their guns from Latvia. There was no law to stop them at the time.

We calculated that an unregistered pool of some four million firearms existed in the UK in 1988. These were (a) pre-regulation – acquired before certificates for them were introduced, (b) war relics, (c) illegal imports or (d) improvised firearms. Murderers might be the owners in one of these categories or might be the beneficiaries of a sale or theft from one of the above.

Forty-six police officers have died as a result of gunshot wounds on the UK mainland since 1945: most were either responding to emergency calls from the public or stopped a suspect who shot his way out. One was shot by a diplomat firing at protesters from within his embassy and one by a firearm certificate holder in the 1987 Hungerford massacre.

What may be owned?

Firearms fall into four categories, viz:

    a. Exempted from certification: This includes low-powered

air guns, antiques, deactivated firearms, airsofts, replicas and ornaments.

b. 'Section 1' firearms are those that require a firearm certificate and a 'good reason' for each.

c. 'Section 2' is shotguns that are exempted from 'section 1' but need to be on a shotgun certificate because they are shotguns. A 'section 2' shotgun has a barrel more than 61cm long and a bore of less than 2 inches. It either has no magazine, or a fixed magazine that holds no more than two cartridges. If it's pump action or semi-automatic it must also be more than 40 inches long overall, measured with any non-rigid stock in the collapsed position.

d. 'Section 5' is the prohibited weapons category, which includes air pistols generating more than 6 foot pounds at the muzzle, pump action or semi-automatic shotguns that have barrels less than 61 cm long, any 'small firearm' having a barrel of less than 30cm, any semiautomatic rifle chambered for any cartridge other that .22 rimfire, any machine gun, burst fire weapon and about three dozen other categories by type, action, etc.

This is a dog's breakfast, obviously. Consider my Mossberg 500ATP, acquired in 1979. This is a pump action shotgun with a 61cm (24-inch) barrel. The magazine is a tube beneath the barrel and in 1979 this was legally a shotgun requiring a section 2 certificate.

In 1988, legislative changes made it a 'firearm' requiring a 'firearm certificate' – section 1. This was because its magazine capacity was more than two shells. I could have had it converted to limit it to two shells in the magazine and kept it on the shotgun certificate, but I didn't because I had a 'good reason' for having the higher capacity.

I'd actually bought it for 'pest control' – pigeons over decoys – but I also used it for 'practical shotgun' and had won the 1988 National Match at Diggle Ranges with it. The 1988 legislative complications were that IF the barrel had been a bit shorter, or IF I'd had one of those swanky folding stocks on it, the reduced dimensions would have put it in section 5 – the (until then) machinegun category.

Summary of what's allowed

Centrefire rifles	Single shot mechanisms, bolt action and lever action repeaters are allowed. No fully automatic or semi-automatic allowed. Magazine capacity is not limited.
Rimfire rifles	All kinds (semi-automatic, bolt action, pump action and lever action) are allowed. Barrels must be more than 30cm long and the overall length must exceed 60cm. Magazine capacity is not limited.
Shotguns	Break action, bolt action and lever action are allowed - section 1 if a magazine is detachable or holds more than 2 shells. Pump action and semi-automatic are allowed - section 1 if the magazine capacity is more than 2; section 5 if barrel is less than 61cm. Magazine capacity – limit of 2 in a fixed magazine for shotgun certificate. No upper limit on firearm certificates.
Pistols	Mostly not allowed. There are exemptions for humane dispatch, and the collecting and limited use of some classics where they can be kept on a firearm certificate. The handgun ban actually prohibits 'small firearms', defined as having a barrel of less than 30cm and/or an overall length of 60cm. This has resulted in the trade building long-barrel revolvers with a counter-balance bar to make the overall length more than two feet, which are sold on section 1 firearm certificates but can't be owned by clubs.
Paintball	Paintball is legal although one police force prosecuted a paintball site proprietor for having a 'prohibited weapon': a smoothbore semiautomatic carbine contrary to section 5 and obtained a conviction because he pleaded guilty. Other police forces didn't follow suit and the same paintball carbine was still on open sale two years later, so aside from destroying one life and livelihood it appears the Forensic Science Service attack on that hobby didn't get off the ground.

How shooters responded

After the 1988 Act banned semi-automatic rifles, some owners either exported their rifles or took them to friendlier jurisdictions such as Belgium, France, Jersey, the Isle of Man, Norway and Switzerland. The United States was closed to such imports at the time. Some of these schemes are still operating; others were gradually closed by local legislative or administrative changes, or by aging shooters giving up.

The main driver for keeping guns abroad was the government attitude, including a lack of trust, the derisory buy-in scheme (half the value of the rifle as determined by auction prices, or £150 and nothing for accessories) and the demeaning of anyone involved in the shooting sports. That said, numbers were small; the overseas escapees collectively accounted for less than 10% of what was handed in, and what was handed in was only 5% of what was out there.

Over half the rifles that I saw at the time going for export or deactivation were British L1A1 self-loading service rifles or the continental equivalents – the FN FAL, G1 and such. The rest were made up of other semiautomatic variants of service rifles of the day – AR15s, Galil, Steyr AUG, Valmet and some 'civilian' models – a Remington .222 pump, Ruger Mini 14s and ranch rifles. I saw just one Norinco type 56 like Michael Ryan's and a handful of M1 carbines.

A lot of owners opted for deactivation, which the legislation recognised, but that led to court cases such as when Horatio Charalambous was prosecuted for possessing his deactivated L1A1 rifle because the serial number on the bolt carrier showed it was from a different rifle. He was acquitted.

The situation and 'atmosphere' after the handgun ban was quite different. The buy-in scheme was more generous in that it recognised accoutrements, with the result that a lot of owners took the opportunity to 'cash-out' of a hobby that had ceased to be acceptable to the government. Owners had more guns and accessories than other shooting sports and thus more to sell to their government, although it welched on many of the claims. While over £100 million was paid out, two manufacturers (Realm Defence Industries Ltd and JSL (London) Ltd received nothing for their tooling, unused component parts or intellectual copyright.

Some shooters, instead of depositing guns abroad, took themselves off to France and elsewhere in Europe into semi-retirement. One collector shifted his Mauser broomhandle pistol collection (worth more than his house) to the USA and then fell afoul of his local police who couldn't 'check' where the guns were.

To this day, Britain is the only European country with a handgun ban.

Postscript

Firearms laws, such as those in Britain, create crime by moving the goalposts. What was legal at one time might not be after a shift in policy or statute: such as the case of the elderly widow prosecuted for possessing her deceased husband's Great War souvenirs as stolen Crown property. The idea that captured enemy weapons were 'Crown property' didn't kick in until 27 years after he took them home and by the time his widow was in the dock they were antiques anyway.

Firearms 'crimes' in the statistics are bolstered by prosecutions of certificate holders over perceived imperfections in paperwork. And it takes a lot of police resources to find such crumbs.

While all this legislation has a direct impact on law-abiding people who try to keep up with it – or who get caught out when the rules change and nobody tells them - it has no effect on those who weren't interested in obeying the law in the first place. Their crimes are buried in the figures and one can't tell which is which.

Britain is a safe place to live, whether you can defend yourself or not, because the risk of being caught up in a violent crime – or a terrorist attack – is rare. However, it is potentially more dangerous to be a firearm certificate holder, as anything you do might be investigated by armed police officers: such as the Burma Star veteran of Wingate's Chindits, arrested outside his home for possessing arms and ammunition in a public place, having left home with his guns to go to his shooting club's monthly meeting.

In my view it's time for a re-think. The regulation and management of the legitimate use of firearms should be by the relevant departments, freeing the Home Office to worry about actual problems in its remit and enabling the police to do something about the crimes that actually impact on the public.

A properly balanced management of our gun laws would see a massive and immediate decline in gun crime statistics without affecting public safety; and general public safety would be much enhanced by our government recognising our common law rights.

IRELAND (EIRE)

FRANK BROPHY

Firearms may be legally owned in Ireland for specific sporting/culling purposes only: clay shooting, game shooting, deer stalking, target shooting, vermin control, etc. Possessing a firearm for self defence is not permitted.

Current licensing conditions are extremely restrictive despite a huge number of successful court challenges in recent years.

It is likely that Ireland's gun laws have been subject to more litigation than those of any other country worldwide.

Since 2009, firearms have been subject to two licensing systems: "non-restricted" and "restricted".

Non-restricted includes shotguns with a maximum magazine capacity of three rounds, all rifles up to .30 calibre, and handguns of .22 calibre.

Restricted firearms include rifles above .30 calibre, semi-automatic shotguns and pump action shotguns with a magazine capacity of more than three rounds and all centre-fire handguns. Garda (Police) Superintendents issue certificates for non-restricted firearms and the Garda Commissioner (Ireland's Top Cop) through Chief Superintendents is responsible for restricted firearms.

Centre-fire handguns may only be licensed to individuals who held certificates for the particular firearm prior to November 2008. The issue of further centre-fire handgun certificates has been banned by law since 2009. When current holders (less than 500) retire from shooting or pass away, no licensed centre-fire handguns will be in the possession of civilians.

Fully automatic firearms of any calibre are banned.

Irish firearms legislation first came into existence in 1925. Prior to that, existing British gun laws applied. These were not intended to be user-friendly to the native Irish. The 1916 Easter Rebellion in Dublin resulted in political upheaval and an ensuing War of Independence (1918 – 1921) which in turn was followed by an even bloodier Civil War (1921 – 1922). Throughout those war years firearms laws would have been irrelevant.

The British mind-set had already been hugely influenced by the Russian revolution of 1917 when vast numbers of trained personnel turned on the Czarist regime. Concerns that millions of British soldiers returning after World War One could have proven a similar threat to the Establishment led to the hasty introduction of new firearms laws. A number of Irishmen who had served in the British forces during WW1 made themselves and their experience available to the Irish movement fighting for independence.

The creation of the new Irish Free State in 1921 necessitated the formation of a Civil Service employing experienced personnel. The newly-formed government retained members of the former Civil Service who imported the anti-gun prejudices of the British administration into the apparatus of the new state.

The firearms act that came into effect in 1925 was not unreasonable given the extent of the previous years' horrors in Ireland. If an applicant for a firearms certificate could show genuine reason for requiring the firearm, a local Garda (Police) Superintendent usually granted the certificate. Each firearm required a separate certificate, which expired annually on July 31st.

Ireland's large agricultural base necessitated a high volume of shotgun and .22 rifle ownership, while pistols and centre-fire rifles numbered less than 3,000. The Act was updated in 1964 to reclassify air guns as firearms, requiring owners to apply for firearms certificates. Air rifles and pistols which were previously available from sweet shops could then only be purchased from a registered firearms dealer.

The 1964 Act also included a number of minor adjustments which did not unduly hinder the licensing process at that time, although the old civil service aspiration of fewer guns in the hands of civilians was always in the background. This increasingly manifested itself more or less depending on which Garda Division an applicant lived in.

Some Superintendents had no difficulty issuing genuine applicants' certificates while others used various ploys to obstruct an applicant. Applications being "lost" was a regular occurrence, prompting some applicants to give up.

In the late 1960s trouble broke out in Northern Ireland. As this crisis deepened the Irish Government invoked a section of the 1964 Act which permitted licensed firearms to be taken into official custody in an emergency. Despite the emergency being in Northern Ireland, not in Ireland (Eire), the government used it to confiscate all handguns plus rifles over .22 cal on July 31st 1972, in accordance with the "One Month Temporary Custody Order" provided for in the Act.

The stated reason was to prevent licensed firearms being stolen by the Provisional IRA from private homes in Ireland for use in Northern Ireland. All firearms certificates coincidentally expired on that same date.

The Act is unambiguous in that firearms taken up under this particular section must be returned to their owners at the end of a one month period. In fact none were returned and all efforts to have the firearms returned were rejected on the grounds that the owners did not hold a current firearm's certificate; therefore firearms could not be given back.

This was seen by those who had previously held licences as sharp practise but apparently little could be done about it. Meetings during the early 1970s with Department of Justice officials and, on one occasion with the Justice Minister, were to no avail. The state was not prepared to hand back the private property that had been confiscated, citing "public safety" as a priority. In subsequent years approximately half a dozen individuals managed to secure firearms certificates for rifles of a calibre larger than .22, while the majority of deer hunters were restricted to using .22/250 calibre rifles until 1992.

As a result of an EU Directive obliging member states to permit a humane calibre for deer culling, rifles up to a maximum of .270 were then permitted in Ireland. This situation continued until 2004 - a total of 32 years - when a High Court challenge for a pistol licence (by this writer) brought it to an end. The case was successful and the Garda authorities were obliged to issue certificates for all sporting firearms including handguns irrespective of calibre as provided for in the 1925 Act.

However, this "honeymoon" period lasted only a few short years. The Garda and the Department of Justice commenced a campaign to have the issue of firearms certificates severely restricted. Many Superintendents made firearms licensing as difficult as possible and the "lost applications" syndrome returned. Anti-firearm articles and reports began to appear in newspapers.

A Firearms Consultative Panel was established with Ministerial agreement. Chaired by a senior official from the Justice Department and comprising Garda officers plus representatives from the various shooting organisations, the Committee's mandate was to produce a suitable regulatory licensing framework agreeable to all sides. Proposals which eventually emerged included a three-year firearms licensing system, range construction specifications, plus the issue of range operational certificates by a newly appointed Range Inspector.

Shooting clubs catering for rifle shooting, pistol shooting or both, were to be subject to the issue of a Garda Authorisation by the district Superintendent. Substantial costs to clubs would accrue in the issue of these certificates. .22 pistols would continue to be licensed but no further licences would be issued for centre-fire pistols. Smallbore pistols were to be restricted to 5-shot magazines and a list of "suitable" pistol makes/models was to be prepared and published by the

Garda Commissioner.

Gun-safes and monitored alarms became a requirement in most instances while all handguns would be restricted to use solely on authorised ranges. It was understood by shooting representatives on the FCP that current holders of centre-fire pistols would continue to have them licensed for the lifetime of the individual shooter. Anyone who did not hold a firearms certificate for a specific centre-fire pistol prior to November 2008 would be unable to obtain a certificate for that or any other centre-fire pistol.

It was then arranged to extend the then current certificate expiry date on a once off basis - from July to October 2009 - to facilitate the introduction of the new three-year licensing system. On a point of information, no legislation exists which permits this extension of the duration of firearms certificates.

This mostly unsatisfactory situation was accepted by Shooting Organisation representatives against an unspoken threat of draconian firearms legislation otherwise.

Unfortunately the State did not live up to the expectations of shooters. Most certificate renewal applications for centre-fire pistols during October 2009 were refused on the grounds that the applicants did not have sufficient reason to possess the firearm. (This writer's .22 pistol renewal applications were also refused although that matter was resolved at a later date).

A massive programme of litigation ensued nationwide, in both District Courts at local level and the High Court in Dublin. The latter's decisions create precedents which can only be overturned in the Supreme Court. The bulk of the District Court hearings ended in favour of the individual shooters but these decisions applied only to each specific case and could not be cited as precedent.

A total of 168 applications for judicial review were lodged in the High Court with all granted leave for a hearing. Such a large number of hearings would have taken months to process so both sides – the State and the individual appellants' legal team – agreed to proceed with three test cases in January 2012.

Three Garda Chief Superintendents involved were required to appear in court to answer Senior Counsel's questions. The State's position collapsed within a very short period after two of the Chief Superintendents had been questioned. Both had been negligent in complying with their statutory obligations in processing firearms certificate applications. The second Chief Superintendent was proven to have altered a number of documents after legal proceedings had commenced.

The High Court Judge immediately stopped the proceedings and in a matter of months all outstanding centre-fire firearms certificates had been issued to the 168 appellants.

In the midst of all this it transpired that the relevant Statutory Instrument authorising the inspection/certification of shooting ranges had not been signed by the Minister for Justice. The legal team was again obliged to go to the High Court seeking an order compelling the Minister to sign the Statutory Instrument. This was successful – inspection and authorising of shooting ranges nationwide commenced immediately.

That action had to be taken because the amendments to the firearms act specified that handguns could only be used on authorised ranges. Without authorised ranges, refusing to renew all firearms certificates would be a simple matter of "no authorised ranges, no pistols"!

The Garda authorities hit back within a short period, calling for the banning of all handguns, pump and semi-automatic shotguns and rifles above .30 calibre. Fresh problems for gun owners were invented. Licences were refused on spurious grounds including statements that .22 pistols on the recommended list were now "restricted" although the list remained unchanged and "restricted" licences could not be issued. This resulted in even more court challenges.

Officialdom further reacted by issuing statements and making public claims about the huge volume of licensed firearms being stolen and used in crime. Statistics presented by police to the Minister, possibly to convince her to take punitive action, were grossly inflated. Opposition members in the Dail (Parliament) challenged these figures on our behalf. Replicas, starting pistols, deactivated guns, a toy pistol, even a gun-safe were all recorded as "stolen firearms". Ammunition, stolen mainly from licensed dealers, was recorded often with each individual round of ammunition being classed as a stolen firearm.

The situation degenerated into further chaos with official statements being made about licensed firearms "known" to have been used in crime. When challenged, this claim morphed into "believed" they "might" have been used in criminal activity. No "stolen" firearm was ever recovered at a crime scene, nor was any evidence produced to support any of these claims.

On examining the eventual "genuine list" of five licensed handguns known to have been stolen in a 5-year period it emerged one was a Garda 9mm Sig pistol issued to a detective which was stolen from under a pillow in his house, and another was a 9mm Glock stolen from an Officer in Northern Ireland which was illegally imported into Ireland and held illegally by persons unknown.

Finally, in desperation, a decision was taken in conjunction with the shooters' legal team to serve a witness summons on the Minister for Justice requiring her to appear before a High

Court judge to be questioned about the behaviour of senior Garda Officers, who are ultimately responsible to her and the Department of Justice. Within days of the summons being served the Minister signed a Statutory Instrument which recognised the right of shooting clubs to exist and citizens to have access to licensed firearms for lawful sporting purposes.

She also re-convened the Firearms Consultative Panel which meets several times yearly. Areas of contention which may arise can now be dealt with before they reach crisis status. The Author served on this Panel for a period before retiring.

The licensing situation in Ireland, as described at the top of this chapter, is currently peaceful.

Shooting enthusiasts may apply for permits for all classes of rifles up to .30 calibre. Rifles above .30 calibre require a "restricted" certificate. There was uncertainty in relation to semi-automatic centre-fire rifles as a consequence of the European Union introducing a new policy banning certain types of centre-fire rifles. However, the Justice Minister signed Statutory Instrument 420 of 2019 on August 2nd 2019 which gave effect to the European Community Firearm Regulations from September 1st 2019.

Briefly, apart from storage, transport and other regulations, this confirms that owners of all semi-automatic rifles are restricted to using magazines with a maximum capacity of 10 rounds. Short centre-fire firearms (pistols) are restricted to using magazines with a maximum capacity of 20 rounds. The restriction of 5 rounds only remains for .22 pistols.

Only .22 pistols may be licensed – strictly for target shooting. Centre-fire pistols cannot be licensed unless the owner held a firearms certificate for the specific firearm prior to November 19 2008. Many consider this to be unconstitutional and only a Supreme Court challenge will bring it to a final conclusion.

The only abuse of firearms in this country today is as always by criminal gangs using illegally imported unlicensed weapons – usually along with equally illegal drug shipments.

Footnote 1:

Between 2014 and 2017, two Ministers for Justice and two Garda Commissioners resigned. The current Garda Commissioner, a former senior officer in the Police Service of Northern Ireland, is engaged in restructuring the Garda Siochana - Ireland's National Police Service.

The Government's Central Statistics Office (CSO) publishes data annually on various areas of Government activity - however to date the CSO adds a rider to Garda Statistics to the effect that it (the CSO) cannot stand over these figures.

Footnote 2:

One of my many experiences with the Irish licensing system:

I had been involved in African big game hunting since the 1990s and used my Irish-licensed .270 Mauser to hunt plains game, occasionally borrowing a locally owned larger calibre rifle.

In the early 2000s I enquired about purchasing a .375 H&H rifle in South Africa to be stored there and used when hunting in that country. Local laws did not permit this so I decided to buy a .375 from the UK and applied for an Irish firearms certificate.

The application was refused on spurious grounds – it would have been the first such calibre rifle to be licensed in Ireland – and in 2003 I challenged the refusal in Dublin's High Court. Shortly afterwards I challenged the refusal to licence a pistol I had stored in France and both cases commenced running concurrently. The pistol case was conceded in June 2004 with full costs in my favour, while the .375 case was constantly adjourned at the State's request.

Eventually the matter came up for a hearing in February 2008 and the State conceded the licence and full costs - outside the door of the courtroom. It took five long years during which others had applied for .375 licences and received them without difficulty!

Two days later, I travelled to the UK and purchased a Sako .375H&H Safari model rifle. My deposit on the original rifle purchased in 2003 was forfeit! A firearms dealer in Dublin was to arrange the rifle's importation into Ireland and I was issued a firearms licence for the rifle by the local Garda Superintendent.

Regrettably, the Department of Justice began stalling the issue of an Import Licence to the Dealer on the grounds of requiring more information about this rifle. It dragged on relentlessly despite the fact that the State had conceded the licence in the High Court and I possessed a current licence for the firearm.

I applied to the Police Service of Northern Ireland (PSNI) to have the rifle's details added to my PSNI Visitor's permit – occasionally I competed in pistol competitions in Northern Ireland. The dealer in Wales where the rifle was purchased had it transferred to a firearms dealer in Northern Ireland – it stayed within the UK. The Police in my district in the Republic (Eire) entered the rifle in my European Union Firearms Permit – they have no discretion where EU permits are concerned. So, with Ireland plus Northern Ireland (at that time) being members of the European Union I was covered on the island of Ireland, complying with all local and national firearm laws.

Early one morning I made the four hour journey to the Northern Ireland Dealer's premises, collected my new Sako rifle, and was back home in the South East by 2pm, armed with all the relevant firearms licences, backed by EU law plus the Good Friday Agreement relating to trade etc between the two jurisdictions. Also the 1964 Firearms Act includes a section which states that if a concurrent firearms certificate is in existence for a firearm, an Import Licence is not required to bring that firearm into Ireland – the same 1964 Act that permitted the "temporary" take-up of our firearms in 1972! I legally brought my rifle home. It's not unreasonable to speculate that the Department of Justice was not amused.

The saga didn't quite end there. When the firearms certificate expired in 2009 it was renewed under the new 3-year licensing system with an added condition attached stating that the rifle could only be used "outside the Jurisdiction". Abroad! This was completely illegal and it was pointed out to the issuing officer that the Firearms Act licensed firearms for use within the State only, and this condition was in breach of the law.

The request to remove the condition was refused so it was back to the High Court again. It took almost four more years for that condition to be removed – once again the State conceded with full costs.

The Irish taxpayer paid total costs for all appellants during those years of non-stop litigation.

INDIA
ABHIJEET SINGH

Who can own guns

The private ownership of firearms in India is governed by the Arms Act of 1959 and its subordinate rules.

Any person legally resident in India may apply for an Arms Licence for the type of firearm he/ she wishes to acquire so long as that person is not barred/ prohibited by the Arms Act. There is also a provision for temporary arms licences for bona fide target shooters who are visiting India to participate in a recognised shooting tournament.

The following categories of persons are barred from acquiring or having in their possession or carrying any arms or ammunition:

    i. Anyone who has not reached the age of twenty-one years, or
    ii. Anyone sentenced to imprisonment for any offence involving violence or moral turpitude and for a period of five years after the expiration of the sentences, or
    iii. Anyone subject to a bond for keeping the peace or for good behaviour.

There is a further prohibition on selling or transferring arms or ammunition to any person suspected to be of unsound mind.

A colonial era exemption (that has been continued) allows people belonging to a certain community (called Kodavas), belonging to a particular district of the state of Karnataka, to own firearms without an Arms Licence so long as they do not carry those firearms outside of the district. As a result there is widespread firearm ownership within the district, including firearms in restricted categories. The annual incidence of firearm related crimes varies between zero and one or two!

The law provides Licensing Authorities with substantial flexibility and discretion. While these provisions were retained under the assumption that they would be used judiciously and in the public interest, the real life experience of applicants shows this is not the case.

For example, in many jurisdictions the Licensing Authority requires all applicants to submit property papers and income tax returns for review. This is despite the fact that the Arms Act makes it very clear in section 14(2) that:

> *"(2) The licensing authority shall not refuse to grant any licence to any person merely on the ground that such person does not own or possess sufficient property."*

Since possessing insufficient property cannot be grounds for refusal, why then require such documents? Isn't this a clear indication of a class bias, where the Licensing Authority is seeking to evaluate a person's net worth before grant of licence?

In other jurisdictions applicants are required to make "donations" to the local Red Cross and/or purchase Government bonds of a certain value, before their applications will be considered. The media has also reported on bizarre instances of Licensing Authorities adopting policies of only granting a licence to those who have undergone a vasectomy! Quite obviously the discretion to grant or refuse a licence is being blatantly misused to serve other interests.

Furthermore, for the past few years, in a move that is clearly ultra vires, almost all Licensing Authorities are demanding that applicants prove "grave and imminent threat" to their lives prior to grant of a licence. This is an absolutely ridiculous demand, as most citizens acquire a firearm to protect themselves against random acts of violence (which have been on a consistent upswing over the past few decades) and not based on some pre-existing threat.

Usually it is only persons of prominence or large wealth who are issued "threats" by anti-social elements, indicating this is a clear attempt to ensure that ordinary law abiding citizens are automatically disqualified from acquiring an arms licence and only the high and mighty would be so "blessed".

What may be owned

The following types of firearms may be legally owned against a valid Arms Licence in India:

1) Restricted Category Firearms (Licences for these are next to impossible)
   a) Semi-automatic centrefire rifles
   b) Firearms chambered for service calibres (.303 , 7.62x51, 7.62x39, 5.56x45, 9x19mm, .455 Webley and .38-200)
2) Permissible Category Firearms (Licences for these are difficult but possible)
   a) Breech loading centrefire rifles other than those chambered for service calibres and not semi-automatic
   b) Breech loading .22 calibre rimfire rifles including semi-automatic
   c) Breech loading shotguns including semi-automatic

d) Handguns including semi-automatic other than those chambered for service calibres

e) Muzzle loading guns

f) Airguns with calibre exceeding .177 or muzzle energy exceeding 20 joules

g) Blank firing guns

h) Paintball guns

i) Firearms replicas (replicas of antique firearms are exempt from licensing)

Airguns with calibre up to .177 and muzzle energy below 20 joules are exempt from licensing requirements.

No licences can be issued for fully automatic firearms of any type. These are expressly prohibited under the Arms Act.

What are the conditions of ownership

1. A valid reason must be given at the time of application for an arms licence. Acceptable reasons are:

    a. Self defense/protection – usually evidence of a verifiable threat to life is demanded at the time of application

    b. Shooting sports (proof of participation in one or more recognised events is required at the time of application)

    c. Crop protection (usually only muzzleloader or at best a shotgun licence may be issued for this; proof of ownership of agricultural land must be provided at the time of application)

    d. Transfer of family heirloom – applicable if the original owner dies and his next of kin wish to retain the firearm OR if the original owner is over a certain age and wishes to transfer the firearms (to next of kin) during his lifetime.

2. For each additional firearm that one wishes to acquire a fresh application must be made.

3. No person (barring some special exceptions) may own

or possess more than two firearms. A limit of three was introduced in 1983, but this has been further restricted to only two, per an amendment to the Arms Act made in December 2019.

4. All arms licences are subject to an "area of validity" and the licensee may not take the firearms beyond this area without prior written permission of the authorities. Most commonly this is restricted to the district of residence of the licensee. The licensee may apply for and have the area of validity extended to the entire state, which is usually possible. There is also a provision to have the area of validity extended to the whole of India, although this is usually granted with much difficulty.

5. All licences are subject to a maximum amount of ammunition that may be purchased at any one time as well as in the whole calendar year – colloquially referred to as the "ammunition quota".

    a. The most common quota is 25 rounds at one time and a maximum limit of 50 rounds in a calendar year i.e. 25/50.
    b. The new Arms Rules 2016 have provided for a universal increase in these quotas, to enable arms licence holders to properly train in the use of their firearms, but the individual needs to apply to the authorities for this.
        i. For ordinary citizens the revised quotas (available on application to the relevant authorities) are 100/200
        ii. For shooters affiliated with recognised clubs these new quotas range from 200 to 500 (at one time) up to a maximum of 500 to 1000 in a year (depending on class of firearms).
        iii. For shooters with some level of sporting achievements the quotas increase substantially, ranging from

15,000 to 200,000 depending on level of achievement. This is merely a "permission to purchase"; there is NO government subsidy!

6. A 1980 government notification classified multiple projectile cartridges with individual projectile diameter of 5mm or greater as "Prohibited ammunition", thus effectively banning the possession or use of any type of buckshot ammunition.

7. A licensee is prohibited from carrying his / her firearms in certain places without prior permission. This includes defence installations, educational institutes, areas notified as "disturbed" (this could be a district or even an entire state), or any other place which the government may notify.

8. As soon as an election is called (local, municipal, state, central government, etc.) until the results are declared, all arms licence holders residing in the area where the election is being held are asked to deposit their firearms with the police or a licensed arms and ammunition dealer. While this practice is constantly (and successfully) challenged in the courts by individual arms licence holders, the administration persists with it.

The history of gun control

Pre-colonial period

Prior to the advent of colonial rule in India, arms of all manner and types were freely owned and carried by all sections of society. Like any other essential tool, they were an integral part of our myths, legends, rituals and daily life. Almost all our collective legends contain references to weapons being used to trounce evil, and many traditional rituals involve either the use or worship of weapons.

In those times it was unusual for anyone to venture out of their homes without being armed in some manner. Whether it was a simple spear, sword, dagger or musket, almost everyone carried one or more weapons. This was both a part of our culture as well as a reflection of the fact that our ancestors were practical enough to not depend on others for assistance. They were both willing and able to protect themselves, as best they could, with the best tools available to them.

Even the most tyrannical of kings and emperors never thought to disarm their Indian subjects. A disarmed populace was simply an incomprehensible thought! In the early 19th century, as India came under the control of the British, all this was to change drastically.

Colonial Times

The British colonial rulers, with an ingrained distrust of their Indian subjects, from 1841 to 1946 passed numerous stringent Acts, with a set of harsh rules as riders, with the sole objective of initially disarming the Indian population and then discouraging future applicants from seeking a licence for one type of firearm or the other.

This process was given further urgency after the failed mutiny of 1857, which had fallen just short of the complete annihilation of the British presence in India.

Attempts to disarm the Indian population started with Act No. 18 of 1841 followed by Act No. 30 of 1854, Act No. 28 of 1857 and Act No. 31 of 1860. With a view to consolidating the laws relating to arms, ammunition and military stores, the Indian Arms Act of 1878 was passed. This exempted all Europeans while placing strict controls and penalties on Indians owning any type of weapon.

This was roundly condemned by all Indian leaders. Even though changes were later made to enable Indians to acquire arms, it was made very difficult if not impossible for many. Punishments were harsh and applicants had to first convince the licensing authority of their loyalty to the crown before being granted a licence. The process was highly subjective and humiliating to an Indian citizen, who was subjected to probes and inquiries. He had to dance attendance on the District Magistrate and keep the local police in good humour so that they would recommend his case for a licence.

Reaction of Indian national leaders to the Arms Act

The father of the nation, Mahatma Gandhi, observed:

> *"Among the many misdeeds of the British rule in India, history will look upon the Act depriving a whole nation of arms, as the blackest ..."*

The (all party) Motilal Nehru Report of 1928 for the first time introduced a list of Fundamental Rights (for all citizens) which included "the Right to Bear Arms".

The Indian National Congress, in its Karachi Resolution of 1931, adopted a list of Fundamental Rights that it proposed to include in any future Constitution of a free India. This also included the Right to Keep and Bear Arms.

Situation in the erstwhile Princely States of India

While the Arms Act applied to all of British India, the situation in the erstwhile Princely States was somewhat different. Subjects of these states had much greater freedom to own and carry weapons, within the boundaries of their own principalities.

When someone wishes to acquire an antique sword/ spear/ shield to hang on their wall, the first place to go looking is in cities located within one of these erstwhile princely states. This is because in areas which were formerly under direct British administration, all such weapons were confiscated under threat of severe punishment and could only be owned on an Arms Licence!

It is pertinent to note that there was no significant difference in the incidence of violent crime in these areas compared to adjoining areas under direct British administration. Of course, then and now, controlling citizen's access to weapons had/ has little to do with preventing crime and everything to do with maintaining control over the populace!

Post Independence

When the Constitution was framed, the "Right to Keep and Bear Arms" was not incorporated in the list of Fundamental Rights. Responding to an amendment to incorporate it into the list of Fundamental Rights, Dr B. R. Ambedkar observed that though this demand had relevance when India was ruled by an alien power, this was no longer the case.

Even after Indian independence in 1947 the law continued unaltered, making it difficult for law abiding citizens to possess firearms for self-defence or recreation. In 1953 the Indian Arms (Amendment) Bill (49 of 1953) was introduced. It was discussed in the House and circulated for public opinion. On the basis of those opinions the re-drafted Arms Bill was introduced in Parliament in 1958 and, being passed by both Houses of Parliament, received the assent of the President on 23rd December, 1959.

Thus the Right to Keep and Bear Arms was not made a Fundamental Right but was recognised as a Legal Right through the Arms Act of 1959.

Current policies and implementation subvert the Objects and Reasons of the Act

It is an unfortunate fact that in the decades since the Arms Act 1959 was enacted by Parliament, successive Governments have worked to subvert and defeat the very purpose for which it was enacted. Instead they have used it, much like our former colonial masters, as a tool to limit access of the general citizenry to arms as well as to bestow favours upon their own supporters/ favourites.

While the intent of replacing the colonial era law was clearly towards making it easier for ordinary law abiding citizens to own legal firearms, while preventing criminals, terrorists and other anti-social elements from acquiring arms, exactly the reverse has been happening.

CZECH REPUBLIC
DAVID KARASEK

Firearm laws in the Czech Republic are outstanding within the European Community. Few European countries have such liberal laws[81] and few European countries have firearms laws that work so well.

We can own all types of civilian firearms, including semi-automatic rifles with a "politically incorrect" military appearance, and obtain a licence to carry for self-defence on a "shall-issue" basis.[82]

---

[81] Other European countries with laws of this type are Switzerland, Slovakia, Lithuania and Estonia.
[82] "Shall-issue" means that conditions for issuance are set in law and police have no discretionary power to deny it.

Yet this is a very safe country[83], with a low rate of crime[84] including gun crime.[85,86]

Czech firearms law has been described as both liberal and very strict. Surprisingly, both claims are true. This situation evolved over the years and for many reasons. At the beginning of the 1900s Czech land was part of the Austro-Hungarian empire with firearms law that could be described as "absolutist but benevolent", like the empire itself.

Military firearms and small pistols were prohibited, but ordinary firearms were easily available. Permits to carry were issued by the Gendarmerie provided an applicant was not a "suspicious person". Interestingly, no permit to carry was required by foresters, security guards and similar employees working in uniform although it was prohibited to "hoard weapons and ammunition".

The first Czechoslovak republic, established after WWI, basically kept the same laws. All this changed in 1938; within a few hours of occupying our country, the Nazis ordered that all firearms be surrendered. Four months later, some firearms were returned to hunters who were limited to 50 rounds of ammunition each. Illegal possession of firearms was punished by prison or death.

After WWII our country was subject to a communist regime. The communist approach to civilian firearms possession could be summed up as "allow as little as necessary, and control it as much as possible". People could possess hunting or sporting firearms, but had to be members of a state-

---

[83] According to Global Peace Index, Czech Republic is 6th most safe country in the world.
[84] Our violent crime rate is about 15 crimes/ 100 000 people, and slowly but steadily decreasing.
[85] In a country of 10 million people, of which 300,000 are legal firearms owners possessing about 800,000 firearms, the highest number of crimes with legally possessed firearms per year ever was 92 (in 2006).
[86] https://en.wikipedia.org/wiki/List_of_countries_by_firearm-related_death_rate

approved hunting or sporting organization which issued an opinion on each application for a firearm's permit. Even so, the local police chief had total discretionary power to deny or issue the licence for any reason. This applied to defensive or military firearms as well, but in practice only high party officials or state-approved organizations had access to such permits.

The real history of current Czech firearms law began with the overthrow of the communist regime in the 1990s. The right to keep and bear arms, prohibited and restricted for many years, was viewed as one of many civil liberties denied for so long. However, few wanted a "wild west system" with unrestricted access to firearms for anyone. Most people understood the necessity for some security requirements and that this required a new regime of firearms law.

That led to quite tumultuous political and public discussion, which naturally happens during codifying of important civil rights. There were many issues: what kind of firearms would be available for civilian possession, whether the police should retain some discretion over licensing, what conditions would apply to possession, whether carrying would be legal, and so on. The discussions were initially heated but settled as parties slowly lost interest. Many politicians took a neutral stance because gun control proved to be a toxic issue that could bring more political losses than gains. The general public also lost interest as fears of a "Wild West" did not materialize. Eventually only people with a genuine interest in the issue participated in the discussion: police and other law enforcement agencies on the state's side, and firearms owners and manufacturers on the citizens' side.

In the end, the state's position could be summed up as: "You know, we actually don't have any problem with you having guns. Have them. We don't care how many guns you have, or what kind of guns they are, excluding machine guns or bazookas or similar, let's leave those with the military. We have no objection to the law-abiding use of guns provided they are not used in committing crime. It's now a free country. But we have two specific requirements: (1) a screening programme that excludes criminals, psychopaths, alcoholics etc. and (2) we require an overview of ownership of all guns, to prevent their leak onto the black market."

The citizens accepted these conditions as they also wish to prevent firearms getting into the wrong hands. However, they had some conditions too.

First, possession of a firearm must be a right that excludes any "proof of need" or "good cause". It should not be necessary to explain why we require something that is a lawful right, and in a free country any reason that's not contrary to the law is good enough.

Second, security screening is fine with us. But its conditions must be defined by the law. No official shall hold discretionary power over a citizen's rights.

Third, these conditions must be evidence-based and set at a level which normal citizens can satisfactorily comply with. For example, coming to the range and showing ability of safe handling is fine but a mandatory thousand dollar safety course is not.

Thus both sides realised that citizens' rights to keep and bear arms are not contrary in principle to the legitimate security interests of society. A further crucial factor was goodwill on both sides. The state accepted that firearm owners are not a risk, but have a legitimate place in society. Firearm owners accepted that, while entitled to their rights, they too had to consider the safety concerns of their fellow citizens.

Current Czech firearm laws

We all know the old saying *"Guns don't kill people, people kill people."* Statistics of violent crime, including gun crime, vouch for this assertion. No matter which tool they use, perpetrators of murder very often share characteristics uncommon among ordinary citizens (including firearms owners).

Criminal records (often violent and lengthy), alcohol and/or drug abuse, mental health troubles, domestic violence, regular interpersonal conflicts and so on are too often found in people who eventually commit murder or other forms of serious violence. Cases where a person who is "just fine" commits murder out of the ordinary are very exceptional, and even then, usually warning signs were present but overlooked.

In effect the Czech Republic's firearms policy places no limitation on the number of firearms legally held by citizens and few on available technology, but great care is taken in the clearance of people who hold them. A firearms licence is "shall-issue" to applicants fulfilling the conditions required by law, and these conditions are quite strict.

1. Official place of residence in the Czech Republic

This is mainly a requirement to have a permanent address where police and other authorities can contact the firearms owner. He/she is not bound to keep the firearms there. Note that you do not have to be Czech citizen to apply for a firearms licence; issuing licences to people from outside EU and NATO countries is permitted, but in this case the police have discretionary power (i.e. not obliged to issue the licence even if applicant fulfills all conditions of the law).

2. Minimum age

Minimum age for possession of sporting or hunting firearms is 18; minimum age for collecting, professional and self-defence purposes is 21.

There are a few defined exemptions. For possession of sporting firearms by members of a sports shooting club, the age limit is lowered to 15. For students of hunting and conservation schools, the limit for hunting firearms possession is 16. Student gunsmiths are licensed for professional purposes at 18.

Note: handling a licensed firearm by persons as young as 10 years is permitted under the direct supervision of a licence holder.

3. Health conditions

Before applying for a firearms licence, prospective owners must attend a medical examination and provide a certificate confirming their health status. A doctor can, at his/her discretion, request a further examination by a specialist.

Even here, the principle that "conditions must be set in law" applies. A doctor does not give his/her personal opinion as to whether the applicant should be allowed to have a firearm. Instead, firearms laws specify particular medical conditions which preclude safe handling of firearms and the doctor's function is to check whether these are present or not.

A check-up is required every time a firearms licence is renewed.[87] Also, the Police have the power to request an additional medical check at any time if they believe that a firearm owner's health has deteriorated, making them a danger to themselves or others. The police are obliged to provide evidence to a doctor when making such a request.

---

[87] For the last three years, licenses are issued for 10 years; before that, they were for 5 years.

4. Legal capacity

Persons who have been declared legally incompetent are not permitted to hold a firearm.

5. Criminal check

Before issuing a licence, a criminal background check is carried out by Police on the applicant.

As with medical checks, the Law defines exactly what is significant for this purpose. Unlike American law, where a criminal record means a lifetime prohibition which may only be lifted by a court decision, prohibition under Czech law is usually temporary but cannot be shortened.

The "probationary period" varies and depends on the original sentence imposed. Probation without a gaol sentence carries a three year ban. A prison sentence up to two years means prohibition on firearms possession for five years after release. Two to five years behind bars raises that period to 10 years, and a five to twelve year sentence to 20 years. Above that, prohibition is permanent.

However, only premeditated crimes carry this prohibition. Crimes involving negligence with a firearm are exempted from all above although a mandatory three-year ban applies regardless of sentence.

6. Misdemeanours record

Some misdemeanours are also considered as signs of risk and accepted by law as grounds for temporary prohibition. However, as misdemeanours are considered less serious than actual crime, limiting conditions apply.

Firstly, not all misdemeanours count; the law lists

misdemeanours which are considered relevant. Firearms licences may be revoked for violent misdemeanours, poaching, driving under the influence and similar.

Secondly, while misdemeanours are minor breaches of law, repeated offences may provide legal reasons for revocation of firearms licences, "repeated" being defined as "more than once in three years". This also defines duration of the prohibition.

7. Knowledge and skill

Laws apply to acquisition and possession of firearms and necessary safe handling skills.

Unlike some other states, where this condition requires passing a certified course, the Czech Republic adopted a different method, more liberal but also more reliable. No course is required by law; instead, the police organise an official exam which the applicant must pass.

Necessary knowledge and skills, including a method of verifying them, are set down in law. An applicant has a broad choice as to where he/she can acquire the necessary skills: they can take and pass a commercial course, learn from friends or family, or use skills mastered in police or military service. It is basically up to them where they learn the minimum required to pass the examination.

The applicant is examined by a special commissioner appointed by the Ministry of the Interior, not the police. The system for appointing a commissioner is similar to an application for a firearms licence. Any license holder can apply to be a commissioner although the conditions required are far more demanding than the conditions for firearms licence, particularly in skills and knowledge.

The system is also totally corruption-proof. The exams are

organised by the police but not conducted by them. Both commissioner and applicants are selected anonymously and no-one knows who will be examined by whom. Police officers oversee these exams, which consist of a theoretical written test of basic firearms law, firearms, rules for self-defence and first aid. The test is standardized and questions with correct answers are published. With a total of over 400 questions, a commissioner may choose any 30 for the test.

Everyone who passes the theoretical test proceeds to the range, to demonstrate their ability to handle firearms safely – check, loading, unloading, field stripping and solving common jams, all the while following safety rules - always treat firearm as loaded, keep the muzzle in a safe direction and keeping the finger off the trigger.

Next is the target shooting test, which is relatively easy. It should be noted that the purpose of the exam is not to ensure that the applicant can use a firearm to defend themselves. The purpose is to make sure that the applicant has sufficient knowledge and skills so he won't endanger himself or others through inability or negligence. Whether or not one can defend oneself if the need arises is not a criterion.

The exam is only required prior to issuing the firearms licence; it is not required for renewals. However, if a licence expires through revocation or allowing it to expire, the exam must be retaken.

More on duties

Firearms ownership involves a duty of safe storage. There is no limit *per se* on the number of firearms possessed, but as the number held increases, the demand for safe storage also increases. Possession of one or two firearms involves storing them safely to prevent theft or unauthorised access. Three to ten firearms must be stored in a safe. Eleven to twenty firearms must be stored in a gun vault. With over twenty firearms, the gun vault must be fitted with an alarm.

The Czech Republic assumes that people with this security clearance can be trusted and expects them to obey the law and the police do not have the power to enter peoples' homes. The privacy of a citizen's home is a basic civil liberty.

Carrying or handling a firearm while under the influence of alcohol (or drugs) is forbidden. However, entering a premises where alcohol is served while in possession of a firearm is not forbidden, as long as the carrier does not drink. An important precept in Czech law requires rules to make sense. It is forbidden to carry a firearm openly although there are exemptions for municipal police - they count as civilians, and possess civilian firearms licences. Hunters can transport firearms openly but they may only be loaded while hunting. It is also forbidden to use a firearm outside of a shooting range, except for hunting or situations of self-defence.

"Gun-free zones"

Gun-free zones are a grey area in the Czech Republic. Theoretically, they are almost everywhere; in practice, they almost don't exist. The Firearms Act prohibits carrying (without explicit permission from the police) at "public meetings and celebrations, sports events or folk fairs". Since our civil code defines "public meeting" as "more than two people together", it would be almost impossible to carry if the law were to be interpreted literally.

There's an unwritten but strictly observed rule that guns are not brought to political meetings. Stickers frequently appear in some public places, banks, post offices etc prohibiting the carrying of firearms but they have no legal standing. There are also "hard" gun-free zones like courthouses with metal detectors and security. Entry with firearms is forbidden.

Types of weapons

Some firearms are universally banned, but the limit is quite high. There is an unwritten but accepted consensus that whatever fires with one pull of the trigger is a civilian firearm and should be allowed. On the other hand, anything automatic or high explosive is generally viewed as military hardware and civilian possession should only be permitted for a good reason to well-screened people. As a result, automatic weapons comprise a fraction of civilian firearms and most of them are either historic originals held by collectors or blank-firing replicas used by re-enactors.

"To do what's not forbidden by law"

All law-abiding citizens who can handle a firearm safely can have almost any non-military firearm they wish provided safe storage is available and they can use it for any purpose that is not contrary to the law. There are no limits on calibre, magazine capacity, accessories or the appearance of the firearm.

Semi-automatic rifles of military appearance, often incorrectly referred to as "assault weapons", are treated like any other civilian firearms. A special permit required for carrying firearms for self-defence is issued without conditions beyond those already mandatory for firearms licences. Applicants usually apply for this permit simultaneously with their licence application. About 80% of firearms licence holders possess a permit to carry.

The Czech Firearms Act covers pretty much anything that shoots – firearms, air-guns, bows etc. No licence or registration is required for "non-firearms" replicas etc. But in regard to other forms of weapons we have *no law regulating them*. "What's not forbidden by law is allowed" applies in these cases. Any non-shooting weapon is "just an item" in the eyes of our law. Our criminal law defines "weapon" as "anything that can make a physical assault more effective". You may carry a concealed dagger or have a halberd slung over your shoulder on the street and be perfectly legal. If these are used in an assault this counts as "armed assault" in a court. Our law is ultimately libertarian: you may have whatever you want, carry it, do with it whatever you want with it – provided you do not commit a crime

Why it works

Czech law is quite unique. In some aspects it is very strict, and yet few people break it. In other aspects it is very liberal and the state shows no intent to restrict it. It seems the Czech Republic managed to attain a level that no other state has, striking the right balance.

Czech Republic policy is that if people want to possess and carry firearms, it should be *a priori* allowed because that alone is not a crime. If there are any risks, it shouldn't be forbidden because of these; instead the State should make reasonable rules which eliminate those risks. The State understands that when people want to do something reasonable and the law bans it, people will do it illegally. If the law permits it and establishes rules, people will do it legally according to the rules.

Moreover, the State understands that if it wants people to follow the law voluntarily, then "reasonable rules" must mean "rules which are seen as reasonable *by the people*". This is what many other states fail to recognise. Too often officials and lawmakers make rules in a manner *"we think that this is reasonable and we are lawmakers, therefore we are right."*

This is why the Czech State takes so much effort to communicate with firearms owners and negotiate the law with them rather than making law and enforcing it. When people view law as fair, there's very little to enforce. We

Czechs see this approach as a strong mark of our democracy and believe that its results speak for themselves.

Years of this approach have resulted in a slow but steady growth of mutual trust between firearms owners and the State. The people obey the law which they see as fair and reasonable, demonstrating to the authorities that they can be trusted. Anything viewed as unfair or unreasonable is decisively defeated in the legislative process.

For many years, a clause in our law was a thorn in the eye of law-abiding firearms owners. It was §70, establishing emergency powers for the government. According to this clause, the government in wartime or national emergency (as declared by the Parliament) could order citizens, by simple executive decree, to surrender their private firearms. Two years ago, this emergency clause was repealed – at the government's own proposal. The Prime Minister himself stated that democratic government, which derives its authority from consent of the people, doesn't need any such power; the Minister of Interior added that should such unfortunate times come, he believes that firearms owners would stand with their country, not against it.

There are many illegal (i.e. unregistered) firearms in our country. Following two occupations (Nazi and Soviet) tons of weapons were left here and, throughout the communist times, many firearms were homemade. Fortunately, these firearms are somewhere in drawers and closets of ordinary people. That's why every update of our Firearms Act contains an amnesty clause. Czech-type amnesty means *legalization*. Bring your illegal gun for police checks as to whether any crime was committed with it and, if not, it's legally treated as yours – you can either register and keep it if you have a firearms licence, or you can sell it to someone who has a firearms licence (in which case the police hand it to the new owner).

The State officials who brought this practice explained it this way: since legal firearms are not a problem, every gun legalized means one gun less available for the black market. This requires trust to work; people won't register their firearms if they are suspicious of government motives. So the amnesty must be clear: if you're not a criminal, it's *yours*, and the State shall respect that.

This approach has proved a success as every amnesty yielded more firearms than previously. The people who remembered pre-democratic times were suspicious at first. However, as time passed and the state didn't attempt to restrict firearm ownership by confiscating legally held firearms, the people's trust increased and this form of legalization became more and more common.

Can it work elsewhere?

When I describe our firearms rules, it may sound like utopia to many foreign firearms owners and they wonder whether these rules could apply in their countries. I think that the more important question is whether these rules would actually *work* in their countries. Such rules are based on mutual *trust*: trust by the state that firearms owners are people who can be trusted to obey the law, and trust by the firearms owners that the state won't restrict their rights above what's absolutely necessary for public security. Effectively our firearm laws either stand or fall with this trust. Therefore, the question is whether this mutual trust between citizens and state that has been established can continue to be sustained.

One reason why Czech firearms owners accept reasonable restrictions is that there is no serious anti-gun lobby here. Some demand strict gun control but are not taken seriously by the government. Under these conditions, we can afford to be reasonable; we can accept rules negotiated around established principles and trust the other side to follow them too.

European Directive

The Czech approach to firearms and the trust on which it is based is currently undergoing "trial by fire". Following terror attacks in France, the European commission proposed restrictions to EU firearms regulations. These put the Czech Republic in a difficult position. As a member state of the EU, it is legally bound to implement these restrictions into firearms law. On the other hand, our firearms law is based on unwritten, trust-based agreement that firearms owners shall follow the law as long as the State shall respect their rights.

For many long years, firearms owners honoured their part of this contract. "Assault weapons" and "high-capacity magazines" have been legal in our country for fifteen years; there are tens of thousands of them here with never any problems thanks to their keepers. The people now expect their State to stand in defence of their rights. This places the built up trust between State and citizens in jeopardy.

Presently the Czech Republic holds the line. Czech deputies were loudest and most active in opposition to the European Parliament's proposals. The Czech Republic opposed any bans in the Council and filed a lawsuit against discrimination.

This situation also demonstrated one factor which, in my opinion, is also crucial for keeping firearms ownership as a right. (Actually, I believe that it is important to keep *any* right.) When I wrote that firearms owners are law-abiding people I should have added "to a point". Czech firearms owners in general are careful to follow the law however trivial or technical. However, when the EU Firearms Directive and its bans were published, the general sentiment of people was: *"If my gun is banned, I'm going to hide it and claim that it was lost or stolen."* I heard it many times, even from police officers and soldiers. Even the State recognised this. As one of our officials told an EU representative: *"If this is passed, our citizens will just hide their firearms, because with our totalitarian history, our people don't see hiding guns from the State as inherently wrong."*

One might wonder how the State views this boiling civil disobedience mood and still trust its citizens.

The EU Firearms Directive is an *order*. We followed the law, observed our duties; we pose no threat to society. Yet it was decided in Brussels that our rights shall be restricted. Czech firearms law, even with its restrictions, conditions and penalties, is a *contract*. It was negotiated and agreed upon by both sides. Firearms owners are proud people and the pride that compels them to resist this order also compels them to respect the contract, for of all things they are proud of, their *honour is paramount*. Being honourable involves *keeping one's word*. Our state still trusts us and fights for us; representatives and officials know us, and they know that as long as the State keeps its part of the agreement, we shall do the same.

Czech constitutional amendment

On the domestic front, another wall against said infringement is currently being built. The Ministry of the Interior proposes to update the Constitutional Act on security of the Czech Republic (specifying the place and role of army, police and other security forces) with an amendment that would establish civilian firearms possession as part of the security doctrine of the Czech Republic. It is legal, since founding treaties of the European Union explicitly state that national defence and internal security of member states is their sole responsibility.

However, the purpose of the constitutional amendment is not just to avoid unjustified infringement brought by the Firearms Directive. From the start, the right to keep and bear arms in Czech Republic was purely *individual*. It was the individual's right to possess and carry firearms for self-defence and any other legal purpose, based on a right of self-defence and the right of personal liberty, which are individual by definition. National security was considered to be an exclusive monopoly for professional forces, only in time of emergency to be supplemented by draft.

However, this might change, and hopefully it shall. As much as we want to keep the right to possess and carry firearms, an individual right in itself, it would be also beneficial for society to extend it to common defence. The system of our national defence would change to that of a professional army backed up by numerous, Swiss-style volunteer reserves.

It is not certain whether this amendment will be passed or not; it passed overwhelmingly through the House of Deputies, but its fate in the Senate is uncertain. Let's just hope that it will pass, for it would be one more foundation stone in the bridge of social contract between people and the state.

MALAYSIA

Malaysia has very severe penalties including both the death penalty and corporal punishment for criminal use of firearms. Despite that, illegal guns are available and used for criminal purposes.

Malaysians require a licence to manufacture, import, export, repair or own firearms. Applicants must be over 18, have no criminal record and no history of physical or mental disability. An application requires a background check including employment and tax records.

Firearms licences are issued at the discretion of the police and can take months or years. It was reported that there were about 90,000 licences issued in 2016.[88]

There are four main purposes for owning a firearm – to protect a farm from pests, to protect yourself and property, sport, and hunting. Permits to carry a gun, either concealed or open, may be granted. Full automatic firearms are prohibited.

Licences expire on June 30 every year, requiring an application for a renewal. There are often restrictions on the type and quantity of ammunition that may be purchased without police permission (and a requirement to return spent cases to the police), and a requirement to use the gun for a specific purpose or at a specific place. For example, you may be permitted to use the gun only at a designated shooting range or during working hours for the purposes of your employment.

There are severe penalties for use of firearms in crime. Discharging a firearm in crimes such as extortion, robbery, resisting arrest and house-breaking is punishable by the death penalty. The death penalty also applies to an accomplice.

Exhibiting a firearm for any of the scheduled offences (without discharging) carries a penalty of life imprisonment and caning of not less than six strokes.

Possession of unlawful firearms carries a sentence of up to fourteen years in prison and caning.

Notwithstanding the severe penalties there is a black market for guns and crime involving the use of guns still occurs. Guns are smuggled into Malaysia from neighbouring countries and an illegal handgun can be bought for as little as RM300. The murder rate is approximately double that of Australia's.

---

[88] https://www.thestar.com.my/news/nation/2016/03/28/nearly-90000-malaysians-licensed-to-carry-guns/

9

GUN CONTROL IN AMERICA

FEDERAL LAW

Although the right to keep and bear arms is protected by the Second Amendment to the United States Constitution, this does not mean there are no laws relating to firearms. In fact, there are both federal and state laws controlling firearm ownership.

Federal laws regulate the manufacture, trade, possession, transfer, record keeping, transport, and destruction of firearms, ammunition, and firearms accessories. They are enforced by both state agencies and the federal Bureau of Alcohol, Tobacco, Firearms and Explosives (ATF).

In particular, federal laws regulate the possession of fully automatic firearms, heavy weapons (eg artillery), explosive ordnance, suppressors and disguised or improvised firearms. A special federal licence is required for these, while fully automatic firearms manufactured post 1986 are not permitted. Transfer of pre-1986 automatic firearms requires ATF approval.

Federal law requires gun manufacturers, importers and retailers to have a federal firearms licence and prohibits the transfer of firearms to certain classes of people.

Interstate trade in firearms is restricted to licensed manufacturers, dealers and importers.

Under federal law, the minimum age to buy a handgun is 21.

Firearms with less than 3.7 oz of metal content are prohibited.

Firearms are not permitted in school zones, although some states have implemented laws contrary to this.

Federal law makes it unlawful for certain categories of people to ship, transport, receive, or possess firearms or ammunition, including any person:

- convicted in any court of a "crime punishable by imprisonment for a term exceeding one year";
- who is a fugitive from justice;
- any person under indictment for a "crime punishable by imprisonment for a term exceeding one year"
- who is an unlawful user of or addicted to any controlled substance
- who has been adjudicated as a mental defective or has been committed to any mental institution;
- who is an illegal alien;
- who has been discharged from the Armed Forces under dishonourable conditions;
- who has renounced his or her United States nationality/ citizenship;
- who is subject to a court order restraining the person from harassing, stalking, or threatening an intimate partner or child of the intimate partner; or
- who has been convicted of a misdemeanour crime of domestic violence

According to the US Sentencing Commission, approximately 5,000 to 6,000 people a year are convicted of receiving or possessing a firearm against one of the prohibitions above.

Current and former law enforcement officers are permitted to carry a concealed firearm in any jurisdiction, regardless of state or local laws, with certain exceptions.

Federal law also prevents firearms manufacturers and licensed dealers from being held liable for negligence when crimes have been committed with their products.

Additionally, the U.S. Supreme Court held in McDonald v. Chicago that the protections of the Second Amendment to keep and bear arms for self-defence in one's home apply against state governments and their political subdivisions.

THE SECOND AMENDMENT

The right to keep and bear arms in the United States is protected by the Second Amendment to the Constitution. While there have been contentious debates on the nature of this right, there was a lack of clear court rulings defining the right until the two Supreme Court cases of District of Columbia v. Heller (2008) and McDonald v. City of Chicago (2010).

An individual right to own a gun for personal use was affirmed in the District of Columbia v. Heller decision, which overturned a handgun ban in the federal District of Columbia. In this decision, the court's majority opinion was that the Second Amendment protects "the right of law-abiding, responsible citizens to use arms in defence of hearth and home."

However, in delivering the majority opinion, Justice Antonin Scalia wrote that the Second Amendment was not an unlimited right:

> Like most rights, the Second Amendment right is not unlimited. It is not a right to keep and carry any weapon whatsoever in any manner whatsoever and for whatever purpose: For example, concealed weapons prohibitions have been upheld under the Amendment or state

analogues. The Court's opinion should not be taken to cast doubt on longstanding prohibitions on the possession of firearms by felons and the mentally ill, or laws forbidding the carrying of firearms in sensitive places such as schools and government buildings, or laws imposing conditions and qualifications on the commercial sale of arms.

In McDonald v. City of Chicago, the Supreme Court ruled that, because of the incorporation of the Bill of Rights, the guarantee of an individual right to bear arms applies to state and local gun control laws and not just federal laws.

The Supreme Court has not ruled on whether the Second Amendment protects the right to carry guns in public for self-defence. Federal appeals courts have issued conflicting rulings on this point. For example, the United States Court of Appeals for the Seventh Circuit ruled in 2012 that it does, saying, "The Supreme Court has decided that the amendment confers a right to bear arms for self-defence, which is as important outside the home as inside."

However, the Tenth Circuit Court ruled in 2013 that it does not, saying, "In light of our nation's extensive practice of restricting a citizen's freedom to carry firearms in a concealed manner, we hold that this activity does not fall within the scope of the Second Amendment's protections."

STATE LAW

All state governments and some local governments have their own laws that regulate firearms. These vary greatly and, as a result, there is no such thing as "American gun laws". Even within a state they can be different.

Each state has laws determining who is allowed to own or possess firearms, with both state and federal laws potentially applying to background checks.

Controversy continues over which classes of people, such as convicted felons, people with severe or violent mental illness, and people on the federal no-fly list, should be excluded. Laws in these areas vary considerably, and enforcement is in flux.

Forty-four states have a provision in their state constitutions similar to the Second Amendment which protects the right to keep and bear arms. The exceptions are California, Iowa, Maryland, Minnesota, New Jersey, and New York. In New York, however, the statutory civil rights laws contain a provision virtually identical to the Second Amendment.

Firearm related matters that are often regulated by state or local laws include the following:

- Some states and localities require that a person obtain a licence or permit in order to purchase or possess firearms.
- Some states and localities require that individual firearms be registered with the police or with another law enforcement agency.
- All states have provisions for some form of concealed carry in public for self defence.
- Many states allow some form of open carry ie the carrying of an unconcealed firearm in public on one's person or in a vehicle.
- Some states have state pre-emption for some or all gun laws, which means that only the state can legally regulate firearms. In other states, local governments can pass their own gun laws that are more restrictive than those of the state.
- Some states and localities place additional restrictions on certain semi-automatic firearms that they have defined as assault weapons, or on magazines that can hold more than a certain number of rounds of ammunition.
- Some states and localities place additional restrictions on weapons that are regulated by federal law.
- Some states have enacted Castle doctrine or stand-your-ground laws, which provide a legal basis for individuals to use deadly force in self-defence in certain situations,

GUN CONTROL

without a duty to flee or retreat if possible.
- In some states, peaceable journey laws give additional leeway for the possession of firearms by travellers who are passing through to another destination.
- Some states require a background check of the buyer when a firearm is sold by a private party. (Federal law requires background checks for sales by licensed gun dealers, and for any interstate sales.)
- Some states have enacted red flag laws that enable a judge to issue an order to temporarily confiscate the firearms of a person who presents an imminent threat to others or to themselves.

This table illustrates some of the key differences between the states.[89]

	Licence to own[1]	Permit to purchase[2]	Firearm registration[3]	Permit for concealed carry[4]	Permit for open carry[5]	Assault weapon law[6]
Alabama	No	No	No	Yes	No	No
Alaska	No	No	No	No	No	No
Arizona	No	No	No	No	No	No
Arkansas	No	No	No	No	No	No
California	No	Yes	Yes	Yes	Yes	Yes
Colorado	No	No	No	Yes	No	No
Connecticut	No	Yes	Yes	Yes	Yes	Yes
Delaware	No	No	No	Yes	No	No
DC	Yes	Yes	Yes	Yes	Not permitted	Yes
Florida	No	No	No	Yes	Not permitted	No
Georgia	No	No	No	Yes	Yes	No
Hawaii	No	Yes	Yes	Yes	Yes	No
Idaho	No	No	No	No	No	No
Illinois	Yes	Yes	No	Yes	Not permitted	No
Indiana	No	No	No	Yes	Yes	No
Iowa	No	Yes	No	Yes	Yes	No
Kansas	No	No	No	No	No	No
Kentucky	No	No	No	No	No	No
Louisiana	No	No	No	Yes	No	No
Maine	No	No	No	No	No	No
Maryland	No	Yes	Yes	Yes	Yes	Yes
Massachusetts	Yes	Yes	No	Yes	Yes	Yes

[89] https://en.wikipedia.org/wiki/Gun_laws_in_the_United_States_by_state

Michigan	No	No	Yes	Yes	No	No
Minnesota	No	Yes	No	Yes	Yes	No
Mississippi	No	No	No	No	No	No
Missouri	No	No	No	No	No	No
Montana	No	No	No	Yes	No	No
Nebraska	No	Yes	No	Yes	No	No
Nevada	No	No	No	Yes	No	No
New Hampshire	No	No	No	No	No	No
New Jersey	No	Yes	Yes	Yes	Yes	Yes
New Mexico	No	No	No	Yes	No	No
New York	Yes	Yes	Yes	Yes	Not permitted	Yes
North Carolina	No	Yes	No	Yes	No	No
North Dakota	No	No	No	No	Yes	No
Ohio	No	No	No	Yes	No	No
Oklahoma	No	No	No	No	No	No
Oregon	No	No	No	Yes	No	No
Pennsylvania	No	No	Yes	Yes	No	No
Rhode Island	No	Yes	No	Yes	Yes	No
South Carolina	No	No	No	Yes	Not permitted	No
South Dakota	No	No	No	No	No	No
Tennessee	No	No	No	Yes	Yes	No
Texas	No	No	No	Yes	Yes	No
Utah	No	No	No	Yes	Yes	No
Vermont	No	No	No	No	No	No
Virginia	No	No	No	Yes	No	Yes
Washington	No	Yes	Yes	Yes	No	Yes
West Virginia	No	No	No	No	No	No
Wisconsin	No	No	No	Yes	No	No
Wyoming	No	No	No	No	No	No

HISTORY OF GUN CONTROL IN AMERICA

Important events regarding gun legislation occurred in the following years.

In 1791 the United States Bill of Rights was ratified which included the Second Amendment to the Constitution. It stated that "A well regulated Militia, being necessary to the security of a free State, the right of the people to keep and bear Arms, shall not be infringed."

After the abolition of slavery in 1865 Southern Democrats quickly rushed to put blacks 'back in their place'. Southern states enacted many 'black codes' which imposed laws on African-Americans which did not apply to whites, amongst other things forbidding black people from possessing firearms[90].

In 1934, in response to gang related crime such as the Saint Valentine's Day Massacre, the National Firearms Act (NFA) was signed into law under President Franklin D. Roosevelt's Administration. The NFA is considered to be the first legislation to enforce gun control in the United States, imposing a $200 tax, equivalent to nearly $4,000 in 2019, on the manufacture and transfer of Title II weapons (machine guns, short or "sawed-off" shotguns and rifles, and so-called "destructive devices" including grenades, mortars, rocket launchers, large projectiles, and other heavy ordnance).

It also mandated the registration of machine guns, short-barreled rifles and shotguns, heavy weapons, explosive ordnance, suppressors, and disguised or improvised firearms.

In 1938, President Franklin D. Roosevelt signed the Federal Firearms Act of 1938 into law, requiring that all gun related businesses must have a Federal Firearms Licence (FFL).

In 1939, through the court case United States v. Miller, the Supreme Court ruled that Congress could regulate interstate selling of sawn-off shotguns, deeming that such a weapon has no reasonable relationship with the efficiency of a well regulated militia.

In 1968, following the spree of political assassinations including John F. Kennedy, Robert F. Kennedy and Martin Luther King Jr, President Lyndon B. Johnson pushed

---

[90]   https://thelibertarianrepublic.com/the-racist-history-of-gun-control/

Congress for the Gun Control Act of 1968 ("GCA"). It repealed and replaced the Federal Firearms Act, regulated "destructive devices" (such as bombs, mines, grenades, and other explosives), expanded the definition of machine gun, required the serialization of manufactured or imported guns, banned importing military style weapons, and imposed a 21 age minimum on the purchasing of handguns from FFLs. The GCA also prohibited selling of firearms to felons and the mentally ill.

In 1986 the Firearm Owners Protection Act passed under the Ronald Reagan administration, introducing protections for gun owners. It prohibited a national registry of dealer records, limited ATF inspections to conduct annual inspections (unless multiple infractions have been observed), allowed licensed dealers to sell firearms at "gun shows" in their state, and loosened regulations on the sale and transfer of ammunition. However the Act also prohibited civilian ownership or transfer of machine guns made after May 19, 1986, and redefined "silencer" to include silencer parts.

In 1993, the Brady Handgun Violence Prevention Act, named after a White House press secretary who was disabled during the attempted assassination of Ronald Reagan, was signed into law under the presidency of Bill Clinton. This required background checks on gun purchasers and established a criminal background check system maintained by the FBI.

In 1994 the Violent Crime Control and Law Enforcement Act, signed into law under the presidency of Bill Clinton, included the Federal Assault Weapons Ban, which effectively banned the manufacture, sale and possession of specific military-style assault weapons such as AR-15 style rifles and banned high-capacity ammunition magazines that held over 10 rounds. Banned arms that were previously legal were grandfathered. The ban expired in September 2004.

In 2003 the Tiahrt Amendment limited the Bureau of Alcohol, Tobacco and Firearms (ATF) to only releasing information from its firearms trace database to law enforcement agencies or prosecutors in connection with a criminal investigation.

In 2005 The Protection of Lawful Commerce in Arms Act was signed into law under the presidency of George W. Bush. This protected gun manufacturers from being named in federal or state civil suits by those who were victims of crimes involving guns made by that company.

In 2008 the Supreme Court ruled in the case District of Columbia v. Heller that the Second Amendment is an "individual right to possess a firearm unconnected with service in a militia" and struck down Washington D.C.'s handgun ban. The Court also stated "that the right to bear arms is not unlimited and that guns and gun ownership would continue to be regulated."

In 2010 the Supreme Court ruled in the case McDonald v. Chicago that the Second Amendment is incorporated and thus applies against the states.

In 2016, the Supreme Court ruled in the case Caetano v. Massachusetts that "the Second Amendment extends, prima facie, to all instruments that constitute bearable arms, even those that were not in existence at the time of the founding".

CONCEALED CARRY[91]

Many guns in America are owned for the purpose of self defence. All states and territories allow guns for self defence in the home, but rules regarding self defence outside the home vary. Depending on the location, both concealed and open carry of firearms are permissible.

---

[91] https://en.wikipedia.org/wiki/Concealed_carry_in_the_United_States

Concealed carry or carrying a concealed weapon (CCW) is the practice of carrying a weapon (such as a handgun) in public in a concealed manner, either on one's person or in close proximity.

As of 2018 there have been 17.25 million concealed weapon permits issued in the United States.[92]

Experts believe that carriage of a concealed firearm has a deterrent effect on criminals, who cannot know who is armed and likely to resist. Even when only a small proportion of people are actually carrying, the deterrent effect is said to apply.

Open Carry is an overt way of carrying a gun where the gun can be seen in public. It includes routine carriage of a firearm, to and from a shooting range or hunting location for example, but is also preferred by some for self defence.

Open carry is practised by uniformed law enforcement and clearly has a deterrent effect. However, its support among members of the public is sometimes more about exercising a civil and constitutional right than crime control.

There is no federal law concerning the issuance of either concealed-carry or open-carry permits. All 50 states have passed laws allowing qualified individuals to carry certain concealed firearms in public, either without a permit or after obtaining a permit from a designated government authority at the state and/or local level. However, there are still some states that, though they have passed concealed carry permit laws, either do not issue permits or make it extremely difficult to obtain one.

The states that are fully unrestricted and allow those who are not prohibited from owning a firearm to carry a concealed firearm without a permit in any place not deemed off-

---

[92] https://en.wikipedia.org/wiki/Concealed_carry_in_the_United_States

limits by law are Alaska, Arizona, Arkansas, Idaho, Kansas, Kentucky, Maine, Mississippi, Missouri, New Hampshire, North Dakota, Oklahoma, South Dakota, Vermont, West Virginia and Wyoming.

Idaho, North Dakota and Wyoming only allow permitless carry by residents of the state; non-residents must still have a permit issued by their home state to legally carry concealed in these states.

Most of these states also allow the open carry of a handgun without a permit. In Oklahoma you must have a permit or licence to Open Carry a handgun; Missouri has restrictions on where you can and cannot Open Carry; and Kansas allows Open Carry for all of its citizens, regardless of their possession of a valid licence or permit.

Most states that require a permit have "shall-issue" statutes, which means that if a person meets the requirements to obtain a permit, the issuing authority (typically the state police) must issue one, with no discretion involved.

Typical licence requirements include residency, minimum age, submitting fingerprints, passing an instant background check (or a more comprehensive manual background check), attending a certified handgun/firearm safety class, passing a practical qualification demonstrating handgun proficiency, and paying a fee.

Requirements vary widely by jurisdiction, with some having few or none of these and others having most or all.

There are many training courses including some developed by the National Rifle Association that combine classroom and live-fire instruction to meet state training requirements. Some states recognize prior military or police service as meeting training requirements.

When in contact with a police officer, some states require

holders to inform that officer that they are carrying a handgun.

States with may-issue statutes typically allow authorities (usually, the county sheriff or police chief in the jurisdiction) to issue permits based upon a demonstrated need. In practice this means rural jurisdictions typically allow many more carry permits than urban ones.

Certain states and jurisdictions, while "may-issue" by law, direct their issuing authorities to issue licences to all or nearly all qualified applicants and are considered "shall-issue" in practice. Connecticut, certain cities and counties in California, Massachusetts and New York are examples.

Hawaii, Maryland and New Jersey are considered restrictive may-issue jurisdictions, where issuing authorities are directed to deny most or all applications, either based on hard-to-meet "good cause" requirements or agency policies specifically prohibiting issue.

In addition, Maryland and New Jersey require the applicant to provide substantive evidence of a clear and immediate threat to their lives that exists outside of their home at the time the permit application is filed. Rhode Island further requires applicants for the statewide permit to submit to a mental health records check at the applicant's expense.

In some may-issue jurisdictions, permits are only issued to individuals with celebrity status, political connections or significant wealth, resulting in accusations of systematic corruption. Additionally, issuing authorities may charge arbitrarily high fees, making the CCW permit unaffordable to most applicants. For example, applying for a New York City concealed carry permit typically costs around $5,000.

Recognition of permits between the states is complex. There are several popular combinations of resident and non-resident permits that allow carry in more states than the original issuing state; for example, a Utah non-resident permit allows carry in 25 states. Some states do not recognize permits issued by other states to non-residents of the issuing state, and some states do not recognize any permit from another state.

Vermont has no provision for issue of concealed-carry licences, as none has ever been necessary. Thus Vermont residents wishing to carry handguns in other states must acquire a licence from a state which is valid in their destination. A popular choice is Florida's concealed handgun permit, which is valid for non-resident holders in 28 other states.

Not all weapons that fall under CCW laws are lethal. For example, in Florida, carrying pepper spray in more than a specified volume (2 oz) of chemical requires a CCW permit, whereas everyone may legally carry a smaller "self-defence chemical spray" device hidden on their person without a CCW permit.

While generally a concealed carry permit allows the permit holder to carry a concealed weapon in public, federal law prohibits carriage of a firearm in certain locations. This includes federal government facilities such as post offices, IRS offices, federal court buildings, military/VA facilities and/or correctional facilities, Amtrak trains and facilities, and Corps of Engineers-controlled property (carry in these places is prohibited by federal law and preempts any existing state law).

A state may restrict carry of a firearm on certain properties, facilities or types of businesses that are otherwise open to the public. These vary by state and can include:

- State and local government facilities, including courthouses, DMV/DoT offices, police stations,

correctional facilities, and/or meeting places of government entities (exceptions may be made for certain persons working in these facilities such as judges, lawyers, and certain government officials both elected and appointed)
- Venues for political events, including rallies, parades, debates, and/or polling places
- Educational institutions including elementary/secondary schools and colleges. Some states have "drop-off exceptions" which only prohibit carry inside school buildings, or permit carry while inside a personal vehicle on school property. Campus carry laws vary by state.
- Certain sporting events and/or venues.
- Amusement parks, fairs, parades and/or carnivals
- Businesses that sell alcohol (sometimes only "by-the-drink" sellers like restaurants, sometimes only establishments defined as a "bar" or "nightclub", or establishments where the percentage of total sales from alcoholic beverages exceeds a specified threshold)
- Hospitals (even if hospitals themselves are not restricted, "teaching hospitals" partnered with a medical school are sometimes considered "educational institutions"; exceptions are sometimes made for medical professionals working in these facilities)
- Churches, mosques and other "houses of worship," usually at the discretion of the church clergy (Ohio allows with specific permission of house of worship)
- Municipal mass transit vehicles or facilities
- Sterile areas of airports (sections of the airport located beyond security screening checkpoints, unless explicitly authorized)
- Non-government facilities with heightened security measures (nuclear facilities, power plants, dams, oil and gas production facilities, banks, factories, unless explicitly authorized)
- Aboard aircraft or ships unless specifically authorized by the pilot in command or ship captain
- Private property where the lawful owner or lessee has

posted a sign or verbally stated that firearms are not permitted

- Any public place, while under the influence of alcohol or drugs (including certain prescription or over-the-counter medications, depending on jurisdiction)

THE EFFECT ON GUN VIOLENCE

Like most aspects of the gun control debate, views on the impact of right to carry guns for self defence tend to be highly partisan, with many studies starting from the conclusion rather than the data. A common criticism of many studies is the inclusion of gun suicides in the figures for gun violence.

Here are some summaries of published work.[93]

A comprehensive 2004 review of the existing literature by the National Academy of Sciences found that the results of existing studies were sensitive to the specification and time period examined, and concluded that a causal link between right-to-carry laws and crime rates cannot be shown.

Quinnipiac University economist Mark Gius summarized literature published between 1993 and 2005, and found that ten papers suggested that permissive CCW laws reduce crime, one paper suggested they increase crime, and nine papers showed no definitive results.

A 2017 review of the existing literature concluded, "Given the most recent evidence, we conclude with considerable confidence that deregulation of gun carrying over the last four decades has undermined public safety—which is to say that restricting concealed carry is one gun regulation that appears to be effective."

A 2016 study in the European Economic Review which examined the conflicting claims in the existing literature

---

[93] https://en.wikipedia.org/wiki/Concealed_carry_in_the_United_States

concluded that the evidence CCW either increases or decreases crime on average "seems weak"; the study's model found "some support to the law having a negative (but with a positive trend) effect on property crimes, and a small but positive (and increasing) effect on violent crimes".

The *Washington Post* fact-checker concluded that it could not state that CCW laws reduced crime, as the evidence was murky and in dispute.

In a 2017 article in the journal Science, Stanford University law professor John Donohue and Duke University economist Philip J. Cook write that "there is an emerging consensus that, on balance, the causal effect of deregulating concealed carry (by replacing a restrictive law with an RTC law) has been to increase violent crime". Donohue and Cook argue that the crack epidemic made it difficult to determine the causal effects of CCW laws and that this made earlier results inconclusive; recent research does not suffer the same challenges with causality.

A 2019 study in Journal of American College of Surgeons found "no statistically significant association between the liberalization of state level firearm carry legislation over the last 30 years and the rates of homicides or other violent crime."

A 2013 study of eight years of Texas data found that concealed handgun licensees were much less likely to be convicted of crimes than were non-licensees. The same study found that licensees' convictions were more likely to be for less common crimes, "such as sexual offenses, gun offenses, or offenses involving a death."

This is also in line with a 1997 study researching county level data from 1977 to 1992 concluding that allowing citizens to carry concealed weapons deters violent crimes and appears to produce no increase in accidental deaths.

A 2018 study in The Review of Economics and Statistics found that the impact of right-to-carry laws was mixed and changed over time. RTC laws increased some crimes over some periods while decreasing other crimes over other periods. The study suggested that conclusions drawn in other studies are highly dependent on the time periods that are studied, the types of models that are adopted and the assumptions that are made.

A 2015 study that looked at issuance rates of concealed-carry permits and changes in violent crime by county-level in four shall-issue states found no increases or decreases in violent crime rates with changes in permit issuances.

A 2019 study in the *International Review of Law and Economics* found that with one method, right-to-carry laws had no impact on violent crime, but with another method led to an increase in violent crime; neither method showed that right-to-carry laws led to a reduction in crime.

One study conducted in 2014 found states with more permissive conceal carry laws had lower murder rates than states with restrictive laws.

A 2019 study in the *Journal of Empirical Legal Studies* found that right-to-carry laws led to an increase in overall violent crime.

A 2017 study in the *American Journal of Public Health* found that "shall-issue laws" (where concealed carry permits must be given if criteria are met) "are associated with significantly higher rates of total, firearm-related, and handgun-related homicide" than "may-issue laws"

A 2017 study in Applied Economics Letters found that property crime decreased in Chicago after the implementation of the shall issue concealed carry law.

In 1996, economists John R. Lott, Jr. and David B. Mustard

analyzed crime data in all 3,054 counties in the United States from 1977 to 1992, finding counties that had shall-issue licensing laws overall saw murders decrease by 7.65 percent, rapes decrease by 5.2 percent, aggravated assaults decrease by 7 percent and robberies decrease by 2.2 percent.

Georgetown University Professor Jens Ludwig, Daniel Nagin of Carnegie Mellon University and Dan A. Black of the University of Chicago in The Journal of Legal Studies, said of the Lott-Mustard study, "once Florida is removed from the sample, there is no longer any detectable impact of right-to-carry laws on the rates of murder and rape".

CITIZENS PREVENTING CRIME

In 2016 the FBI analyzed 40 "active shooter incidents" in 2014 and 2015 where bystanders were put in peril in on-going incidents that could be affected by police or citizen response.

Six incidents were successfully ended when citizens intervened. In two stops citizens restrained the shooters, one unarmed, one with pepper spray. In two stops at schools, the shooters were confronted by teachers: one shooter disarmed, one committed suicide. In two stops citizens with firearms permits exchanged gunfire with the shooter. In a failed stop attempt, a citizen with a firearms permit was killed by the shooter.

In 2018 the FBI analyzed 50 active shooter incidents in 2016 and 2017. This report focused on policies to neutralize active shooters to save lives. In 10 incidents citizens confronted an active shooter. In eight incidents the citizens stopped the shooter.

Four stops involved unarmed citizens who confronted and restrained or blocked the shooter or talked the shooter into surrender. Four stops involved citizens with firearms permits: two exchanged gunfire with a shooter and two detained the shooter at gunpoint for arrest by responding police. Of the two failed stops, one involved a permit holder who exchanged gunfire with the shooter but the shooter fled and continued shooting and the other involved a permit holder who was wounded by the shooter.

The FBI report concluded: "Armed and unarmed citizens engaged the shooter in 10 incidents. They safely and successfully ended the shootings in eight of those incidents. Their selfless actions likely saved many lives."[94]

GUN VIOLENCE IN AMERICA

Suicide Dominates

In 2017, 39,773 Americans were killed by guns, the highest absolute number of gun deaths in nearly 50 years. When adjusted for population size, the rate of gun deaths also increased slightly, to 12 deaths for every 100,000 people, up from 11.8 per 100,000 in 2016. By this measure, 2017 had the highest rate of firearm deaths since the mid-1990s.

This increase in the firearm death rate was driven by suicides, with 60% of these gun deaths self-inflicted. While the rate of gun homicides has fluctuated over the last decade, the rate of gun suicides has steadily increased. Indeed, the suicide rate rose 3.7 percent in 2017 and Americans make up a full third of the people worldwide who die by gun suicide each year.

Men outnumber women in the suicide rate by a factor of three to one, but they outnumber closer to 7 to 1 in gun suicides. Suicide by men between 25 and 64 is particularly significant, accounting for 37% of all firearm deaths. That's

---

[94] https://www.fbi.gov/file-repository/active-shooter-incdents-us-2016-2017.pdf

partially attributable to men's proclivity to choose more violent methods of suicide, and partially to men making up 62% of gun owners.

Intentionally killing yourself with a firearm is over 38 times more likely than accidentally killing yourself with one.

The data suggest suicide by firearms increases with increased firearm ownership and that the overall rate of suicide also increases, but only for men (ie not women). Appropriate interventions to address suicide in men have been suggested as a means of addressing this.[95]

Many reports on "gun violence" in the media, particularly in Australia, fail to distinguish between suicides and criminal shootings.

Crime Rates

Violent crime in the U.S. has fallen sharply over the past quarter century.[96] [97] The two most commonly cited sources of crime statistics both show a substantial decline in the violent crime rate since it peaked in the early 1990s.

One is an annual report by the FBI of serious crimes reported to police in approximately 18,000 jurisdictions around the country. The other is an annual survey of more than 90,000 households conducted by the Bureau of Justice Statistics, which asks Americans ages 12 and older whether they were victims of crime, regardless of whether they reported those crimes to the police.

Using the FBI numbers, the violent crime rate fell 49%

---

[95] https://medium.com/handwaving-freakoutery/the-left-is-making-the-wrong-case-on-gun-deaths-heres-a-better-case-1429e7ad2f25
[96] https://www.pewresearch.org/fact-tank/2019/01/03/5-facts-about-crime-in-the-u-s/
[97] https://en.wikipedia.org/wiki/Crime_in_the_United_States

between 1993 and 2017. Using the BJS data, the rate fell 74% over that period. (For both studies, 2017 is the most recent full year of data.)

There are large geographic variations in crime rates. The BJS data do not allow for specific geographic comparisons, but the FBI data show big differences from state to state and city to city.

In 2017 there were more than 600 violent crimes per 100,000 residents in Alaska, New Mexico and Tennessee. By contrast, Maine, New Hampshire and Vermont had rates below 200 violent crimes per 100,000 residents. And while Chicago has drawn widespread attention for its soaring murder total in recent years, its murder rate in 2017 – 24.1 murders and non-negligent manslaughters per 100,000 residents – was less than half the rates in St. Louis (66.1 per 100,000) and Baltimore (55.8 per 100,000).

In contrast to violent crime rates, drug overdose deaths have been surging, a trend that continued in 2017. About 70,000 people died from drug overdoses — almost double the number that died from guns including suicide by shooting.

Gun Homicide

A 2013 report by the United Nations Office on Drugs and Crime (UNODC) concluded that, between 2005 and 2012, the average homicide rate in the U.S. was 4.9 per 100,000 people. This was lower than the average rate globally, which was 6.2, but much higher than countries identified in the report as "developed", which all had average homicide rates of 0.8 per 100,000. South American countries and Russia are the main exceptions.

Almost two-thirds of gun deaths are due to suicide.

Of murders, FBI data shows 73 percent of these were committed with a firearm in 2013. Knives are regularly in second place, at about 10 percent. The remaining gun deaths are accidents or classified as undetermined.

There has been a substantial drop in the annual rate of homicides using a firearm, from 7.0 per 100,000 population in 1993 to 3.6 per 100,000 in 2014. This has occurred despite a significant increase in the sales of firearms since 1994 and substantial liberalisation of gun laws (particularly with respect to concealed carry).

More than half of all gun homicide victims are young men, two thirds of them black, and overwhelmingly located in cities such as New Orleans, Chicago and Washington DC. A very small percentage of the population is responsible for 50 percent to 60 percent of the shootings; 31 percent of gun murders occurred in the 50 cities with the highest murder rates, though only 6 percent of Americans live in these cities.

In fact, half of all gun homicides took place in just 127 cities, which represented nearly a quarter of the U.S. population.

There are wide variations within these cities too. An example is St. Louis, where 28 of the city's 88 neighborhoods had either zero or one murder in the last five years while 41 percent of murders and 35 percent of all gun assaults occurred in just nine neighborhoods.

Women are far less likely to be gun homicide victims — about 1,700 are killed each year, many in domestic violence incidents.

The rate of gun deaths, both homicides and suicides, varies substantially according to race.[98]

---

[98] https://fivethirtyeight.com/features/gun-deaths/

Racial group	Gun homicides per 100,000	Gun suicides per 100,000
Whites	1.5	9.4
Blacks	16.7	2.9
Hispanic	3.5	2.0
Asians	1.1	1.5
Native Americans	1.1	1.9

From this it can be seen that white people are killing themselves with guns, black people are killing each other with guns, and Asians are neither killing themselves nor each other, making the availability of guns not very satisfactory as an explanation.

Notwithstanding their high profile, mass shootings account for just 0.3% of gun deaths and mass school shootings make up just 0.03%.

Analysis of mass shootings in the period 1998 though June 2019 showed that only 13% of mass public shootings involved the use of a rifle alone, including so-called assault rifles. By contrast, more than half (56%) only involved a pistol.[99]

Of the perpetrators of mass shootings, over 80 percent were at least 21 and more than half were over 30, 96% were male and 58% were white. (For reference, whites including white Hispanics constituted 72% of the population in the 2010 Census.) The vast majority of these killers had no known religious or political views.

Also significant is that about 9 in 10 of the attacks (89%) occurred in gun-free zones - that is, areas in which it is prohibited to carry a firearm for self-defence. Many times, mass shootings have either been prevented or stopped with

---

[99] https://crimeresearch.org/2019/07/breaking-down-mass-public-shooting-data-from-1998-though-june-2019-info-on-weapons-used-gun-free-zones-racial-age-and-gender-demographics/

fewer casualties by civilians legally carrying firearms.[100]

Mass Shootings

Former President Barack Obama claimed, "The one thing we do know is that we have a pattern now of mass shootings in this country that has no parallel anywhere else in the world." To justify this claim and many other similar quotes, Obama's administration cited a then-unpublished paper by criminologist Adam Lankford.

Others have been unable to confirm the findings of Lankford. A study by the Crime Prevention Research Centre found[101]:

> *Of the 86 countries where we have identified mass public shootings, the US ranks 56th per capita in its rate of attacks and 61st in mass public shooting murder rate. Norway, Finland, Switzerland and Russia all have at least 45 percent higher rates of murder from mass public shootings than the United States.*
>
> *When Lankford's data is revised, the relationship between gun ownership rates and mass public shooters disappears.*
>
> *How could that be? One possibility is that guns don't just enable mass shooters; gun owners can also deter and prevent such shootings. Another is that culture — not gun ownership — is a bigger factor in shootings.*

Other data also suggest that, notwithstanding the enormous publicity they attract, mass shootings are no more common now than in the past.[102]

---

[100] https://crimeresearch.org/2019/05/uber-driver-in-chicago-stops-mass-public-shooting/
[101] https://crimeresearch.org/2018/08/new-cprc-research-how-a-botched-study-fooled-the-world-about-the-u-s-share-of-mass-public-shootings-u-s-rate-is-lower-than-global-average/
[102] https://theconversation.com/mass-shootings-arent-growing-more-common-and-evidence-contradicts-common-stereotypes-about-the-killers-121471

GUN CONTROL

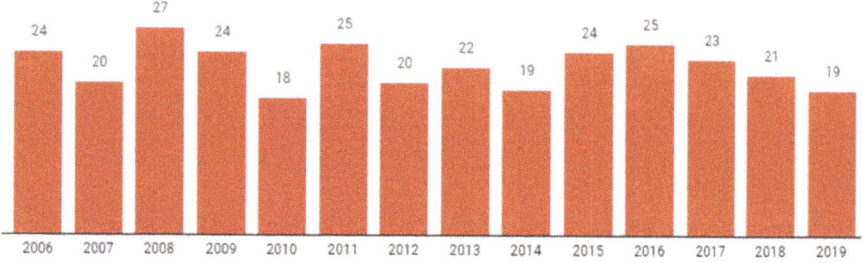

Mass shooting incidents, by year

Despite the common perception that mass homicides are occurring more frequently, the data suggests they've happened at a fairly steady rate over the past decade or so. In the U.S., 1,714 people have been killed in 311 mass shootings since 2006.

Data is current as of Aug. 5, 2019.
Chart: The Conversation, CC-BY-ND · Source: The USA TODAY/AP/Northeastern University mass killings database · Get the data

As to the causes and possible solutions to mass shootings one study argues:[103]

> Contrary to popular belief, the people who commit mass murder aren't necessarily mentally ill, at least not in the sense of having a diagnosable condition. Some do, but most don't. So that's not the common thread.
>
> What is a common thread is that they are almost all frustrated losers. The anguished virgin. The disgruntled husband who explodes and kills the extended family. The racist killing the outgroup that he feels is threatening his ingroup. The religious zealot doing the same. And, for that matter, the impoverished high schooler who kills a classmate after school over some trivial slight ...
>
> The shape changes but the mass stays constant: a hopeless loser who feels like he or his group are losing, thinks he spots who's to blame, and decides he's going to show everyone that damn it, he's not the loser that you (and, subconsciously, he) think he is.

It also suggests:

> That the (extremely understandable) hysteria about mass shootings is tragically self-reinforcing. And that the lurid details the media perseverates on are providing a specific template that draws in lower-threshold murderers in the future.

---

[103] https://opensourcedefense.org/blog/what-is-going-on-with-mass-shootings-lessons-from-past-solved-problems

THE NATIONAL RIFLE ASSOCIATION[104]

The National Rifle Association (NRA) claims a current membership of nearly five million target shooters, hunters, gun collectors, gunsmiths, police, and other gun enthusiasts.

It was established in 1871 with the primary goal of improving the marksmanship of American civilians in preparation for war. The organisation continues to teach firearm safety and competency, publishes several magazines, and sponsors competitive marksmanship events.

The NRA is also the leader in firearms education. Over 125,000 certified instructors now train about 1,000,000 gun owners a year. Courses are available in basic rifle, pistol, shotgun and muzzle loading firearms, personal protection and even ammunition reloading.

Additionally, nearly 7,000 certified coaches are specially trained to work with young competitive shooters. Since the establishment of the Eddie Eagle GunSafe Program in 1988, more than 28 million pre-kindergarten to fourth grade children have learned that if they see a firearm in an unsupervised situation, they should "STOP. DON'T TOUCH. RUN AWAY. TELL A GROWNUP."

Over the past seven years, Refuse To Be A Victim seminars have helped more than 100,000 men and women develop their own personal safety plan using common sense strategies.

Since 1977 the NRA has been a dedicated defender of the Second Amendment. Many now see it as one of the top three most influential lobbying groups in Washington, D.C. The organization has influenced legislation, participated in or initiated lawsuits, and endorsed or opposed various candidates at local, state and federal levels. Its rating of candidates each election is often highly influential with

---

[104] https://home.nra.org/

voters.

Former Clinton spokesman George Stephanopoulos said, "Let me make one small vote for the NRA. They're good citizens. They call their congressmen. They write. They vote. They contribute. And they get what they want over time."

10

MORAL AND PHILOSOPHICAL ARGUMENTS FOR GUN OWNERSHIP

ARM THE WORKERS

"Arm the workers" has always been a key demand of revolutionary anti-capitalists, whether communist or anarchist. Without arms, the class struggle and overthrow of the power of the ruling class would not be possible.[105]

Karl Marx and Frederick Engels, the fathers of communism, wrote in 1850:

> To be able forcefully and threateningly to oppose this party, whose betrayal of the workers will begin with the very first hour of victory, the workers must be armed and organized. The whole proletariat must be armed at once with muskets, rifles, cannon and ammunition, and the revival of the old-style citizens' militia, directed against the workers, must be opposed.

---

[105] https://www.reddit.com/r/Firearms/comments/3iabp9/karl_marx_on_gun_control/

> ......
>
> Under no pretext should arms and ammunition be surrendered; any attempt to disarm the workers must be frustrated, by force if necessary. The destruction of the bourgeois democrats' influence over the workers, and the enforcement of conditions which will compromise the rule of bourgeois democracy, which is for the moment inevitable, and make it as difficult as possible – these are the main points which the proletariat and therefore the League must keep in mind during and after the approaching uprising.

This is from the Address of the Central Committee to the Communist League and came at a time when a major anti-capitalist revolt had just taken place, but also when Marx saw the workers movement being co-opted by "petty bourgeois democrats."

Marx believed that a combination of worker inexperience (both in the context of organization and armed defence) and the influence of the German petty bourgeois were leading a true proletarian movement away from self-realization through an alliance with traditional authoritarian state powers.

He also believed that a revolution "will not take this peaceful course", being sparked by the hands of workers or by counter-revolutionary feudalist violence. As such, an armed proletarian population, equipped and able to fight, was essential for the future workers movement.

VI Lenin was also in favour of arming the workers, although once communism had been achieved throughout the world he believed there would be no need for nations to have arms.

He was particularly opposed to leftists who advocated complete disarmament. In 1916 in "On the 'Disarmament'

Slogan," Lenin wrote[106]:

> In a number of countries, mostly small and not involved in the present war—Sweden, Norway, Holland and Switzerland, for example—there have been voices in favour of replacing the old Social-Democratic minimum-programme demand for a "militia", or the "armed nation" by a new demand: "disarmament". ....
> Let us take a closer look at the position of the disarmament advocates.
> One of the principal premises advanced, although not always definitely expressed, in favour of disarmament is this: we are opposed to war, to all war in general, and the demand for disarmament, is the most definite, clear and unambiguous expression of this point of view.
> We showed the fallacy of that idea in our review of Junius's pamphlet, to which we refer the reader. Socialists cannot be opposed to all war in general without ceasing to be socialists. We must not allow ourselves to be blinded by the present imperialist war. Such wars between "Great" Powers are typical of the imperialist epoch; but democratic wars and rebellions, for instance, of oppressed nations against their oppressors to free themselves from oppression, are by no means impossible. Civil wars of the proletariat against the bourgeoisie for socialism are inevitable. Wars are possible between one country in which socialism has been victorious and other, bourgeois or reactionary, countries.
> Disarmament is the ideal of socialism. There will be no wars in socialist society; consequently, disarmament will be achieved. But whoever expects that socialism will be achieved without a social revolution and the dictatorship of the proletariat is not a socialist. Dictatorship is state power based directly on violence. And in the twentieth century—as in the age of civilisation generally—violence means neither a fist nor a club, but troops. To put "disarmament" in the programme is tantamount to making the general declaration: We are opposed to the use of arms. There is as little Marxism in this as there

---

[106] https://www.marxists.org/archive/lenin/works/1916/oct/01.htm

would be if we were to say: We are opposed to violence!

......

An oppressed class which does not strive to learn to use arms, to acquire arms, only deserves to be treated like slaves. We cannot, unless we have become bourgeois pacifists or opportunists, forget that we are living in a class society from which there is no way out, nor can there be, save through the class struggle and the overthrow of the power of the ruling class.

In every class society, whether based on slavery, serfdom, or, as at present, on wage-labour, the oppressor class is always armed. Not only the modern standing army, but even the modern militia—and even in the most democratic bourgeois republics, Switzerland, for instance—represent the bourgeoisie armed against the proletariat. That is such an elementary truth that it is hardly necessary to dwell upon it. Suffice it to recall that in all capitalist countries without exception troops (including the republican-democratic militia) are used against strikers. A bourgeoisie armed against the proletariat is one of the biggest, fundamental and cardinal facts of modern capitalist society.

....

The whole of social life is now being militarised. Imperialism is a fierce struggle of the Great Powers for the division and redivision of the world. It is therefore bound to lead to further militarisation in all countries, even in neutral and small ones. How will proletarian women oppose this? Only by cursing all war and everything military, only by demanding disarmament? The women of an oppressed and really revolutionary class will never accept that shameful role. They will say to their sons:

"You will soon be grown up. You will be given a gun. Take it and learn the military art properly. The proletarians need this knowledge not to shoot your brothers, the workers of other countries, as is being done in the present war, and as the traitors to socialism are telling you to do. They need it to fight the bourgeoisie of their own country, to put an end to exploitation, poverty and war, and not by pious wishes, but by defeating and disarming the bourgeoisie."

.....

In working out a concrete and practically necessary answer on the question of a militia we should say: We are not in favour of a bourgeois militia; we are in favour only of a proletarian militia. Therefore, "not a penny, not a man", not only for a standing army, but even for a bourgeois militia, even in countries like the United States, or Switzerland, Norway, etc.

In real world movements, it has been fairly common to see communists securing arms for themselves, recruiting regular people into armed groups, and subverting state prohibitions or restrictions on arms possession and use. Castro, Lenin, Mao, Tito and others had periods when they operated in this mode.[107]

However, in practice communist movements have tended to follow a Leninist model on their pathway to revolution and power. That is, a cadre, the communist party, serves as the leaders and organizers of the masses. They 'guide' the revolution and educate workers on what is in the interest of their class, to 'jump start' the revolution. Once the old government is removed and the party has a monopoly on power, they rule on behalf of the proletariat until enough transformation in the means of production and overall society has taken place to produce ideal conditions for communism and the elimination of coercive power.

This is where the relationship with arms changes. None of the communist movements that gained power (all of them being Leninist to a greater or lesser degree) felt secure enough to continue to allow the masses to hold arms unfettered. All prioritized control of the means of force by the party, seeing themselves as having internal as well as external threats. All had needed to overcome resistance not just from wealthy elites and their paid soldiers, but from large sectors of

---

[107] https://www.quora.com/What-is-the-communist-perspective-on-gun-control

regular people who just never bought into communist goals.

Thus they instituted their own controls on arms possession and use, or borrowed and expanded the restrictions in place under prior regimes. Needless to say, none of them ever felt like they had reached the point, or would even soon reach it, where coercive power was no longer needed.

Usually they allowed designated groups of party members to have arms to secure the revolution, whether armed force strictly controlled by the party, loyalists militias, or armed police and Chekists. Some allowed hunting guns where they were seen as practical to support agricultural or remote communities. Some also pursued competition in international shooting events as a means of showing off the prowess of communist societies in human endeavours.

We have yet to see a communist movement that espouses revolution by the masses, and then lets the masses keep their guns.

Many modern day leftists continue to insist that communism can be achieved without the possession of arms by the people. However, this view is controversial in modern American Marxist circles:[108]

> The recent attacks in Colorado, Connecticut, Boston, and across the country have shocked everyone. As has been previously explained in the pages of Socialist Appeal, these repeated incidents of violence signify the decay of American capitalism. The decline of capitalism offers no future for today's youth, only distractions, desperation, and escapism. High unemployment, debt, lack of healthcare facilities, alienation, and a widespread feeling of insecurity is enough to push some over the edge. Only by changing society to one which will give everyone hope of a better future; only by engaging people in a way that they will want to live their lives rather than escape from

---

[108] https://www.marxist.com/gun-control-and-class-struggle.htm

them, can we put an end to these horrible crimes.

However, many capitalist politicians are telling us that there is a quick and easy solution: stricter gun control laws. This "solution" flies in the face of actual experience. Alcoholism is as prevalent and intractable a problem today as it was in the 1920s. In January 1920, the 18th Amendment was put into effect, prohibiting the production and sale of alcohol. The argument was put forward that by banning alcohol, alcoholism would fade away. Nothing of the kind happened. Prohibition strengthened organized crime, giving criminal gangs a monopoly over all aspects of the production and distribution of alcohol, and alcoholism continued as before.

Today, states with tough gun control laws like New York, Massachusetts, New Jersey, and California are still among those that experience the most violent crime involving firearms. Illegal guns are most commonly acquired from other states, by individuals who can legally purchase firearms, and from the illegal sale of guns by licensed dealers. Although this seems like an argument to broaden the strict gun laws to the federal level, there is no reason to assume firearms won't make their way into the hands of those with malicious intent.

At the time of the signing of the Constitution, despite the reining in of the revolutionary energy of the masses by the ruling class, the capitalist system was still young and historically progressive. A strong state apparatus had not yet been developed. The ruling class did not yet need one, as the proletariat had not yet developed into a powerful and massive force constituting the vast majority of society, as is the case today. It could depend on geography and local armed militias for national defense and to put down local uprisings, supplemented by a small standing army, and above all, a strong navy.

But things have changed in the United States. The slogan "we are the 99%" is a close approximation to the actual class balance of forces today, with a tiny minority of capitalists on one side, and a mass of workers on the other. The working class has tremendous potential power in its hands—the ability to bring production and society as a whole to a grinding halt. With the capitalist crisis deepening, the ruling class can no longer rely on ideology or a few concessions to keep class peace. In the face of such a threat, the capitalists have developed an imposing state apparatus in order to maintain their rule.

Frederick Engels, in his classic work The Origin of the Family, Private Property, and the State, explains the role of the state: "The state is therefore by no means a power imposed on society from without... Rather, it is a product of society at a particular stage of development; it is the admission that this society has involved itself in insoluble self-contradiction and is cleft into irreconcilable antagonisms which it is powerless to exorcise. But in order that these antagonisms, classes with conflicting economic interests, shall not consume themselves and society in fruitless struggle, a power, apparently standing above society, has become necessary to moderate the conflict and keep it within the bounds of 'order'; and this power, arisen out of society, but placing itself above it and increasingly alienating itself from it, is the state."

When capitalist politicians call for "gun control," they are really saying that the working class majority should give more power to the bourgeois state in determining who should have access to arms. The capitalist class would breathe a sigh of relief at the complete disarmament of the working class. The capitalist state would then have a complete monopoly of arms, on top of its monopoly of the courts, prisons, police, spy agencies, military, etc.

Therefore, from the point of view of the capitalist class, the real essence of "gun control" is not the disarming of criminal elements or unstable individuals—who would still have access to guns through illegal channels—it is the disarming of the working class on the whole.

The United States has a long history of gun violence on the part of the state against immigrants, blacks, and against the working class on the whole, especially when they dare to struggle. Nearly every major labor battle in the U.S. has been marked with violent attacks by the state against the striking workers. As one boss infamously put it, his striking workers needed to be "shot back to work." Against this overwhelming force of the capitalist state, the working class must defend its basic democratic right to defend itself and its organizations, including its right to access arms.

There are no quick fixes to the problem of gun violence, and no solutions within the limits of capitalism, a system based on the organized exploitation and violence of one class against another. Only the organized and united working class can offer a solution to the violence of class society, whether it be perpetrated by the capitalist state when breaking a strike, or by unstable and alienated individuals on a killing rampage.

The labor movement, by organizing a political party of its own, could begin to deal with the ills of our society— but only if that party is armed with a socialist program. Corporations like Colt and Smith & Wesson make huge profits from the sale of weapons. A workers' government would nationalize the arms industry and place it under democratic workers' control.

Under a workers' government, the working class would democratically organize itself to protect society. As socialism spreads worldwide, and relations between nations are increasingly based on solidarity, not exploitation, the need for national defense and the military will fade away, along with national borders themselves. Here at home, the need for a special police force standing above society, with special powers and privileges, would likewise disappear.

With the immense wealth and resources of our society geared towards providing jobs and raising everyone's standard of living, we could eliminate the instability, alienation, and inhuman conditions of capitalism that give rise to the senseless violence that plagues our society.

THE HARM PRINCIPLE

John Stuart Mill's famous 'harm principle', articulated in *On Liberty* (1859), states:

> The object of this Essay is to assert one very simple principle, as entitled to govern absolutely the dealings of society with the individual in the way of compulsion and control, whether the means used be physical force in

the form of legal penalties, or the moral coercion of public opinion. That principle is, that the sole end for which mankind are warranted, individually or collectively, in interfering with the liberty of action of any of their number, is self-protection. That the only purpose for which power can be rightfully exercised over any member of a civilized community, against his will, is to prevent harm to others. His own good, either physical or moral, is not a sufficient warrant. He cannot rightfully be compelled to do or forbear because it will be better for him to do so, because it will make him happier, because, in the opinion of others, to do so would be wise, or even right... The only part of the conduct of anyone, for which he is amenable to society, is that which concerns others. In the part which merely concerns himself, his independence is, of right, absolute. Over himself, over his own body and mind, the individual is sovereign..

An equivalent was earlier stated in France's *Declaration of the Rights of Man and of the Citizen* of 1789:

> Liberty consists in the freedom to do everything which injures no one else; hence the exercise of the natural rights of each man has no limits except those which assure to the other members of the society the enjoyment of the same rights. These limits can only be determined by law.

By that standard, the justification for gun control relies on a fundamental question: does gun control lead to reduced harm to others? If a country such as Australia implements more stringent control, will this result in reduced violence? More generally, do countries with more stringent gun control have lower rates of violence than countries with more liberal gun control?

John Stuart Mill (1806-1873) was a British philosopher, political economist and civil servant, and one of the most influential thinkers in the history of classical liberalism.

Mill advocated easing the burdens on Ireland, was the first person in the history of Parliament to call for women to be given the right to vote, became a strong advocate of such social reforms as labour unions and farm cooperatives, and called for various reforms of Parliament and voting, especially proportional representation, the single transferable vote, and the extension of suffrage.

On Liberty addresses the nature and limits of the power that can be legitimately exercised by society over the individual. Mill's conception of liberty justified the freedom of the individual in opposition to unlimited state and social control. He believed that "the struggle between Liberty and Authority is the most conspicuous feature in the portions of history".

For him, liberty in antiquity was a "contest ... between subjects, or some classes of subjects, and the government."

Mill defined "social liberty" as protection from "the tyranny of political rulers". He introduced a number of different concepts of the form tyranny can take, referred to as social tyranny, and tyranny of the majority.

Social liberty for Mill meant putting limits on the ruler's power so that he would not be able to use his power on his own wishes and make decisions which could harm society; in other words, people should have the right to have a say in the government's decisions. He said that social liberty was "the nature and limits of the power which can be legitimately exercised by society over the individual". It was attempted in two ways: first, by obtaining recognition of certain immunities, called political liberties or rights; second, by establishment of a system of "constitutional checks".

However, in Mill's view, limiting the power of government was not enough. He stated:

> Society can and does execute its own mandates: and if it issues wrong mandates instead of right, or any mandates at all in things with which it ought not to meddle, it

practices a social tyranny more formidable than many kinds of political oppression, since, though not usually upheld by such extreme penalties, it leaves fewer means of escape, penetrating much more deeply into the details of life, and enslaving the soul itself.

Mill states that the only reason rights can be taken away from an individual is to ensure their safety and the safety of society as a whole. This leads some to argue that Mill would therefore support gun control, based on the proposition that without guns at all, society would be a lot safer than it is today. Mill was essentially a utilitarian influenced by Jeremy Bentham.

Clearly it is unrealistic to suggest that all guns might be removed from society. This leaves the argument that taking away guns from some people (the general public, for example) will make it safer. This is highly contested and also contrary to Mill's basic proposition as to the justification for coercive measures.

Furthermore, if it is legitimate for the state to intervene on a precautionary basis in the case of firearms, what else justifies such intervention? This can obviously lead to highly illiberal outcomes: should all Muslims be subject to control orders, on the basis that a small number of them engage in terrorist violence? Should all Catholic priests be barred from contact with children because a small number of them are paedophiles?

Mill would very likely agree with the well known quote "guns don't kill people, people kill people." Guns are only harmful when they are in the hands of people intent on doing harm and, as a supporter of individualism, Mill would not agree with the assumption that all gun owners are potentially harmful and should have their freedom infringed.

CITIZEN OR SUBJECT

A central question in the context of gun control is whether a state can legitimately deny its citizens the ownership of guns while at the same owning them itself.

While it is true that this is more or less the status quo in many countries, that in itself is not a basis for legitimacy. Authoritarian governments often lack legitimacy despite having a complete monopoly on power.

John Howard clearly believes it is acceptable for the government to have all the guns. His famous comment in 2002 made that abundantly clear:

> We will find any means we can to further restrict them because I hate guns. I don't think people should have guns, unless they are police, or in the military or security industry. Ordinary citizens should not have weapons. We do not want the American disease imported into Australia.

Howard clearly believed the government was entitled to disarm the population. It has been suggested that he was only dissuaded from pursuing complete disarmament because of the political consequences, not due to any consideration of the relationship between the state and its people.

At the heart of this issue is whether our rights and freedoms are derived from government, or whether we have rights and freedoms that precede government. This question was considered by two seventeenth century philosophers, John Locke and Thomas Hobbes.

Both were social contract and natural law theorists, but there the resemblance ends.

Locke argued[109] that man is by nature a social animal and that in the state of nature men mostly kept their promises

---
[109] https://jim.com/hobbes.htm

and honored their obligations and, though insecure, it was mostly peaceful, good and pleasant.

In his *Two Treatises of Government* (1690), Locke set forth the view that the state exists to preserve the natural rights of its citizens. Those rights include the protection of life, liberty and property.

He argued that humans know what is right and wrong and are capable of knowing what is lawful and unlawful well enough to resolve conflicts. In particular, and most importantly, they are capable of telling the difference between what is theirs and what belongs to someone else.

However, he acknowledged they do not always act in accordance with this knowledge. Thus we give up our right to exact retribution for crimes ourselves in return for impartial justice backed by overwhelming force. This allows us to retain the right to life and liberty, and gain the right to just, impartial protection of our property

Locke believed peace is the norm, and that we can and should live together in peace by refraining from molesting each other's property and persons; and for the most part we do. The only important role of the state is to ensure that justice is seen to be done

When governments fail in that task, Locke said, citizens have the right—and sometimes the duty—to withdraw their support and even to rebel. And if a ruler seeks absolute power, if he acts both as judge and participant in disputes, he puts himself in a state of war with his subjects and the people have the right and the duty to kill such rulers and their servants.

Hobbes had a very different concept of the state. He maintained that man is not by nature a social animal and that society could not exist except by the power of the state.

In his view, in a state of nature people cannot know what is theirs and what is someone else's. Property exists solely by the will of the state, thus in a state of nature men are condemned to endless violent conflict. In practice, morality is for the most part merely a command by some person or group or God, and law merely the momentary will of the ruler.

Without subjection to a common power, Hobbes believed, men are necessarily at war:

> Hereby it is manifest, that during the time men live without a common Power to keep them all in awe, they are in that condition which is called Warre; and such a warre, as is of every man, against every man.

Indeed, there is:

> no society; and which is worst of all, continual fear, and danger of violent death; and the life of man, solitary, poor, nasty, brutish, and short.

To overcome this we all concede our rights to the government, in return for our life. Whatever the state does is just by definition. All of society is a direct creation of the state, and a reflection of the will of the ruler.

Moreover, civil society is the application of force by the state to uphold contracts and so forth, a creation of the state. What most modern people would call civil society is "jostling", pointless conflict and pursuit of selfish ends that a good government should suppress.

In his view, if you shut up and do as you are told you have the right not to be killed, although you do not even have the right not to be killed, for no matter what the Sovereign does, it does not constitute a violation of the contract. The King can do no wrong, because lawful and unlawful, good and evil, are merely commands, the will of the ruler. There is no right to rebel.

The concept of just use of force is meaningless or cannot be known. Just use of force is whatever force is authorized.

Locke was the seventeenth century precursor of classical liberalism, and Hobbes was the seventeenth century precursor of modern totalitarianism, particularly fascism.

Hobbes favored unlimited power for the state, and he favored it for the purpose of ending all conflict and contention. He saw all non-state society as simply bad happenings that should be suppressed. If people go about their material lives freely they will come in conflict, and Hobbes regards it as the duty of the state to prevent such conflict.

Locke argued that government is legitimate, but only legitimate in so far as it acts within the limits of this implied contract.

Locke heavily influenced the American declaration of independence. As is well known, it says:

> We hold these truths to be self-evident, that all men are created equal, that they are endowed by their Creator with certain unalienable Rights, that among these are Life, Liberty and the pursuit of Happiness. That to secure these rights, Governments are instituted among Men, deriving their just powers from the consent of the governed, That whenever any Form of Government becomes destructive of these ends, it is the Right of the People to alter or to abolish it, and to institute new Government.

When it says, "All men are created equal", it does not mean everyone is the same or that everyone should achieve the same outcome in life, but that no individual or class enjoys moral or legal superiority over other individuals or classes.

When it says, "We are endowed with inalienable rights", it means inherent rights that cannot be taken from us.

Good government can help protect our rights by reflecting them in legislation, but they don't get to dole them out piecemeal. Bad government may seek to legislate away our rights, but only by usurping them.

The Declaration of Independence also says, "Governments are instituted among Men, deriving their just powers..."

That means, when government acts to secure rights they are acting justly. When they move to violate those rights, they are acting unjustly. They derive that legitimacy from the consent of the governed.

The author of the Declaration of Independence, Thomas Jefferson, was a firm supporter of Locke's view of the relationship between the people and the state.

Both Locke and Jefferson focused on the belief that all men are created equal and believed in God-given rights. Locke said humans have natural rights of life, liberty, and property. Jefferson restated this as unalienable Rights of life, liberty, and the pursuit of happiness.

Both state that no one person is above or superior to another person. The natural law of man is not under the authority of man but ruled by the Laws of Nature. They also state that those natural rights cannot be taken away, because humans are born with those rights that are governed by natural laws, and not by a government.

As for keeping the government in its place, Jefferson was all in favour[110]:

> I hold it that a little rebellion now and then is a good thing, and as necessary in the political world as storms in the physical. Unsuccessful rebellions, indeed, generally establish the encroachments on the rights of the people

---

[110] https://www.varsitytutors.com/earlyamerica/early-america-review/volume-1/jefferson-letter-madison

which have produced them. An observation of this truth should render honest republican governors so mild in their punishment of rebellions as not to discourage them too much. It is a medicine necessary for the sound health of government.

Jefferson's perspective is summarised in the now famous quote attributed to him, although apparently not accurately[111]:

> When the people fear the government, there is tyranny.
> When the government fears the people, there is liberty.

It is obviously much easier to fear a government that insists it has a monopoly on the ownership of firearms. Equally, a government that fears the people is unlikely to become authoritarian.

DEFENCE AGAINST GENOCIDE AND OPPRESSION

Every genocide in the twentieth century was preceded by substantial gun control.

The organisation *Jews for the Preservation of Gun Ownership* says that evil governments wiped out 170 million innocent non-military lives in the 20th Century alone, because unarmed defenceless people had no hope against armed aggressors. Following is a chart of the genocides it has documented.[112]

---

[111] https://www.monticello.org/site/research-and-collections/when-government-fears-people-there-liberty-spurious-quotation
[112] http://jpfo.org/filegen-a-m/deathgc.htm#chart

MORAL AND PHILOSOPHICAL ARGUMENTS FOR GUN OWNERSHIP

Government	Dates	Targets	Civilians Killed	"Gun Control" Laws	Features of Overall "Gun Control" scheme
Ottoman Turkey	1915-1917	Armenians (mostly Christians)	1-1.5 million	Art. 166, Pen. Code, 1866 & 1911 Proclamation, 1915	•Permits required •Government list of owners •Ban on possession
Soviet Union	1929-1945	Political opponents; farming communities	20 million	Resolutions, 1918 Decree, July 12, 1920 Art. 59 & 182, Pen. code, 1926	•Licensing of owners •Ban on possession •Severe penalties
Nazi Germany & Occupied Europe	1933-1945	Political opponents; Jews; Gypsies; critics; "examples"	20 million	Law on Firearms & Ammun., 1928 Weapon Law, March 18, 1938 Regulations against Jews, 1938	•Registration & licensing •Stricter handgun laws •Ban on possession
China, Nationalist	1927-1949	Political opponents; army conscripts; others	10 million	Art. 205, Crim. Code, 1914 Art. 186-87, Crim. Code, 1935	•Government permit system •Ban on private ownership
China, Red	1949-1952 1957-1960 1966-1976	Political opponents; Rural populations; Enemies of the state	20-35 million	Act of Feb. 20, 1951 Act of Oct. 22, 1957	•Prison or death to "counter-revolutionary criminals" and anyone resisting any government program •Death penalty for supply guns to such "criminals"
Guatemala	1960-1981	Mayans & other Indians; political enemies	100,000-200,000	Decree 36, Nov 25 Act of 1932 Decree 386, 1947 Decree 283, 1964	•Register guns & owners •Licensing with high fees •Prohibit carrying guns •Bans on guns, sharp tools •Confiscation powers
Uganda	1971-1979	Christians Political enemies	300,000	Firearms Ordinance, 1955 Firearms Act, 1970	•Register all guns & owners •Licenses for transactions •Warrantless searches •Confiscation powers
Cambodia (Khmer Rouge)	1975-1979	Educated Persons; Political enemies	2 million	Art. 322-328, Penal Code Royal Ordinance 55, 1938	•Licenses for guns, owners, ammunition & transactions •Photo ID with fingerprints •License inspected quarterly
Rwanda	1994	Tutsi people	800,000	Decree-Law No. 12, 1979	•Register guns, owners, ammunition •Owners must justify need •Concealable guns illegal •Confiscating powers

The Genocide Chart © JPFO.org 2002

Its publication, *Death by Gun Control*, makes the case for private gun ownership on the grounds that people with guns can defend themselves against government criminals as well as common ones. It also maintains that gun control laws denigrate tolerance and diversity, and that gun control violates the moral principles of the Judeo-Christian tradition.

Others have also pointed out how governments intent on mass murder invariably prioritize victim disarmament. David Kopel describes how the Turks first sought to disarm the Armenians prior to murdering them in their thousands, and that in pitifully few cases the Armenians were able to resist because they had retained their arms.[113]

During the Mao regime in China from 1949-76, more people were murdered than by Hitler and Stalin combined. Mao's arms policies and victim disarmament were integral to his mass killings and are a sine qua non for a communist regime maintaining power.

Kopel and others have also detailed the failures of genocide prevention strategies currently favoured by the United Nations (targeted sanctions, United Nations peacekeepers, etc).[114] They note that the Genocide Convention[115] (which Australia was the first country to ratify in 1949) strongly forbids any form of complicity in genocide and is jus cogens (meaning that it prevails over any conflicting national or international law).

They argue this means the Convention forbids any interference, including interference based on otherwise valid laws, against the procurement of defensive arms by groups which are being victimized by genocide.

---

[113] https://www.nationalreview.com/2007/10/genocide-resistance-dave-kopel-paul-gallant-joanne-d-eisen/
[114] https://papers.ssrn.com/sol3/papers.cfm?abstract_id=1022114
[115] https://www.un.org/en/genocideprevention/genocide-convention.shtml

GUN CONTROL IS RACIST

It is beyond doubt that gun control has a particular egregious history in relation to racism and racist oppression. In an article in the Libertarian Republic[116], Emmanuel Sessegnon writes:

Gun Control is Racist: Here's 2 Reasons Why

> Modern liberals love one word more than any other: racist. They've called Trump racist. They've called tax cuts racist. And last year they even called Paw Patrol, a show about a kid with super-powered dogs, fascist.
>
> Recently they have also made a name for themselves opposing guns. After every single mass shooting they are quick to blame the guns used instead of the people using them. Instead of advocating for more security, they demand that guns be taken from law-abiding citizens.
>
> One problem: gun control laws heavily discriminate against minorities, especially African-Americans. Here's how.
>
> **1. Early gun control laws disarmed African-Americans and encouraged lynchings**
>
> After the abolition of slavery in 1865 Southern Democrats quickly rushed to put blacks 'back in their place'. Southern states enacted many 'black codes' which placed laws on African-Americans which did not apply to whites.
>
> However, after the passage of the 14th amendment and the Civil Rights Act of 1870, these gun laws had to be race-neutral. At least in name.

---

[116] https://thelibertarianrepublic.com/the-racist-history-of-gun-control/

But a black man's right to bear arms would soon be infringed. After a lynching in Florida was thwarted by a group of armed African-Americans, southern states began passing laws requiring licenses for firearms. Naturally, only blacks were ever charged for carrying unlicensed firearms. Whites only received a small fine, if any punishment at all. And blacks almost never received licenses.

In a blatant attempt to disarm African-Americans Tennessee and Arkansas banned all handguns except for 'military handguns'; which former plantation owners could afford and confederate veterans already had. Freedmen's guns were confiscated and destroyed all across the South.

By the 1880s blacks had been effectively disarmed and lynching rates skyrocketed.

These laws quickly spread to the North and the Midwest, robbing countless African-Americans of our second amendment rights. In 1919 a black worker in Ohio was charged with concealing a weapon. Where? In his own bunk bed where he lived.

As the disarmament of black men continued into the 20th century, vicious race riots grew in popularity. The most vicious of these was the Tulsa Race Riot of 1921, in which mobs of armed whites attacked the black area of the city. In fact, they even used bi-planes to drop bombs from the air onto black homes. Over 200 African-Americans were killed.

The end of Jim Crow in 1964 after the passage of the Civil Rights Act did not stop the proliferation of racist gun laws. The Mulford Act was a law that banned the public carrying of firearms. The state legislature passed it almost immediately after the Black Panthers made armed demonstrations protesting the mistreatment of blacks in the region.

2. Today, gun laws disproportionately imprison African-Americans

Today's gun laws are the strictest in democratic strongholds like California and Illinois. Chicago has extremely tough gun laws that have stripped thousands of their second amendment rights, including a handgun ban that was so tough the Supreme Court struck it down.

And unfortunately Chicago doesn't even have the toughest gun laws in America anymore; California, D.C, and other states have now surpassed Chicago.

Not much data is kept on how many black men have been thrown in jail for weapon charges. But the data that does exist is startling. In 1995 the US Department of Justice did its one and only study on how many people are imprisoned for having a gun.

The results were shocking. Black men were five times as likely to be arrested for having a gun. And they were far more likely to be thrown into prison as well.

Why? Likely because urban areas have some of the toughest gun laws, making it almost impossible to legally own a gun. In communities where gangs often roam the streets at night, many black men and women buy guns simply to defend themselves. When it's impossible to get them legally they get them illegally for their own safety.

Even when a black man can get a gun license they are more likely to be harassed by law enforcement. Cops often assume that black men got the gun illegally and often accuse them of doing so. In many cases they shoot first and ask questions later.

It is undeniable that the right to bear arms largely doesn't apply to African-Americans. It is ironic that the same leftists that decry racism continue to support policies rooted in racism in the past and the present.

If you really care about us, don't throw us in prison for exercising our second amendment rights.

A similar argument is presented in this article by Clayton E. Cramer.[117]

The Racist Roots of Gun Control

The historical record provides compelling evidence that racism underlies gun control laws - and not in any subtle way. Throughout much of American history, gun control was openly stated as a method for keeping blacks and Hispanics "in their place," and to quiet the racial fears of whites.

This paper is intended to provide a brief summary of this unholy alliance of gun control and racism, and to suggest that gun control laws should be regarded as "suspect ideas," analogous to the "suspect classifications" theory of discrimination already part of the American legal system.

Racist arms laws predate the establishment of the United States. Starting in 1751, the French Black Code required Louisiana colonists to stop any blacks, and if necessary, beat "any black carrying any potential weapon, such as a cane." If a black refused to stop on demand, and was on horseback, the colonist was authorized to "shoot to kill." Slave possession of firearms was a necessity at times in a frontier society, yet laws continued to be passed in an attempt to prohibit slaves or free blacks from possessing firearms, except under very restrictively controlled conditions. Similarly, in the sixteenth century the colony of New Spain, terrified of black slave revolts, prohibited all blacks, free and slave, from carrying arms.

In the Haitian Revolution of the 1790s, the slave population successfully threw off their French masters, but the Revolution degenerated into a race war, aggravating existing fears in the French Louisiana colony, and among whites in the slave states of the United States. When the first U.S. official arrived in New Orleans in 1803 to take charge of this new American possession, the planters sought to have the existing free black militia disarmed, and otherwise exclude "free blacks from positions in which they were required to bear arms," including such

---

[117] https://www.firearmsandliberty.com/cramer.racism.html

non-military functions as slave-catching crews. The New Orleans city government also stopped whites from teaching fencing to free blacks, and then, when free blacks sought to teach fencing, similarly prohibited their efforts as well.

It is not surprising that the first North American English colonies, then the states of the new republic, remained in dread fear of armed blacks, for slave revolts against slave owners often degenerated into less selective forms of racial warfare. The perception that free blacks were sympathetic to the plight of their enslaved brothers, and the dangerous example that "a Negro could be free" also caused the slave states to pass laws designed to disarm all blacks, both slave and free. Unlike the gun control laws passed after the Civil War, these antebellum statutes were for blacks alone. In Maryland, these prohibitions went so far as to prohibit free blacks from owning dogs without a license, and authorizing any white to kill an unlicensed dog owned by a free black, for fear that blacks would use dogs as weapons. Mississippi went further, and prohibited any ownership of a dog by a black person.

Understandably, restrictions on slave possession of arms go back a very long way. While arms restrictions on free blacks predate it, these restrictions increased dramatically after Nat Turner's Rebellion in 1831, a revolt that caused the South to become increasingly irrational in its fears. Virginia's response to Turner's Rebellion prohibited free blacks "to keep or carry any firelock of any kind, any military weapon, or any powder or lead..." The existing laws under which free blacks were occasionally licensed to possess or carry arms was also repealed, making arms possession completely illegal for free blacks.

But even before this action by the Virginia Legislature, in the aftermath of Turner's Rebellion, the discovery that a free black family possessed lead shot for use as scale weights, without powder or weapon in which to fire it, was considered sufficient reason for a frenzied mob to discuss summary execution of the owner.

The analogy to the current hysteria where mere possession of ammunition in some states without a firearms license may lead to jail time, should be obvious.

One example of the increasing fear of armed blacks is the 1834 change to the Tennessee Constitution, when Article XI, 26 of the 1796 Tennessee Constitution was revised from: "That the freemen of this State have a right to keep and to bear arms for their common defence," to:

> "That the free white men of this State have a right to keep and to bear arms for their common defence."

It is not clear what motivated this change, other than Turner's bloody insurrection. The year before, the Tennessee Supreme Court had recognized the right to bear arms as an individual guarantee, but there is nothing in that decision that touches on the subject of race.

Other decisions during the antebellum period were unambiguous about the importance of race. In State v. Huntly (1843), the North Carolina Supreme Court had recognized that there was a right to carry arms guaranteed under the North Carolina Constitution, as long as such arms were carried in a manner not likely to frighten people. The following year, the North Carolina Supreme Court made one of those decisions whose full significance would not appear until after the Civil War and passage of the Fourteenth Amendment. An 1840 statute provided:

> *That if any free negro, mulatto, or free person of color, shall wear or carry about his or her person, or keep in his or her house, any shot gun, musket, rifle, pistol, sword, dagger or bowie-knife, unless he or she shall have obtained a licence therefor from the Court of Pleas and Quarter Sessions of his or her county, within one year preceding the wearing, keeping or carrying therefor, he or she shall be guilty of a misdemeanor, and may be indicted therefor.*

Elijah Newsom, "a free person of color," was indicted in Cumberland County in June of 1843 for carrying a shotgun without a license - at the very time the North Carolina Supreme Court was deciding Huntly. Newsom was convicted by a jury; but the trial judge directed a not guilty verdict, and the state appealed to the North

Carolina Supreme Court. Newsom's attorney argued that the statute requiring free blacks to obtain a license to "keep and bear arms" was in violation of both the Second Amendment to the U. S. Constitution, and the North Carolina Constitution's similar guarantee of a right to keep and bear arms. The North Carolina Supreme Court refused to accept that the Second Amendment was a limitation on state laws, but had to deal with the problem of the state constitutional guarantees, which had been used in the Huntly decision the year before.

The 17th article of the 1776 North Carolina Constitution declared:

> That the people have a right to bear arms, for the defence of the State; and, as standing armies, in time of peace, are dangerous to liberty, they ought not to be kept up; and that the military should be kept under strict subordination to, and governed by, the civil power.

The Court asserted that: "We cannot see that the act of 1840 is in conflict with it... The defendant is not indicted for carrying arms in defence of the State, nor does the act of 1840 prohibit him from so doing." But in Huntly, the Court had acknowledged that the restrictive language "for the defence of the State" did not preclude an individual right. The Court then attempted to justify the necessity of this law:

> Its only object is to preserve the peace and safety of the community from being disturbed by an indiscriminate use, on ordinary occasions, by free men of color, of firearms or other arms of an offensive character. Self preservation is the first law of nations, as it is of individuals.

The North Carolina Supreme Court also sought to repudiate the idea that free blacks were protected by the North Carolina Constitution's Bill of Rights by pointing out that the Constitution excluded free blacks from voting, and therefore free blacks were not citizens. Unlike a number of other state constitutions with right to keep and bear arms provisions that limited this right only to citizens, Article 17 guaranteed this right to the people -- and try as hard as they might, it was difficult to argue that a "free person of color," in the words of the Court, was not one of "the people."

It is one of the great ironies that, in much the same way that the North Carolina Supreme Court recognized a right to bear arms in 1843 - then a year later declared that free blacks were not included - the Georgia Supreme Court did likewise before the 1840s were out. The Georgia Supreme Court found in Nunn v. State (1846) that a statute prohibiting the sale of concealable handguns, sword-canes, and daggers violated the Second Amendment:

> *The right of the whole people, old and young, men, women and boys, and not militia only, to keep and bear arms of every description, and not such merely as are used by the militia, shall not be infringed, curtailed, or broken in upon, in the smallest degree; and all of this for the important end to be attained: the rearing up and qualifying a well-regulated militia, so vitally necessary to the security of a free State. Our opinion is, that any law, State or Federal, is repugnant to the Constitution, and void, which contravenes this right, originally belonging to our forefathers, trampled under foot by Charles I. and his two wicked sons and successors, reestablished by the revolution of 1688, conveyed to this land of liberty by the colonists, and finally incorporated conspicuously in our own Magna Charta! And Lexington, Concord, Camden, River Raisin, Sandusky, and the laurel-crowned field of New Orleans, plead eloquently for this interpretation!*

Finally, after this paean to liberty -- in a state where much of the population remained enslaved, forbidden by law to possess arms of any sort -- the Court defined the valid limits of laws restricting the bearing of arms:

> We are of the opinion, then, that so far as the act of 1837 seeks to suppress the practice of carrying certain weapons secretly, that it is valid, inasmuch as it does not deprive the citizen of his natural right of self-defence, or of his constitutional right to keep and bear arms. But that so much of it, as contains a prohibition against bearing arms openly, is in conflict with the Constitution, and void...

"Citizen"? Within a single page, the Court had gone from "right of the whole people, old and young, men, women and boys" to the much more narrowly restrictive right of a "citizen." The motivation for this sudden narrowing of the right appeared two years later.

The decision Cooper and Worsham v. Savannah (1848) was not, principally, a right to keep and bear arms case. In 1839, the city of Savannah, Georgia, in an admitted effort "to prevent the increase of free persons of color in our city," had established a $100 per year tax on free blacks moving into Savannah from other parts of Georgia. Samuel Cooper and Hamilton Worsham, two "free persons of color," were convicted of failing to pay the tax, and were jailed.

On appeal, counsel for Cooper and Worsham argued that the ordinance establishing the tax was deficient in a number of technical areas; the assertion of most interest to us is, "In Georgia, free persons of color have constitutional rights..." Cooper and Worsham's counsel argued that these rights included writ of habeas corpus, right to own real estate, to be "subject to taxation," "[t]hey may sue and be sued," and cited a number of precedents under Georgia law in defense of their position.

Justice Warner delivered the Court's opinion, most of which is irrelevant to the right to keep and bear arms, but one portion shows the fundamental relationship between citizenship, arms, and elections, and why gun control laws were an essential part of defining blacks as "non-citizens":

> "Free persons of color have never been recognized here as citizens; they are not entitled to bear arms, vote for members of the legislature, or to hold any civil office."

The Georgia Supreme Court did agree that the ordinance jailing Cooper and Worsham for non-payment was illegal, and ordered their release, but the comments of the Court made it clear that their brave words in Nunn v. State (1846) about "the right of the people," really only meant white people.

While settled parts of the South were in great fear of

armed blacks, on the frontier, the concerns about Indian attack often forced relaxation of these rules. The 1798 Kentucky Comprehensive Act allowed slaves and free blacks on frontier plantations "to keep and use guns, powder, shot, and weapons, offensive and defensive." Unlike whites, however, a license was required for free blacks or slaves to carry weapons.

The need for blacks to carry arms for self-defense included not only the problem of Indian attack, and the normal criminal attacks that anyone might worry about, but the additional hazard that free blacks were in danger of being kidnapped and sold into slavery. A number of states, including Ohio, Indiana, Illinois, Michigan, and Wisconsin, passed laws specifically to prohibit kidnapping of free blacks, out of concern that the federal Fugitive Slave Laws would be used as cover for re-enslavement.

The end of slavery in 1865 did not eliminate the problems of racist gun control laws; the various Black Codes adopted after the Civil War required blacks to obtain a license before carrying or possessing firearms or Bowie knives; these are sufficiently well-known that any reasonably complete history of the Reconstruction period mentions them. These restrictive gun laws played a part in the efforts of the Republicans to get the Fourteenth Amendment ratified, because it was difficult for night riders to generate the correct level of terror in a victim who was returning fire. It does appear, however, that the requirement to treat blacks and whites equally before the law led to the adoption of restrictive firearms laws in the South that were equal in the letter of the law, but unequally enforced. It is clear that the vagrancy statutes adopted at roughly the same time, in 1866, were intended to be used against blacks, even though the language was race-neutral.

The former states of the Confederacy, many of which had recognized the right to carry arms openly before the Civil War, developed a very sudden willingness to qualify that right. One especially absurd example, and one that includes strong evidence of the racist intentions behind gun control laws, is Texas.

In Cockrum v. State (1859), the Texas Supreme Court had recognized that there was a right to carry defensive arms, and that this right was protected under both the Second Amendment, and section 13 of the Texas Bill of Rights. The outer limit of the state's authority (in this case, attempting to discourage the carrying of Bowie knives), was that it could provide an enhanced penalty for manslaughters committed with Bowie knives. Yet, by 1872, the Texas Supreme Court denied that there was any right to carry any weapon for self-defense under either the state or federal constitutions -- and made no attempt to explain or justify why the Cockrum decision was no longer valid.

What caused the dramatic change? The following excerpt from that same decision -- so offensive that no one would dare make such an argument today -- sheds some light on the racism that apparently caused the sudden perspective change:

> *The law under consideration has been attacked upon the ground that it was contrary to public policy, and deprived the people of the necessary means of self- defense; that it was an innovation upon the customs and habits of the people, to which they would not peaceably submit... We will not say to what extent the early customs and habits of the people of this state should be respected and accommodated, where they may come in conflict with the ideas of intelligent and well-meaning legislators. A portion of our system of laws, as well as our public morality, is derived from a people the most peculiar perhaps of any other in the history and derivation of its own system. Spain, at different periods of the world, was dominated over by the Carthagenians, the Romans, the Vandals, the Snovi, the Allani, the Visigoths, and Arabs; and to this day there are found in the Spanish codes traces of the laws and customs of each of these nations blended together in a system by no means to be compared with the sound philosophy and pure morality of the common law.*

This particular decision is more open than most as to its motivations, but throughout the South during this period, the existing precedents that recognized a right to open carry under state constitutional provisions were being narrowed, or simply ignored. Nor was the reasoning that led to these changes lost on judges in the North. In 1920, the Ohio Supreme Court upheld the conviction of a Mexican for concealed carry of a handgun--while asleep in his own bed. Justice Wanamaker's scathing dissent criticized the precedents cited by the majority in defense of this absurdity:

> *I desire to give some special attention to some of the authorities cited, Supreme Court decisions from Alabama, Georgia, Arkansas, Kentucky, and one or two inferior court decisions from New York, which are given in support of the doctrines upheld by this court. The southern states have very largely furnished the precedents. It is only necessary to observe that the race issue there has extremely intensified a decisive purpose to entirely disarm the negro, and this policy is evident upon reading the opinions.*

While not relevant to the issue of racism, Justice Wanamaker's closing paragraphs capture well the biting wit and intelligence of this jurist, who was unfortunately, outnumbered on the bench:

> *I hold that the laws of the state of Ohio should be so applied and so interpreted as to favor the law-abiding rather than the law-violating people. If this decision shall stand as the law of Ohio, a very large percentage of the good people of Ohio to-day are criminals, because they are daily committing criminal acts by having these weapons in their own homes for their own defense. The only safe course for them to pursue, instead of having the weapon concealed on or about their person, or under their pillow at night, is to hang the revolver on the wall and put below it a large placard with these words inscribed:*
>
> *"The Ohio Supreme Court having decided that it is a crime to carry a concealed weapon on one's person in one's home, even in one's bed or bunk, this weapon is hung upon the wall that you may see it, and before you commit any burglary or assault, please, Mr.*

Burglar, hand me my gun."

There are other examples of remarkable honesty from the state supreme courts on this subject, of which the finest is probably Florida Supreme Court Justice Buford's concurring opinion in Watson v. Stone (1941), in which a conviction for carrying a handgun without a permit was overturned, because the handgun was in the glove compartment of a car:

> I know something of the history of this legislation. The original Act of 1893 was passed when there was a great influx of negro laborers in this State drawn here for the purpose of working in turpentine and lumber camps. The same condition existed when the Act was amended in 1901 and the Act was passed for the purpose of disarming the negro laborers and to thereby reduce the unlawful homicides that were prevalent in turpentine and sawmill camps and to give the white citizens in sparsely settled areas a better feeling of security. The statute was never intended to be applied to the white population and in practice has never been so applied.

Today is not 1893, and when proponents of restrictive gun control insist that their motivations are color-blind, there is a possibility that they are telling the truth. Nonetheless, there are some rather interesting questions that should be asked today. The most obvious question is, "Why should a police chief or sheriff have any discretion in issuing a concealed handgun permit?" Here in California, even the state legislature's research arm - hardly a nest of progunners - has admitted that the vast majority of permits to carry concealed handguns in California are issued to white males. Even if overt racism is not an issue, an official may simply have more empathy with an applicant of a similar cultural background, and consequently be more able to relate to the applicant's concerns. As my wife pointedly reminded a police official when we applied for concealed weapon permits, "If more police chiefs were women, a lot more women would get permits, and be able to defend themselves from rapists."

Gun control advocates today are not so foolish as to openly promote racist laws, and so the question might be asked what relevance the racist past of gun control laws has. One concern is that the motivations for disarming blacks in the past are really not so different from the motivations for disarming law-abiding citizens today. In the last century, the official rhetoric in support of such laws was that "they" were too violent, too untrustworthy, to be allowed weapons. Today, the same elitist rhetoric regards law-abiding Americans in the same way, as childlike creatures in need of guidance from the government. In the last century, while never openly admitted, one of the goals of disarming blacks was to make them more willing to accept various forms of economic oppression, including the sharecropping system, in which free blacks were reduced to an economic state not dramatically superior to the conditions of slavery.

In the seventeenth century, the aristocratic power structure of colonial Virginia found itself confronting a similar challenge from lower class whites. These poor whites resented how the men who controlled the government used that power to concentrate wealth into a small number of hands. These wealthy feeders at the government trough would have disarmed poor whites if they could, but the threat of both Indian and pirate attack made this impractical; for all white men "were armed and had to be armed..." Instead, blacks, who had occupied a poorly defined status between indentured servant and slave, were reduced to hereditary chattel slavery, so that poor whites could be economically advantaged, without the upper class having to give up its privileges.

Today, the forces that push for gun control seem to be heavily (though not exclusively) allied with political factions that are committed to dramatic increases in taxation on the middle class. While it would be hyperbole to compare higher taxes on the middle class to the suffering and deprivation of sharecropping or slavery, the analogy of disarming those whom you wish to economically disadvantage, has a certain worrisome validity to it.

Another point to consider is that in the American legal system, certain classifications of governmental discrimination are considered constitutionally suspect, and these "suspect classifications" (usually considered to be race and religion) come to a court hearing under a strong presumption of invalidity. The reason for these "suspect classifications" is because of the long history of governmental discrimination based on these classifications, and because these classifications often impinge on fundamental rights.

In much the same way, gun control has historically been a tool of racism, and associated with racist attitudes about black violence. Similarly, many gun control laws impinge on that most fundamental of rights: self-defense. Racism is so intimately tied to the history of gun control in America that we should regard gun control aimed at law-abiding people as a "suspect idea," and require that the courts use the same demanding standards when reviewing the constitutionality of a gun control law, that they would use with respect to a law that discriminated based on race.

ANIMAL WELFARE AND CONSERVATION

It is sometimes said that the level of civilisation of a society is shown by its concern for the welfare of animals. It is certainly true that Australians, like most people in the developed world, are acutely aware of the importance of animal welfare.

In the case of domesticated animals this involves their environment, housing and diet, their ability to exhibit normal behaviour patterns, and the need to be protected from pain, suffering, injury and disease.

For animals in the wild, minimising the infliction of pain and suffering are the key concerns.

Farmers have a vested interest in the welfare of their animals. They are valuable property with a substantial impact on their finances, whether livestock or working dogs. In addition to humanitarian considerations there is a strong economic incentive to ensure they are healthy and in good condition.

However, there are times when animals are injured or sick and cannot be effectively treated. A broken leg in a horse, cow or sheep, for example, usually cannot be repaired as if it were a human. Difficulty giving birth, serious illness, burning following a fire or insufficient food or water during a drought may be impossible to rectify.

In such cases the humane response may be to end their suffering by shooting. Done correctly, death by shooting is quick and painless. No other method can compare.

It is fundamental to the welfare of animals that farmers, their employees and others with responsibility for the care of animals have access to firearms for this purpose.

The killing of pest animals, from camels and deer to foxes, pigs, wild dogs and rabbits, should also occur humanely. While the elimination of these animals is desirable for both economic and environmental reasons, this does not justify inflicting pain and suffering. Shooting is absolutely the most humane method of killing them and infinitely more humane than poisoning or trapping.

For this to occur, obviously it is important that those engaged in hunting have access to firearms of appropriate size and utility. This should not be limited to professional hunters, as some people argue quite naively. The only difference between a professional and a recreational hunter is that the former is being paid. The types of firearms used and the end results are the same.

In fact there are relatively few professional hunters in Australia, and nowhere near enough to make a serious dent in the feral animal population. Volunteer hunters, by contrast, are relatively numerous and also capable of effectively controlling feral animal populations.

SELF DEFENCE

In the latter part of the Roman Empire, the people had been disarmed by law as the emperors sought to control every aspect of life.

In 455 AD the Vandals, a Germanic tribe from where we get our term for wanton destruction, invaded Italy and sacked the city of Rome. There were not enough soldiers to protect the people from the depredations of the Vandals, and having no means of defending themselves, they were brutalized and plundered without mercy.

The emperor at the time, Petronius Maximus, was killed trying to defend the city. Fortunately, his main general, Majorian succeeded him. He immediately instituted a series of reforms. One of which was the restoration of the right of the Roman people to bear arms once again. A strong leader, Majorian might have revived the western part of the Roman Empire, but he was betrayed and killed by his leading general who was of Germanic origin.

Then, as now, our right to express ourselves freely and redress the government for any grievances, is tied directly to our ability to defend ourselves. With the talk of "national emergencies" making it possible to confiscate guns from people, the government must be closely monitored.

No government, no matter how benign, will listen as closely to its people if they have no means of defending their position. What happens if we have no means of defending our position? Then we will be at the mercy of whatever comes from the top. We would then be in the same situation as the citizens of Rome in 455 A.D.

- *Greg Woods*[118]

---

[118] https://www.courierpress.com/story/opinion/2019/05/01/letter-need-self-defense/3647037002/

Modern self-defence laws build on the Roman Law principle of *dominium*, where any attack on the members of the family or the property it owned was a personal attack on the *pater familias*.

In *Leviathan* (1651), Hobbes argues that although some may be stronger or more intelligent than others in their natural state, none are so strong as to be beyond a fear of violent death, which justifies self-defence as the highest necessity.

Article 12 of the Universal Declaration of Human Rights states:

> No one shall be subjected to arbitrary interference with his privacy, family, home or correspondence, nor to attacks upon his honour and reputation. Everyone has the right to the protection of the law against such interference or attacks.

Combined with the principle of the state's monopoly of legitimate force, this means that those authorized by the state to defend the law (in practice, the police) are charged with the use of necessary force to protect such rights. The right to personal self-defence is limited to situations where the immediate threat of violence cannot be prevented by those authorized to do so (in practice, because no police force is present at the moment of the threat).

The right to self-defence granted by law to the private citizen is strictly limited. Use of force that goes beyond what is necessary to dispel the immediate threat of violence is known as excessive self-defence (also self-defence with excessive force). The civil law systems have a theory of "abuse of right" to explain denial of justification in such cases.

In English law, the general common law principle is stated in *Beckford v R* (1988) 1 AD 130:

> A defendant is entitled to use reasonable force to protect himself, others for whom he is responsible and his property. It must be reasonable.

Similar provisions are found in legislation throughout the western world. They derive historically from article 6 of the French Penal Code of 1791, which ruled that "manslaughter is legitimate if it is indispensably dictated by the present necessity of legitimate defence of oneself or others." The modern French penal code further specifies that excessive self-defence is punishable due to "disproportion between the means of defence used and the gravity of the attack" defended against.

In international law, the right to personal self-defence can be found in a number of areas including international humanitarian law, international criminal law, the law of the sea, and the law of diplomatic relations.

Article 51 of the United Nations Charter recognises the right of both individual and collective self-defence in the context of a threat to a member country.

> Nothing in the present Charter shall impair the inherent right of individual or collective self-defence if an armed attack occurs against a Member of the United Nations, until the Security Council has taken measures necessary to maintain international peace and security. Measures taken by Members in the exercise of this right of self-defence shall be immediately reported to the Security Council and shall not in any way affect the authority and responsibility of the Security Council under the present Charter to take at any time such action as it deems necessary in order to maintain or restore international peace and security.

While some have argued that there is a human right to keep and bear arms for the purposes of self defence, this is disputed by those who oppose private ownership of firearms. Irrespective, it is certainly arguable that Australia's highly restrictive approach to the practical exercise of the right of self defence is contrary to international law.

Libertarianism characterises the majority of laws as intrusive to personal autonomy and, in particular, argues that the right to defend oneself from coercion (including violence) is a fundamental human right.

It follows that laws restricting the ability to exercise the right of self defence are illegitimate and should be opposed.

This does not mean, as some suggest, that everyone should have a gun for self defence. Rather, it means the state should not impose blanket limitations on the ownership of guns for self defence. Restricting or removing the right in relation to individuals who pose a threat to others is not prevented.

The following list shows countries that allow guns for self defence as a right, those that allow them for self defence subject to approval, and those that prohibit them entirely for that purpose.[119]

Allow as a right	May allow	Not allowed
Argentina	Bosnia & Herzegovina	Australia
Czech Republic	Botswana	Brunei
Estonia	Brazil	Cambodia
Lithuania	Canada	China
Honduras	Chile	Cook Islands
Iraq	Croatia	Denmark
Lithuania	Cyrus	East Timor
Pakistan	Egypt	Eritrea
Serbia	France	Fiji
United States	Germany	Finland
Yemen	Guatemala	Iceland
	Hungary	Ireland
	India	Japan
	Indonesia	Malta
	Israel	Marshall Islands
	Italy	Myanmar
	Jamaica	Nauru
	Kuwait	Netherlands
	Malaysia	North Korea
	Mexico	Puerto Rico
	Montenegro	Solomon Islands

---

[119] https://en.wikipedia.org/wiki/Overview_of_gun_laws_by_nation

	Mongolia	South Korea
	Namibia	Turkey
	Nepal	Uganda
	New Zealand	Ukraine
	Norway	United Kingdom
	Philippines	Venezuela
	Poland	Vietnam
	Romania	
	Russia	
	Singapore	
	Slovakia	
	Slovenia	
	South Africa	
	Spain	
	Switzerland	
	Sweden	
	Taiwan	
	Thailand	
	Uruguay	
	Zambia	

From this there are two important observations.

First, quite a few of the countries that do not permit private citizens to own firearms for self-defence are fundamentally authoritarian. This is not surprising – strict gun control is itself inherently authoritarian. Australia's approach places it in some unsavoury company.

Second, of the countries that do allow the ownership of guns for self-defence, whether as a right or subject to approval, many are liberal democracies comparable to Australia. Notwithstanding their approach, they have similar or lower levels of gun violence.

Allowing people to exercise their right to self-defence in practical terms has no adverse impact on society.

11

GUN MYTHS

GUNS ARE ONLY DESIGNED TO KILL

Offence or defence against people and animals has always been a major focus of firearms and played a substantial role in their development. However, this has never been their sole purpose and there are many guns which were designed or adapted for other purposes, particularly sport.

It is the same with all weapons. The modern javelin was derived from the spear and has been used for hunting and as a weapon since the beginning of time. Both the compound bow and crossbow, now used in modern archery, are also both based on weapons originally designed for hunting and war.

Many knives also have a military heritage including the short stabbing sword of the Romans, the kukri of the Ghurkas, military bayonets and daggers of many kinds.

Firearms have a very long history, beginning with the invention of gunpowder by the Chinese in the ninth century. The first device identified as a gun, a bamboo tube that used gunpowder to fire a spear, was seen in China around AD 1000.

Gunpowder came to Europe in the first half of the 13th century. Around the late 14th century, small, portable hand-held cannons were developed, creating in effect the first smooth-bore personal firearm. The earliest surviving firearm in Europe was found at Otepää, Estonia, and dates to at least 1396.

The Ottoman empire adopted gunpowder early and is said to have been the first to use firearms as part of its regular infantry, although this was not necessarily a positive experience.[120]

> Someone in Vienna is credited with having built the first rifle in 1411. It apparently was modeled on the cannon being used at the time and consisted of a very heavy metal barrel mounted on a wooden block. Like a cannon, it was loaded from the front of the barrel, hence the adjective muzzle-loading. By the second half of the 15th century, the Ottomans, as well as other countries, had improved the rifle through the use of the lever and spring and used the firearm in its armies. Breech-loading rifles also appeared but not until the 19th century.
>
> **Ottomans used rifles as early as 1420**
> Tezcan also said it was generally accepted that the Ottomans were using rifles as early as 1420; however, he referred to the following anecdote from the 16th century:
>
> Ogier Ghiselin de Busbecq, an ambassador to the Ottomans for the Austrians, relates in his memoirs how Süleyman the Magnificent's son-in-law, Rüstem Pasha, "went on campaign against Iran (1553-54). He armed some of the soldiers with rifles and brought out a cavalry unit. The pasha was thinking that he would frighten and terrify the enemy with this. However, while he was having the soldiers taught, not even one day passed before parts of most of the weapons were broken and destroyed.

---

[120] http://www.hurriyetdailynews.com/firearms-among-the-ottomans-23818

> The powder and oil that had to be replaced every time the rifle was fired dirtied their hands and clothing. The powder horn that hung at their sides was the butt of their friends' jokes. As a result they persuaded the pasha that this weapon that the soldiers couldn't get used to was not helpful and they would take back their bows and arrows."

Along with the potential for military use, firearm technology has also been driven by the quest for food. Indeed, shotguns owe their development almost entirely to this, having limited military application. There are many millions of families that owe their survival to the ability to shoot rabbits, hares, ducks, quail and other edible game with a shotgun.

From the 20th century, with the replacement of live pigeons with clay targets, shotgun development was primarily concerned with sport although law enforcement also had an influence. While any shotgun can be used as a weapon (particularly for self-defence), many modern shotguns are not particularly suited to that purpose.

Pistols have always had a very minor role in the military, their development being driven by self-defence and law enforcement. However, like shotguns, sporting uses have dominated development for well over a century. Indeed, modern small calibre pistols are not even recommended for self-defence due to their low power. High technology pistols, such as those used in the Olympic Games, cost thousands of dollars and have no purpose other than sport. Air pistols, many of which are highly sophisticated, are essentially ineffective as weapons.

Modern rifles have also moved far beyond military applications, although military considerations remain a factor in the development of centrefire calibres. Air rifles and rimfire rifles have no military uses and are only vaguely useful in either a defensive or offensive context. Some sporting rifles even lack a magazine and can only fire a single shot before being reloaded, with very heavy barrels to enhance accuracy. Such characteristics make them quite unsuitable for use by the military.

Hunting ammunition has also been developed to kill the quarry with a single well-aimed shot, while this ammunition is not permitted for military use.

In reality, the development of military firearms has relied on non-military innovations far more than vice versa.

SEMI-AUTOMATIC GUNS ARE NEW TECHNOLOGY

The assumption that semi-automatic firearms are relatively recent technology is a myth.

The first successful rapid-fire firearm was the Gatling Gun, used by Union forces during the American Civil War in the 1860s.

The world's first submachine gun (a fully automatic firearm which fires pistol cartridges) was invented by Theodor Bergmann and introduced into service in 1918 by the German Army during World War I, primarily for trench combat.

The first selective fire rifle (ie selectable for fully automatic or semi-automatic) was introduced during World War II by the Germans. Known as the Sturmgewehr 44 "assault rifle 44" (StG44, also known as the MP44 and MP45) it had a relatively short cartridge (7.92x33 Kurz), controllable automatic fire, a more compact design than a battle rifle with a quicker rate of fire, and was intended for hitting targets within a few hundred metres.

Semi-automatic rifles also had military origins, although not exclusively so. In 1903 and 1905, the Winchester Repeating Arms Company introduced the first low-power blowback (non-gas operated) semi-automatic rimfire and centrefire rifles.

By the early 20th century, several manufacturers had introduced semi-automatic .22 rifles, including Winchester, Remington, Fabrique Nationale and Savage Arms, all using the direct blow-back system of operation.

Winchester introduced a medium calibre semi-automatic rifle, the Model 1907, as an upgrade to the Model 1905, utilizing a blowback system of operation, in calibres such as .351 Winchester. Both the Model 1905 and Model 1907 saw limited military and police use.[121]

In 1906, Remington Arms introduced the "Remington Auto-loading Repeating Rifle", renamed it the "Model 8" in 1911, and promoted it as a sporting rifle.

The first successful gas operated semi-automatic rifle is attributed to Mexican General Manuel Mondragon in 1885. In 1908 he patented the rifle, the Mondragón rifle M1908, and Mexico was the first nation to use a semi-auto rifle in battle in 1911; the rifles being issued to regular troops during the Mexican revolution. This would be the basis of all future semi-automatic firearms to date.

France introduced a semi-automatic rifle, the Fusil Automatique Modele 1917, during the latter stages of WWI but it did not receive a favourable reception and the army retained bolt action rifles for many years subsequently.

In 1937 the American M1 Garand was the first semi-automatic rifle to replace a nation's bolt-action rifle as the standard-issue infantry weapon. During World War II the M1 Garand gave American infantrymen an advantage over their opponents, most of whom were issued slower firing bolt-action rifles.

---

[121] https://en.wikipedia.org/wiki/Semi-automatic_rifle

The Soviets and Germans issued semi-automatic gas-operated rifles during World War II in relatively small numbers - the Soviet AVS-36, SVT-38, and SVT-40 and the German Gewehr 43. In practice, they did not replace the bolt-action rifle as a standard infantry weapon of their respective nations.

The United Kingdom had intended to replace the bolt-action Lee–Enfield with a self-loading rifle but discarded that plan when the Second World War became imminent, shifting its emphasis to speeding-up re-armament with existing weapons.

THE AR-15 IS A MILITARY ASSAULT RIFLE

The AR-15 has never been issued to military forces because it is semi-automatic. While that may not have been a barrier previously, by the time of its release in 1964 military forces were only issuing rifles capable of full automatic action.

The military assault rifle version is the M16, first issued to US forces in 1964 to replace the M14. The M16 has now been mostly replaced by the M4.[122]

The generally accepted definition of an assault rifle includes having selective fire (ie a selector switch which allows automatic firing). The first rifle to be referred to as an assault rifle, the German Sturmgewehr 44, was defined by this characteristic.

The AR design was developed by the Armalite company and AR is an abbreviation of Armalite Rifle, not automatic rifle as some claim. Armalite was acquired by Colt's Manufacturing Company in 1959, which still owns the brand, but there are numerous other manufacturers making similar rifles and using the 'AR-15 style' term.

---

[122] https://en.wikipedia.org/wiki/M16_rifle

The first mass production version of the AR-15 was the Colt AR-15 Sporter, in .223 Remington, with a 20-inch barrel and issued with 5-round magazines.

The AR-15 uses the same .223 ammunition as many other rifles, both semi-automatic and bolt action. It is neither more powerful nor more lethal than any other rifle that uses the same ammunition.

These two rifles have identical firepower.

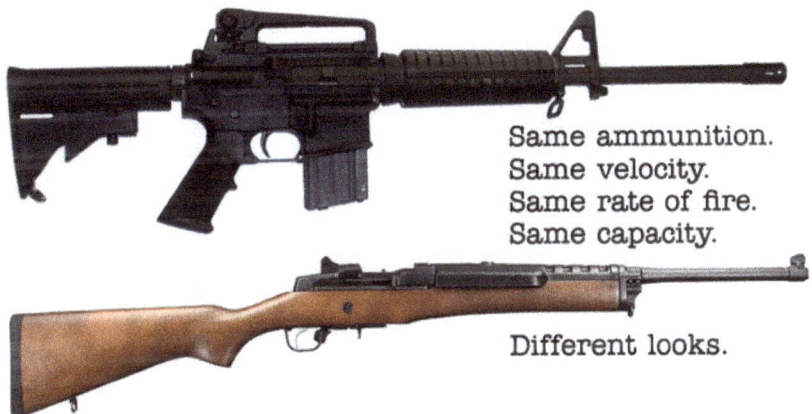

Same ammunition.
Same velocity.
Same rate of fire.
Same capacity.

Different looks.

The AR design has also been applied to other calibres - the AR-10 in .308 calibre and the AR-7[123] in .22, both semi-automatics.

GUN OWNERSHIP IS A PRIVILEGE, NOT A RIGHT

This is the myth that underpins Australia's National Firearms Agreement. It is based on the proposition that governments have a right to limit or revoke the freedoms of those they govern by defining those freedoms as "privileges".

The philosophical context of this is discussed in Chapter 10. The central issue is whether the government is our servant

---

[123] https://en.wikipedia.org/wiki/ArmaLite_AR-7

or our master. Needless to say, it is controversial and highly contested.

Australians are at a particular disadvantage in relation to the exercise of government power due to few constitutional protections. Most other democratic countries have some form of limit on government power, of which the US Bill of Rights is most well-known. Australia remains the only Western democratic country with neither a constitutional nor federal legislative bill of rights to protect its citizens.[124]

Australia's Constitution contains just five explicit individual rights. These are the right to vote (Section 41), protection against acquisition of property on unjust terms (Section 51 (xxxi)), the right to a trial by jury (Section 80), freedom of religion (Section 116) and prohibition of discrimination on the basis of State of residency (Section 117).

The High Court has found that certain additional rights for individuals may be inferred from the Constitution. In 1992 it decided that Australia's form of parliamentary democracy (dictated by the Constitution) necessarily requires a degree of freedom for individuals to discuss and debate political issues.

While it is true that the protection of individual liberty is not completely guaranteed even with a bill of rights, at least it provides a benchmark from which actual rights can be compared. In Australia our governments can declare almost anything a privilege and place limits on access to it, with the only dispute being whether it is a state or federal responsibility.

Those who believe governments are inherently benign are likely to agree that it can declare gun ownership to be a privilege, to be granted or removed as it chooses. They will

---

[124] https://www.creativespirits.info/aboriginalculture/law/human-rights-are-not-protected-in-australia

most likely never even question that notion unless and until the government restricts their right to something which they value personally.

However, anyone who believes in individual rights, inherent rights, in governments serving the people rather than vice versa, in the principle that the government has no right to restrict anyone's activities unless it is to prevent harm to others, will find the proposition that gun ownership is a privilege to be a complete myth.

MORE GUNS MEANS MORE CRIME

This myth is what leads to the conclusion that reducing the number of firearms in the community, which is only possible by restricting their availability to law-abiding people (because criminals, by definition, do not obey the law), will reduce the level of crime, particularly gun homicides.

Those who seek civilian disarmament argue this point very strongly, often including suicides in cited levels of "gun violence" in order to reinforce their case. There are a number of such dishonest publications which are quoted by gun control advocates.

The evidence overall shows there is simply no correlation between the number of guns and the crime rate. Rates of violence (ie not including suicides) are not correlated with firearm ownership rates either in the United States or globally, whether in peaceful countries or among violent countries.

Moreover, people who own a hundred guns are no more likely to use them for criminal purposes than those who own just one or two guns.

The reason is that gun ownership and crime are independent variables. That is, they move independently of each other;

one does not influence the other apart from the fact that perceptions of danger may prompt the acquisition of guns for self defence.

If a country like America was to impose gun control laws like Australia's (ignoring whether that was possible), there would be no change in the rate of violent crime. If Australia was to adopt gun control laws like America, its crime rates would also not change. (Noting that there are parts of America (eg Vermont) that are safer than Australia notwithstanding virtually no gun control laws, and parts of Australia with quite high levels of violence notwithstanding few guns.)

This is explained by the fact that violent crime is committed by individuals, not by the implements they choose. The availability of a firearm does not transform a non-violent person into a violent person. The people who commit violent crime will still be criminals whether or not they have a firearm.

A graph of firearm murder rates against gun ownership shows a correlation (r^2) of just 0.0031 for the states of America[125] and 0.0107 on a country by country basis. Some countries with high levels of gun ownership also have high rates of gun homicide while some have low rates, and vice versa.

There is simply no correlation between the two. Gun murder rates among US states is not correlated with gun ownership rates, and there is also no correlation between firearm homicide rates and guns per capita on a country to country basis.

---

[125] https://medium.com/handwaving-freakoutery/everybodys-lying-about-the-link-between-gun-ownership-and-homicide-1108ed400be5?

To further reinforce the point, here is a summary of data on murder rates for the countries discussed in this book plus several US states.[126] [127] [128]

Country/State	Gun ownership (per 100,000)	Overall Homicide Rate (per 100,000)	Gun Homicide Rate (per 100,000)	Gun Laws
Australia	13.7	0.80	0.18	Strict
Czech Republic	16.3	0.60	0.15	Relaxed
India	4.2	3.22	0.30	Strict
Ireland	7.2	0.90	0.21	Strict
New Zealand	30	0.70	0.11	Moderate
UK	2.8	1.20	0.06	Strict
Switzerland	24.4	0.50	0.15	Relaxed
USA	120.5	5.30	4.46	Relaxed
Vermont		1.6	0.3	Very relaxed
Michigan		5.5	4.2	Relaxed
New Hampshire		1.5	0.4	Very relaxed
Missouri		9.9	5.4	Very relaxed
District of Columbia		21.8	16.5	Strict

LEGAL GUNS SUPPLY ILLEGAL USERS

This myth is based on the proposition that stolen legal guns are the primary source of illegal guns. It assumes that if guns are removed from the law-abiding, the non law-abiding will be unable to obtain them.

Legal firearm owners obviously do not want their property stolen and have an inherent interest in preventing it. However, they do not agree it is legitimate to deny them the use of firearms in order to prevent others from using them

---

[126] https://en.wikipedia.org/wiki/List_of_countries_by_firearm-related_death_rate
[127] https://en.wikipedia.org/wiki/List_of_countries_by_intentional_homicide_rate
[128] https://en.wikipedia.org/wiki/Firearm_death_rates_in_the_United_States_by_state

illegally. This would be comparable to denying access to money because it might be stolen and used for criminal purposes.

In any case, there are far more important sources of illegal firearms than the theft of legal firearms. Australia imports over eight million containers a year, of which only a relatively small number are checked in sufficient detail to detect firearms. The widespread availability of drugs such as heroin and cocaine, despite the investment of enormous resources to prevent their importation, shows the difficulty.

Police advise that the firearm of choice for criminals is pistols rather than rifles or shotguns. These are obviously small enough to be easily concealed. For criminals, the risks involved in stealing guns from private homes is much greater than importing them or buying them on the black market from importers.

APPEARANCE MATTERS

A replica gun that cannot fire bullets, or a gun that only fires plastic pellets, gel balls or water, cannot be used for mass shootings or even individual homicides. They are harmless.

There is nonetheless a perception that banning such guns, if they look like real guns, serves a useful purpose. This is a myth.

While it is true that some of them can be mistaken for real guns, and might be used in armed holdups, it is also true that armed robbers use pieces of soap, wood and other items hidden under a garment to look like pistols.

It is sometimes claimed that police will mistake a replica for a real gun and act accordingly, potentially with lethal consequences.

On 22 September 1999, a man in the UK[129] was returning home from the pub carrying a table leg that had been repaired by his brother earlier that day, in a plastic bag . Someone phoned the police to report "an Irishman with a gun wrapped in a bag". A police crew challenged the man from behind. As he turned to face them, they shot him dead at a distance of 15 feet. The police claimed self defence and no charges were laid.

If this argument is followed to its natural conclusion, carrying virtually anything should be prohibited. Who knows what mistakes the police will make?

The suggestion that people should be denied ownership of harmless objects that look like firearms, to avoid police shooting them, is absurd. The onus must be on the police to distinguish between merely carrying a firearm (or something that looks like a firearm) and using a firearm in a dangerous manner.

The National Firearms Agreement allows firearms registries to reclassify any firearm to a more restrictive category where it "substantially duplicates those rifles in design, function or appearance". There is no qualification or guidance as to how this should be applied.

As a consequence, bolt-action Category B firearms are being reclassified as Category D or denied import permits for the sole reason that they vaguely resemble semi-automatic or full automatic firearms.

It was once common for firearms to be carried in public with no consequences. Sporting shooters in Sydney would travel to the Malabar rifle range on the tram, carrying their rifles with them. The Swiss still frequently and openly carry their firearms on public transport.

---

[129] https://en.wikipedia.org/wiki/Death_of_Harry_Stanley

GUN CONTROL

It is now illegal to carry a firearm in public unless it is in a bag or carry case, with police and security guards the only exceptions. This is legislation based on emotion rather than public safety.

To do harm, guns require an individual to use them in a harmful manner. A replica cannot be used to do harm even if it is in the possession of a homicidal maniac, and a gun does not become a different gun just because it resembles one.

Laws based on appearance do nothing to improve public safety. They are authoritarian, based on fear and emotion, and should have no place in a free society.

In Switzerland, carrying real guns on public transport is common. In Australia, even owning replicas is highly regulated and carrying them in public could get you shot.

JUST BAN THEM

A popular myth among those who find guns scary and just want them "gone" is that they can be banned. All it requires, they say, is for the government to take decisive action.

Leaving aside the compatibility of that view with a liberal democratic society, it should be abundantly clear that it is not achievable.

There are millions of guns in Australia, including around three million or so that are not known to the government. Even with searches of every single house in the country (including the houses of those who hate guns), it could never hope to find them all. Indeed, it is unlikely it could even find most of them.

A ban could not prevent the smuggling of guns into the country. This is already the main source of illegal firearms.

Unless the ban includes the police and security guards, guns will be stolen from them. This already occurs from time to time but would inevitably increase. Thefts from military armouries also occur.

Finally, a ban could not prevent local manufacture of guns. This has always been possible with appropriate metal working equipment, but is now becoming even easier as a result of 3D printing. With printers readily available and the programs for constructing gun parts accessible online, it is only the availability of conventional guns that reduces the incentive to produce 3D guns on a widespread basis.

12

SENSIBLE GUN LAWS

A common refrain from those who support gun control is that they are only seeking 'sensible' measures.

What they regard as sensible tends to be different from the views of those who own and use guns. Gun owners are very conscious of creeping gun control: so-called 'sensible' measures have a tendency to be replaced by something even more 'sensible' down the track, none of it making much objective sense. The ultimate objective in most cases is complete civilian disarmament.

Moreover, laws based on an assumption that innocent people who own guns are inherently a risk to others are never likely to be acceptable to either gun owners or those who value personal freedom generally.

That said, firearm owners readily acknowledge that some people should not have access to firearms. The shooting sports are exceptionally conscious of safety and well aware of risks posed by certain individuals. Hunters are also very cautious about who they hunt with, if anyone.

The challenge is to keep firearms out of the hands of those who are dangerous, without infringing the rights of those who are not. There are both sensible and non-sensible approaches to that.

LICENCES

Many jurisdictions seek to keep firearms out of the wrong hands through licensing, with denial of licences to those regarded as inherently risky.

Australian gun owners generally have no objection to the requirement for a licence, at least for genuine firearms (ie not including air-powered firearms and replicas). It is well accepted that some people are fundamentally dangerous and should not have access to firearms of any kind. Denial of a licence to such people is one means by which this might be achieved, notwithstanding the availability of guns via the black market.

If denial of a licence was restricted to those with a history of violence, making threats of violence, or who suffer from conditions that predispose to violence, most firearm owners would have few concerns. However, the history of gun control is that it never stops at that point. Inevitably, the conditions on the issuing of licences are ratcheted up based on assertions of risk for which there is no evidential basis.

For example, we hear claims by gun control advocates that those involved in divorce or custody proceedings are liable to resort to violence, that verbal confrontations indicate potential violence, or that those with a potential for violence can be screened out by psychological assessments or the opinion of family doctors. Some even insist that men are inherently violent.

None of these is true. However, they are often presented as "sensible" in order to justify additional gun control measures.

The most acceptable approach is for every adult to be entitled to a licence if they want one, but for that entitlement to be forfeited on specific, objective grounds. That said, with appropriate background checks (see subsequent section), even the need for a licence can be questioned.

RESTRICTIONS ON FIREARM TYPES

A measure regularly described as "sensible" is to restrict the types of firearms that may be owned. This is based on the assumption that there is a higher potential for gun violence with certain firearms, particularly firearms capable of firing rapidly.

This is the rationale for restrictions on automatic and semi-automatic firearms and limits on magazine capacity. Both are based on an assumption that these either somehow deter people from using firearms to commit violence, or result in fewer victims.

This is entirely conjecture driven by emotion; there is no objective evidence to support it.

For example, there is no evidence that an individual intent on gun violence might have a change of heart because there are no rapid firing firearms available, or because the only magazines available hold 10 rounds rather than 15 or 30.

There is no evidence that the few seconds required to swap magazines (ie replace a 10 round magazine with another 10 round magazine) provides a realistic opportunity to take down a spree shooter who would otherwise use a 20 or 30 round magazine.

There is no evidence that because a firearm can be fired rapidly, more people will be shot.

In fact, a firearm capable of firing multiple shots rapidly will not be accurate if fired that way. Even highly trained and experienced shooters find it very difficult to combine speed and accuracy. In untrained hands, automatic and semi-automatic firearms fired rapidly typically fail to hit their target after the second or third shot.

This has been shown many times by poorly trained militia using AK47 assault rifles in automatic mode. Only the first two or three bullets have much possibility of hitting the intended target, the remainder typically passing overhead.

It is also not true that only automatic and semi-automatic firearms can be fired rapidly. Prior to the first World War, the British army had an exercise known as "Practice number 22, Rapid Fire, The Musketry Regulations, Part I, 1909" which required riflemen to fire 15 rounds at a target from 300 yards (270m) in one minute using their service Lee Enfield rifles. Loading was from a pouch or bandolier in five round clips.

The practice, known as the 'Mad Minute', was one of several exercises used to grade a soldier as a marksman, first-class or second-class shot, depending on the scores achieved. The rapid aimed fire was accomplished by using a 'palming' method where the rifleman used the palm of his hand to work the bolt rather than his thumb and forefinger, while maintaining his cheek weld and line of sight.

It developed into a contest to see how many shots could hit the target. The first record was set in 1908 with 36 hits on a 48 inch target at 300 yards. Another world record of 38 hits on a 24 inch target at 300 yards was set in 1914. Similar competitions are still held today.

The Lee-Enfield .303 rifle is a bolt-action rifle with a 10 round magazine that served as the main firearm of the military forces of the British Empire (including Australia) during the first half of the 20th century. It was the British Army's standard rifle from its official adoption in 1895 until 1957.

This rifle is now classified as Category B and owned by tens of thousands of Australians. Up to 1997 it was available without a licence in some states. Many other types of bolt action rifles are also available, owned by hundreds of thousands of Australians.

The assumption that a modern semi-automatic rifle capable of firing a shot with each pull of the trigger represents a greater risk to public safety than a 120 year old rifle that can accurately fire a shot every two seconds is simply false. Both can be fired either rapidly or accurately, but only highly trained and practised users can fire either of them both rapidly and accurately.

One of the victims of the negative attitude to certain guns is the AR-15 rifle, which has long been demonised as a "military-style assault rifle". In reality it has never been issued to the military anywhere. Moreover, the ammunition it uses, and thus its potential lethality, is no different to a .223 bolt action hunting rifle.

In 1994 the US implemented a Federal Assault Weapons Ban[130] (the Public Safety and Recreational Firearms Use Protection Act). This prohibited the manufacture or importation of certain semi-automatic firearms that it defined as "semi automatic assault weapons" and banned the manufacture or importation of magazines that could hold more than ten rounds of ammunition.

The Act defined certain firearms as assault weapons based on features including semi-automatic action, a detachable magazine and at least two of a pistol grip, a folding or telescoping stock, a flash suppressor or threaded barrel, a bayonet mount, or a muzzle-mounted grenade launcher.

It included semi-automatic pistols with a detachable magazine and at least two of a magazine that attaches outside the pistol grip, a threaded barrel, a barrel shroud, or an unloaded weight of 50 ounces or more.

Additionally defined as assault weapons were semi-automatic shotguns with a rotating cylinder, or with at

---

[130] https://en.wikipedia.org/wiki/Assault_weapon

least two of a pistol grip, a folding or telescoping stock, a detachable magazine, or a fixed magazine that can hold more than five rounds. The ban also specifically named 19 models of firearms, as well as copies of those guns.

The Act lapsed in 2004 and the bans were not restored. A study by the Department of Justice in 2004[131] concluded:

> *In sum, AWs and LCMs were used in up to a quarter of gun crimes prior to the 1994 AW-LCM ban. By most estimates, AWs were used in less than 6% of gun crimes even before the ban. Some may have perceived their use to be more widespread, however, due to the use of AWs in particularly rare and highly publicized crimes such as mass shootings (and, to a lesser extent, murders of police), survey reports suggesting high levels of AW ownership among some groups of offenders, and evidence that some AWs are more attractive to criminal than lawful gun buyers.*
>
> *In contrast, guns equipped with LCMs – of which AWs are a subset – are used in roughly 14% to 26% of gun crimes. Accordingly, the LCM ban has greater potential for affecting gun crime. However, it is not clear how often the ability to fire more than 10 shots without reloading (the current magazine capacity limit) affects the outcomes of gun attacks. All of this suggests that the ban's impact on gun violence is likely to be small.*
>
> Note: AW = assault weapon   LCM = large capacity magazine

There is nothing sensible about restricting the types of firearms that can be used by a safe shooter. If a person is safe with one type of firearm, that person is safe with all kinds of firearms. Conversely, a person who is dangerous with one type of firearm will be dangerous with all kinds.

---

[131] https://www.ncjrs.gov/pdffiles1/nij/grants/204431.pdf

There is also nothing sensible about restricting the types of firearms or magazines as a means of reducing suicide. A single shot firearm, even a simple .22 rifle, is just as suitable for this as a machinegun. Even if the first shot is not fatal, the victim will be in no condition to keep firing.

In the USA, eight states and a number of local governments ban or regulate magazines that they have defined as high-capacity (ie more than 10 rounds). The majority of states (42) do not.[132]

However, unlike Australia, states with large capacity magazine bans or restrictions typically do not apply these to firearms with fixed magazines (eg lever and pump actions).

In the UK, notwithstanding its relatively strict gun controls, there is no ban, restriction or other legal limit on the possession, purchase, sale or import of high capacity magazines that are designed for use in rifles, shotguns and pistols.

GUN REGISTRATION

A measure often described as "sensible" is the registration of individual firearms. Individual pistol registration has been the law in Australia since the 1930s but registration of rifles and shotguns was only introduced nationally in 1997 with the Howard gun laws.

It is likely that registration has never saved a single life. Some suggest it may have helped solve a crime, but even that is questionable. On the rare occasions that legal owners commit crimes with a registered firearm, the fact that it is registered is of no consequence.

At most, a registered firearm that has been stolen, used in a

---

[132] https://en.wikipedia.org/wiki/High-capacity_magazine_ban

crime and recovered can be traced back to its original owner. The police then typically look for a way to prosecute the original owner for allowing it to be stolen.

In fact, rifles and shotguns are only rarely used in crime. Pistols are far more popular with criminals. If registration really was of benefit in preventing or solving gun crime, it would have been apparent from the decades-long registration of pistols.

In reality, registration is about control rather than crime or safety. A register is an almost irresistible temptation to those who want to prohibit civilian gun ownership as it identifies all the legally owned guns, their owners and where they are stored.

A register is not cost free; the establishment and maintenance of an accurate registry of firearms is complex and expensive. It costs hundreds of millions of dollars annually for each Australian state and territory to maintain a registry, each of them notorious for errors and inaccuracies. Proposals to establish a central national registry will inevitably be more expensive and no more accurate.

Both New Zealand and Canada have recognised the lack of benefit from registration, of rifles and shotguns at least. Canada introduced universal registration of guns, including rifles and shotguns, in 1995.[133] Proponents said the central registry would give law-enforcement agencies a powerful new tool for tracking guns used in crimes. They also claimed it would help reduce domestic violence and suicide.

The body responsible for the registry, the Canada Firearms Center, quickly rose to 600 employees and the cost climbed past $600 million. In 2002 Canada's auditor general issued a report saying initial cost estimates of C$2 million had

---

[133] https://www.forbes.com/sites/danielfisher/2013/01/22/canada-tried-registering-long-guns-and-gave-up/#64aef33d5a1b

increased to C$1 billion as the government tried to register the estimated 15 million guns owned by Canada's 34 million residents.

The registry was plagued with complications such as duplicate serial numbers and millions of incomplete records. One person managed to register a soldering gun, demonstrating the lack of precise standards. Overshadowing the effort was the suspicion of misplaced effort: pistols were used in 66% of gun homicides in 2011, yet they represent about 6% of the guns in Canada. Legal rifles and shotguns guns were used in 11% of killings that year, according to Statistics Canada, while illegal weapons like sawn-off shotguns and machineguns, which by definition cannot be registered, were used in another 12%.

The government was spending the bulk of its money trying to register long guns when the statistics showed they weren't the problem.

There was also the question of how registering guns was supposed to reduce crime and suicide in the first place. From 1997 to 2005, only 13% of the guns used in homicides were registered. Police studies estimated that 2-16% of guns used in crimes were stolen from legal owners and thus potentially in the register. The bulk of the guns, Canadian officials concluded, were unregistered weapons imported illegally from the U.S. by criminal gangs.

Finally, in 2011 the government voted to abolish the long-gun registry and destroy all its records. Pistols and automatic firearms continue to be registered.

The bigger lesson of Canada's experiment, according to Canadian researcher Gary Mauser, is that gun registration rarely delivers the results proponents expect. In most countries the actual number registered settles out at about a sixth of the actual number. Germany required registration during the Baader-Meinhof reign of terror in the 1970s, and recorded 3.2 million of the estimated 17 million guns in that country; England tried to register pump-action and semi-automatic shotguns in the 1980s, but only got about 50,000 of the estimated 300,000 such guns stored in homes around the country

Some Canadian police officers also questioned the efficacy of the registry in protecting them on domestic violence calls, since the registry was riddled with inaccuracies and did not say where guns are located, only who owns them. Either way, long guns are only involved in about 18% of female spousal killings in Canada. Knives account for 31%, according to Mauser.

The experience in New Zealand was similar.[134] Registration of individual firearms was first introduced in 1920, although shotguns were exempted in the 1930s.

During the 1960s, with the police attempting to make more frequent use of the register, widespread issues were identified. The police concluded that the validation of existing records was too big a task and would detract from other work. Thus in 1983 registration of longarms was abandoned in favour of tighter screening of firearms licence applicants. Registration of pistols and restricted weapons was retained.

In 1992, following a massacre at Aramoana, registration of "military style semi-automatics" was reintroduced. In 1997 a proposal to ban such firearms and reintroduce registration of all others was considered in response to pressure from Australia following the Port Arthur massacre, but did not proceed.

Following the Christchurch massacre in April 2019, military style semi-automatics were banned along with

---

[134] https://www.loc.gov/law/help/firearms-control/newzealand.php

centrefire semi-automatic firearms and certain pump action shotguns.[135] The government has also announced an intention to reintroduce a register of all rifles and shotguns. All the evidence indicates it will similarly fail to achieve any useful purpose.

PREVENTION OF THEFT

One of the few areas of agreement between gun prohibitionists and gun owners is the need to prevent the theft of firearms. While stolen guns are not the main source of guns used to commit gun violence, it is agreed that any level of theft is undesirable.

However, measures designed to minimise the theft of legally owned firearms almost invariably go well beyond what is sensible.

For example, for many years the law in NSW specified that a gun could not be left outside a gun safe unless it was being used or transported to a gunsmith. This meant that a gun owner could only legally clean it while it was in a safe.

This might have been ignored on the basis of triviality but for the fact that countless owners of firearms have been prosecuted or had their licences revoked because they did not comply with storage obligations.

That includes firearm owners who had their guns out of the safe for cleaning or were tinkering with them at the time they were visited by police. It also includes farmers who kept a shotgun handy in case they encountered a snake close to their house or in anticipation of seeing a rabbit or fox.

Failure to lock up ammunition has also been grounds for prosecution or revocation of licences, despite ammunition

---

[135] https://www.loc.gov/law/foreign-news/article/new-zealand-legislation-banning-certain-firearms-magazines-and-parts-passed/

being harmless in the absence of a working firearm.

It may be sensible for firearm owners to have a general obligation to take reasonable steps to prevent theft of their firearms, but petty rules that have no influence on the misuse of firearms are clearly not sensible.

GUN AMNESTIES

A popular measure to those who advocate "sensible" gun laws is gun amnesties, in which gun owners are encouraged to surrender firearms with an assurance that they will not be prosecuted if they do not own them legally.

Australia has had several of these since 1997, mostly at state level although one was co-ordinated and undertaken nationally.

Amnesties rely on the assumption that by removing guns from the community, there are fewer guns overall and society is safer. In fact, there is no evidence that either the number of guns is actually reduced or that the removal of those guns results in an increase in safety.

Fairly obviously, criminals never surrender their guns. Moreover, the guns surrendered in amnesties are almost never used in crime. Typically they are old, many are inoperable and owned by people (via inheritance mostly) who are not interested in them. At most, gun amnesties reduce the risk that a tiny number of guns will fall into the wrong hands through theft. Whether that actually occurs has never been proven.

Law abiding gun owners generally do not oppose gun amnesties, although they view them with cynicism and do not regard them as sensible.

GUN BUYBACKS

A gun buyback is a government program to purchase privately owned firearms. The term "buyback" is misleading, as the guns were never owned by the government. When accompanied by legislation prohibiting certain types of firearms, a more correct term is confiscation with compensation.

The goal is to reduce the total number of firearms, or certain types of firearms, owned by civilians. Like amnesties, it relies on the assumption that this will result in fewer guns in the community and thus less gun violence.

Gun owners do not regard buybacks as 'sensible' for reasons previously discussed. There is no evidence that reducing the number of firearms in the community, either by this method or any other, changes the misuse of firearms.

At most it may result in the substitution of other methods in suicide. There is no evidence, from Australia or other countries where they have been tried, that buybacks have had any effect on gun violence.[136]

In Australia the buyback associated with the introduction of the Howard gun laws in 1997 was intended to remove semi-automatic rifles and shotguns and pump action shotguns from civilian ownership. As discussed in Chapter 7, this failed to have any impact on either gun violence or mass murders.

The buyback was undertaken at the instigation of John Howard, the Prime Minister at the time. However, it was the state governments that legislated and implemented it. There were two reasons for this. First, regulation of guns is a state responsibility, although the Commonwealth generally manages to find a head of power to overcome this when it wants to.

---

[136]_https://en.wikipedia.org/wiki/Gun_buyback_program

Second and most importantly, the Commonwealth Constitution requires proper compensation to be paid for any property confiscated by the government. There is no such obligation on the state governments, which meant that they could set the levels of compensation without risk of legal challenge.

In the event, the compensation paid was relatively generous and there were few complaints about that aspect of the program from gun owners. This is not the case with the 2019 buyback in New Zealand, where inadequate compensation is reported to have contributed to a significant lack of interest by gun owners.

WAITING PERIODS

A waiting period law requires a certain number of days to elapse between the purchase of a firearm and when the buyer can actually take possession of it.

Proponents of waiting periods argue that by delaying immediate access to firearms, a "cooling off" period is created that can help prevent impulsive acts of gun violence, including gun homicides and suicides.

In practice, there are two types of waiting periods - one applied to those who currently own no firearms and have never previously owned them, and one applied to people who own at least one firearm and are seeking to obtain more.

The second kind of waiting period is clearly irrational. If someone already owns a gun, it makes no sense to compel them to wait before obtaining another one. If they are going to misuse a gun, the opportunity is already available.

For over a decade in NSW post 1997 the legislation obliged Firearms Registry to wait 28 days before issuing a permit for an additional firearm, irrespective of whether the applicant already owned firearms.

The argument is different when a waiting period is applied to those who do not already own a gun.

If a gun is being obtained in order to commit murder, the key question is whether that intention will change as a result of waiting. Some speculate that should be the case but there is no objective evidence to confirm it. In the United States, where background checks are undertaken in a matter of minutes prior to purchasing a gun, impulse murders or robberies upon legal acquisition of a first gun are not a concern.

Suicide attempts are sometimes impulsive, singular episodes that involve little planning. Some studies suggest that suicide survivors may contemplate their actions for only a brief period of time—often less than 24 hours—before making a suicide attempt. If that is the case, the requirement to wait before obtaining a gun may mean suicide is not attempted. However, it is also likely that an alternative method will be found.

The anti-gun Giffords Law Centre argues:

Waiting period laws, which create a buffer between the time of gun purchase and gun acquisition, can help to prevent impulsive acts of gun violence. In particular, studies suggest that waiting period laws prevent firearm suicides and firearm homicides.

- *Studies suggest that waiting period laws are associated with reduced rates of firearm suicide. By one estimation, waiting period laws may reduce firearm suicide rates by 7–11%.*

- *Waiting period laws also appear to reduce gun homicide rates. One study found that waiting period laws that delay the purchase of firearms by a few days can reduce gun homicides by roughly 17%.*

This statement is significant because it does not claim an overall reduction in suicides or homicides. Firearms are just one method of committing suicide or murder. The reality is, there is no evidence to show a reduction in the total numbers of either.

A GOOD GUY WITH A GUN

A law that many gun owners would find sensible is having the right to shoot back, whether at a criminal intent on robbery or a mass murderer.

As the saying goes, the only sure way to stop a bad guy with a gun is a good guy with a gun. This is the basis for arming the police, something gun control advocates never dispute. However, they never explain why others are not equally capable of using guns to protect themselves and others.

It is simply irrational to argue that those who wear a badge and government uniform are the only people capable and entitled to do so. Indeed, in many cases the only difference between police and law-abiding members of the community is the badge and uniform. Firearms expertise, knowledge of the law and general responsibility are shared by many others.

Using a gun for protection is not for everyone, but it is certainly not sensible to insist it is not for anyone. Very few countries take such an attitude.

BACKGROUND CHECKS

Keeping firearms out of the wrong hands is clearly desirable. The question is, can it be achieved in a manner that does not involve authoritarian impositions on law-abiding firearm owners?

In the US, even those states that do not require a licence or permit nonetheless seek to ensure firearms are kept out of the wrong hands. This occurs by means of background checks which are undertaken each time a firearm is purchased from a firearms dealer.

In 30 states, five U.S. territories and the District of Columbia this is achieved via the National Instant Criminal Background Check System (NICS), operated by the FBI[137]. Dealers contact the NICS via telephone or internet to request a background check on prospective customers. An answer is provided within minutes and the service operates 17 hours a day, seven days a week.

Between November 30, 1998 and May 31, 2016 the NICS denied 1,323,172 transactions. The top reasons for denials include: "Convicted of a crime punishable by more than one year or a misdemeanour punishable by more than two years", "Fugitive from Justice", "Misdemeanor Crime of Domestic Violence Conviction" and "Unlawful User/Addicted to a Controlled Substance."

In 2019, over 28.4 million background checks were performed. The FBI says more than 230 million such checks have been made in total.

The FBI database is updated by local, state, tribal and federal agencies. In addition it receives calls, often in emergency situations, from mental health care providers, police departments and family members requesting placement of individuals into the NICS Index.

Those states that do not use the NICS system all have a system for background checking. There are no exceptions.

As explained in Chapter 8, Switzerland has a licensing system but also undertakes a background check with every

---

[137] https://www.fbi.gov/services/cjis/nics

purchase of a firearm. A clearance, issued by the police in the applicant's Canton, is required irrespective of prior history. However, there is no central register of firearms including for automatic and semi-automatic firearms. Switzerland saves a lot of money by not adopting ineffective policies.

Firearm owners generally regard background checks prior to each purchase as sensible in theory. However, this is subject to the information upon which the checks are based; the information has to be accurate, objective (ie not subject to bureaucratic interpretation) and the checking process should not be used to develop a register of firearm owners and their property. A register becomes an enormous temptation to authoritarians.

It is also important to ensure the reasons for rejection are valid. An example of misuse was the refusal to approve any ex-military US personnel who had been diagnosed or received treatment for PTSD or depression, affecting hundreds of thousands of people who posed no threat to anyone.

Background checks must be based on individual circumstances, not collective assumptions. The onus must be on government authorities and law enforcement to treat people as individuals rather than numbers, statistics or members of groups. It is individuals who commit crimes, not groups of people and not guns.

ACKNOWLEDGEMENTS

This book was conceived and commenced while I was serving in the Senate, even before I wrote my previous book, *Freedom's Salesman*.

Progress was initially slow – writing and editing a book whilst serving as a member of parliament is a lot more challenging than I anticipated. There were lengthy periods when no progress was possible.

I resigned from the Senate on 1 March 2019 in order to stand for the NSW state parliament. When I narrowly failed to win, I was able to devote time to completing the book. That's not a complaint – I much prefer writing to being a politician.

Quite a lot of the book is my work, and I accept responsibility for any errors, but others have contributed significantly. The chapters on Ireland, Switzerland, India, New Zealand, the Czech Republic and United Kingdom were written by others and I am very grateful to all of them for their contributions. I did no more than edit what they provided.

Grant Bayley, my Switzerland-based friend and author of the chapter on that country, has been helpful in other ways too. Frank Brophy, author of the chapter on Ireland, helped me find authors in the Czech Republic, India and the UK. Oskar Zimmerman assisted with the discussion about Port Arthur.

My thanks to those who helped with proofreading, particularly Max Rheese. I also acknowledge Tom Frame's book, *Gun Control: What Australia got right (and wrong)*, which helped me clarify certain sectors, and by the many unknown authors and photographers who contribute to Wikipedia and whose work I have reproduced.

ABOUT THE AUTHOR

David Leyonhjelm was elected to the Australian Senate in 2013, commencing his term in mid 2014. He was re-elected in 2016 and resigned in March 2019 to contest the NSW state election.

In the Senate he campaigned tirelessly for law-abiding firearm owners. He not only advocated for firearms and non-lethal means of self-defence but fought a long and controversial battle to prevent further tightening of Australia's gun laws. He also assisted firearm dealers facing unhelpful bureaucracy and successfully negotiated permanent tenure for sporting shooters on the Anzac rifle range in Sydney.

He has owned and used firearms most of his life. As a child he shot sparrows with an air rifle and rabbits with a .22 rifle. These days he is a regular target shooter and sporadic hunter of feral animals. He owns rifles, pistols and shotguns and loads his own ammunition.

He is the proprietor of an agribusiness consulting company and has degrees in veterinary science, law and business.

www.ingramcontent.com/pod-product-compliance
Lightning Source LLC
Chambersburg PA
CBHW040421110426
42814CB00007B/322